THE FUTURE
OF THE SUNBELT

THE FUTURE
OF THE SUNBELT

Managing Growth and Change

Edited by
Steven C. Ballard
and Thomas E. James

PRAEGER

PRAEGER SPECIAL STUDIES • PRAEGER SCIENTIFIC

Library of Congress Cataloging in Publication Data
Main entry under title:

The Future of the Sunbelt.

    Includes bibliographies and index.
    1. Sunbelt States—Economic policy. 2. Sunbelt
States—Social policy. I. Ballard, Steven C. II. James,
Thomas E.
HC107.A163F87 1983   338.973   83–13890
ISBN 0-03-063392-3

338.973
F996

Published in 1983 by Praeger Publishers
CBS Educational and Professional Publishing
a Division of CBS Inc.
521 Fifth Avenue, New York, New York 10175, USA

© 1983 by Praeger Publishers

3456789 052 987654321

Printed in the United States of America
on acid-free paper

84-8469

To Philip M. Burgess
For teaching us about the real world
and for his continuing contributions
to the policy sciences.

Acknowledgments

The theme of this book and some of the research reported herein originated with a two-year study, the "Sunbelt Project," funded by the U.S. Environmental Protection Agency, Office of Research and Development (Cooperative agreement CR 808418-01-0). We are particularly indebted to John Reuss, Acting Director of the Environmental Protection Agency's Office of Strategic Assessment and Special Studies, and Charles Oakley, Project Officer.

We are also indebted to our colleagues in the Science and Public Policy Program for their contributions to the Sunbelt Project: Basil Achilladelis, Michael A. Chartock, Michael D. Devine, Elizabeth M. Gunn, Richard L. Johnston, Rebecca S. Roberts, and Karen J. Selland. We are particularly grateful to Michael D. Devine, Project Director, for his support of this book and assistance in its development. Elizabeth Gunn provided valuable help during the final stages of development.

Several members of our support staff were helpful in the production of this book: Lennet Bledsoe, Ellen Ladd, Deborah Kasbaum, and Emily Terrell. Lennet Bledsoe deserves special thanks for the overall coordination and typing of the manuscript. Emily Terrell was a significant help in preparing the index and bibliography for the volume.

Contents

CHAPTER

CHAPTER

LIST OF TABLES AND FIGURES

TABLES

FIGURES

Introduction

Growth in the Sunbelt has received considerable public attention in recent years. Much of this attention has focused on the rise of the Sunbelt, its relationship to the decline of the Northeast, and the impact of governmental policies — particularly federal spending policies — on promoting these changes. Many have viewed regional imbalances in the amount of federal money spent compared to the amount of tax revenue collected as a primary force behind the rapid development of the South.

Although federal spending policies have been and will continue to be influential with respect to Sunbelt growth, they are only one of many reasons for the rapid growth of this region. Further, the emphasis on federal spending and tax policies has drawn attention away from other important issues, particularly federal-state relationships, state innovations in growth management capacity, and long-term needs to balance the benefits of growth with its costs and risks.

MYTHS ABOUT THE SUNBELT

Although the Sunbelt is a diverse and changing area, some overall characterizations can be made about the region. Unfortunately, many of the popular generalizations about the Sunbelt are not accurate. At least four of these myths are particularly important to the issues discussed in this volume.

Myth 1: Sunbelt growth is only significant in Florida and Texas. While Florida and Texas clearly are two of the key Sunbelt states, economic and population growth are pervasive across most of the region. For example, all states of the Sunbelt are experiencing increases in population and manufacturing employment rates that are greater than the national average, and these trends are expected to continue (see Chapter 2). For manufacturing employment, the largest percentage increases are occurring in Louisiana, New Mexico, Oklahoma, and Texas. For total employment, states with traditionally low growth rates (Kentucky, Mississippi, South Carolina, and

Tennessee) are expected to experience the more rapid increase typical of the Sunbelt as a whole.

Myth 2: The states in the South are attracting growth because they are more willing to sacrifice natural resources. Public opinion polls indicate that residents of the Sunbelt strongly support environmental goals, and support comes from a broad base of society rather than special geographic or demographic subgroups. Sunbelt residents view the costs of environmental protection to be worthwhile, interest group activity supporting environmental protection has increased throughout the Sunbelt, and state agencies responsible for protecting the environment have become stronger over the past decade (see Chapter 5).

Myth 3: Economic growth is a uniform advantage to the Sunbelt. While Sunbelt states generally view industrial growth positively, they also clearly recognize the need to manage this growth to balance the benefits with potential negative consequences. For example, for the first time environmental problems typically associated with the industrialized Northeast, such as acid rain, are being experienced in the South; consequently, many southeastern states are recognizing the need to protect their air and water resources. Further, states increasingly recognize that short-term economic gains may turn to long-term economic losses — out-of-state investment may quickly turn to job flight beyond the borders with a potential for net loss of jobs.

Myth 4: State governments are neither willing nor able to manage rapid growth. Across the Sunbelt, states are developing long-term planning and research capabilities and innovative institutional approaches to actively manage growth and to foster conditions that will maximize the benefits of continued growth. For example, Mississippi is actively developing strategies to decrease their dependency on imported (out-of-state) energy; Florida has one of the most innovative water management strategies in the country; and Texas has institutionalized long-term strategic planning.

PURPOSE AND SCOPE

Little question exists that the Sunbelt will continue to be an important region in the future. Its size, voting strength, and relative cohesion suggest that this region is likely to continue to grow in political power. Economically, the Sunbelt will continue to be a major energy consumer and producer; it is expected to rank first in manufacturing employment by the end of the century, and agricultural earnings are projected to increase faster than the U.S. average in most of the Sunbelt states. The Sunbelt is also rich in natural resources, including forests, wetlands, coastal resources, prime farmland, and energy sources.

This book addresses several issues associated with the rapid growth of this region. Specifically, its purposes are to:

- identify the primary causes of growth in the Sunbelt and the relative importance of factors associated with this growth;
- anticipate future growth patterns, including those which may require active management in order to maximize benefits and minimize negative impacts;
- characterize several of the issues related to the management of growth and change that the states in the Sunbelt are facing or are likely to face over the next several decades.

The first two chapters of the volume provide the foundation for the remaining chapters — they demonstrate the past, current, and future reality of growth in the Sunbelt and describe several specific driving forces that will increase the need for more systematic and comprehensive growth management strategies. In Chapter 1, *The Sunbelt Phenomenon: Causes of Growth*, Rebecca S. Roberts and Lisa M. Butler provide a comprehensive overview of the causes of Sunbelt growth based on an extensive review of the literature on regional growth. By describing the factors which have encouraged the economic and population growth of the Sunbelt, the authors provide a clear perspective about the relative importance of several growth factors, as well as an assessment of the probable importance of these factors for future growth.

In Chapter 2, *Anticipating Future Growth in the Sunbelt*, Thomas E. James, Jr. extends the overview presented in Chapter 1 by discussing projections of population, employment, industrial development, and income trends in the Sunbelt through the year 2010. Based on projections developed by the U.S. Department of Commerce, Bureau of Economic Analysis, the South is expected to continue to be one of the two fastest growing regions in the country for the forseeable future. This growth will create substantial benefits, including increases in the employment to population ratio and in wage rates which will, in turn, increase the economic well-being of virtually every state.

Chapters 3 through 9 discuss several of the growth management issues that are of particular importance to the Sunbelt. In Chapter 3, *Capital Flight: Anticipating Sunbelt Problems*, Daniel McGovern tests three explanations of capital movement — geographic constraints, regional cost differences, and individual firm characteristics. Among his findings is the virtual absence of support for the idea that regional cost differences influence capital movement. Thus, while economic incentives may do nothing to attract new investment and jobs, they may have several negative consequences, including damage to the tax base and reduction of public services.

Chapter 4, *Urban Health Care Delivery in the Sunbelt*, begins a series of articles which address state and local growth management. Mary G. Almore and Frances Richardson discuss the impact of federal budget reductions on discretionary health programs. Because of rapid population growth and existing inadequacies in the health care delivery systems in many Sunbelt states, quality of health care in the Sunbelt can be expected to be a significant issue in the 1980s.

In Chapter 5, *State Government Capacity for Managing Sunbelt Growth*, Steven C. Ballard and Elizabeth M. Gunn examine the capacity of Sunbelt states to balance the management of natural resources with the desire for economic growth. The authors emphasize nonfinancial elements of problem-solving capacity — anticipatory capability, political will, institutional development, and management capacity. Examination of these indicators across the region challenges the conventional wisdom that Sunbelt states are somehow less able than others to manage their resources; rather capacity building efforts are being undertaken by all states.

In Chapter 6, *Managing Urban Growth: Citizen Perceptions and Preferences*, Susan A. MacManus examines the rapid population and economic growth in Houston and the usefulness of citizen perceptions as a growth management tool. She finds that citizens typically express positive perceptions of growth from a personal perspective but an increasingly negative perspective toward growth in general. Also, a high degree of public consensus exists about the seriousness of urban problems resulting from the rapid growth of the area. She discusses five alternative strategies for managing growth, the preferences of Houston residents for each, and the impact of citizen preferences on the development of growth management strategies and mechanisms.

Chapter 7, *Intergovernmental Issues in Managing Sunbelt Growth*, examines the implications of the Reagan Administration's failure to link science and technology policy to the needs of states in managing growth. James L. Regens and Robert Rycroft conclude that science and technology mechanisms will be particularly important to the future of the Sunbelt states. The management of environmental problems is discussed as an example of an area that will be especially difficult, given recent budget cutbacks and modifications in science and technology policy.

Chapters 8 and 9 look at what two Sunbelt states have done to develop a long-term growth management capacity. In *Energy Management and Economic Development in Mississippi*, Timothy A. Hall examines the economic advantages of lignite development in Mississippi. He discusses five areas of research and development activities which will be required if the state is to meet its energy needs while still preserving environmental and other values.

In Chapter 9, *Long Range Planning for Managing Growth and Change*, Victor L. Arnold characterizes the development of the Texas 2000 Project and Commission as mechanisms to anticipate future development issues. The Commission represents one of the most innovative and successful attempts to form a consensus among public and private sector interests about the future direction of a state.

In Chapter 10, *Policy and Research Needs*, Dwight F. Davis integrates several ideas found in the preceding nine chapters. He emphasizes factors which make the Sunbelt unique, problems in managing Sunbelt growth, and the research needs for providing a better understanding of regional growth. Problems associated with planning, the difficulty in finding historical parallels, and the relative newness of growth are seen as constraints to management.

1 The Sunbelt Phenomenon: Causes of Growth
Rebecca S. Roberts
and Lisa M. Butler

INTRODUCTION

During the first half of this century, the South was a relatively rural region with a small industrial base; per capita incomes were below U.S. averages (Figure 1-1). During the past decade, the centers of economic, population, and per capita income growth in the United States have shifted from the North to the South and West. From 1970 to 1980, the population growth rate in the South was over one and one-half times the overall growth rate of the United States and the growth rate of employment was twice as great. Per capita incomes have been rapidly approaching those of the United States as a whole.

Considerable controversy surrounds almost all interpretations of the causes of regional population and economic growth. Growth in the South has been widely perceived in the popular press as a result of the flight of both industry and people from the Frostbelt to the Sunbelt. Some explanations have emphasized the attractions of the area for industry, with people following on the heels of industry in search of jobs. In this context, low wages, favorable business climates, low taxes and cheap land, the energy boom, and active recruitment of industry by state and local governments are often cited. Other explanations have taken the opposing view, emphasizing the increasing draw of the South for people, with industry parading after the labor force. A mild climate, sunny

1

Figure 1-1: Per Capita Income for the South*.[a]

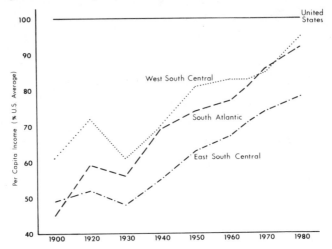

[a]Because of variations in data acquired from different sources, in this chapter the following definitions are used:

Standard Federal Regions

Southeast: Alabama, Florida, Georgia, Kentucky, Mississippi, North Carolina, South Carolina, and Tennessee;

Southwest: Arkansas, Louisiana, New Mexico, Oklahoma, and Texas;

South: Southeast and Southwest.

U.S. Census Regions

South Atlantic: Delaware, District of Columbia, Florida, Georgia, Maryland, North Carolina, South Carolina, Virginia, and West Virginia;

East South Central: Alabama, Kentucky, Mississippi, and Tennessee;

West South Central: Arkansas, Louisiana, Oklahoma, and Texas;

South*: South Atlantic, East Southcentral and West Southcentral.

Source: U.S. Department of Commerce, Bureau of the Census 1981, p. 429; and U.S. Department of Commerce, Bureau of the Census 1975, p. 242.

2

beaches, sports and recreation, relaxed outdoor living, and escape from northern congestion and "big city" life characterize the new image of the South.

Of course, both arguments — industrial attractiveness and population lure — have merit. Indeed, there may very well be a circular process at work. This chapter explores alternative explanations for the causes of growth in the Sunbelt to provide a basis of understanding for dealing with growth-associated problems. It draws from a diverse literature dealing with the causes of growth and regional differentiation, and leads to a number of conclusions at variance with popular wisdom:

- rapid growth of the southern manufacturing sector is not a new phenomenon. The popular perception of a new, resurgent South is more a result of slow economic growth in the North and the eventual absorption of displaced southern agricultural labor by other sectors or regions;
- a net flow of federal dollars to the South has been an important stimulus to southern growth, but its importance has been over-emphasized in the political conflicts over federal spending. Further, federal expenditures per capita in the South are below, and not above, the U.S. average;
- the perception of a favorable business climate that is attached to most southern states has been very important to the ability of these states to attract industry. However, the perception may be more closely related to persistent low wages and low levels of unionization and labor activism than it is to economic development policies of state and local governments. Low taxes and financial incentives to newly locating firms appear to have little impact on choice of state or region; and
- climatic and other amenities have been crucial to the growth of a few areas within the South. Southern Florida, the Ozarks, and the mountains of North Carolina are prominent examples. All in all, however, the gradual disappearance of negative features — racial segregation, inferior schools and public services, and poor access to major metropolitan areas with their entertainment and commercial facilities — may be more important for the region as a whole.

ATTRACTING INDUSTRY

The Importance of Manufacturing

Total employment in the South[*1] grew relatively slowly between 1920 and 1960, with employment growth rates never exceeding 16 percent per decade (U.S. Department. of Commerce, Bureau of the Census 1920-1970; U.S. Department of Commerce, Bureau of Economic Analysis 1980). However, beginning about 1960 the employment growth rate accelerated, increasing to 23 percent in the 1960s and to 43 percent from 1970 to 1978. To a large extent, this sudden acceleration was a result of underlying trends that have been building since at least 1920.[2]

These trends become evident when changes in the structure of the southern economy are examined. Basic industries, or those sectors that serve national markets, form the economic foundation of a region. They are typically defined to include a high proportion of the agriculture, mining, and manufacturing sectors, plus portions of other major sectors. Remaining sectors, termed service or non-basic, serve primarily regional markets and depend for their growth on the strength of the region's basic sector. Generally they are locationally tied to the industries and population they serve. These sectors typically include most government, services, finance, insurance and real estate, retail and wholesale trade, transportation, utilities, and construction. The size of the nonbasic sector, relative to the basic sector, is dependent on the proportion of revenues producers spend on regionally produced services and on the wages paid to employees in basic industries; where spending for services is high the nonbasic sector is more important to the total economy. Trends in total employment are thus related to the success of a region in attracting basic industries and to the wages paid by the basic sector.

In 1920, agricultural employment dominated both basic and total employment in the South* — 69 percent of basic employment was in agriculture, while only 27 percent was in manufacturing (U.S. Department of Commerce, Bureau of the Census 1923). For the rest of the country in 1920, the roles of agricultural and manufacturing employment were almost reversed; manufacturing accounted for 64 percent of basic employment compared to only 31 percent for agriculture.

The agricultural sector thus remained preeminent in the economy of the South longer than in the rest of the country. Numerous reasons have been suggested for the lagging development of the South, including (Sale 1977; Cobb 1982): a cumulative headstart in the North; inadequate transportation and discriminatory railroad rates; a poorly developed urban network; the dominance of cotton and the sharecropper system; a colonial pattern of absentee owner-ship of resources; the destruction and political aftermath of the civil war; a poorly educated labor force; an unequal distribution of income; and racial segregation.

Despite speculation over the reasons for the initial develop-mental lag, three trends have been evident since 1920 which largely explain the slow economic growth from 1920 to 1960 followed by rapid economic growth from 1960 to 1978 (Figure 1-2). First, agri-cultural employment in the South* declined precipitously in the 1920s, influenced by the fall of cotton prices, the decline of the sharecropping system, and the technological and economic changes leading to farm consolidation throughout the nation. Because of this dramatic decline, total basic employment actually fell during every decade between 1930 and 1960.

Figure 1-2: *Employment in Basic Industries in the South* 1920-1980*

Source: U.S. Department of Commerce, Bureau of the Census 1923, 1933, 1943, 1952, 1963, 1973; and U.S. Department of Commerce, Bureau of Economic Analysis 1980.

In spite of the overall slow growth in total employment, manufacturing employment grew at a rapid rate throughout the entire period. The South* has experienced a steady rise in manufacturing employment of 20 to 40 percent during each decade from 1920 to 1970, with the exception of the depression years. Although the rapid growth rate in manufacturing capacity in the South is a trend of long duration, not until 1960 was the absolute increase enough to offset agricultural employment decline and to produce an increase in basic employment. The acceleration of total employment growth coincided with the upturn in basic employment.

The third important trend is the rise in the percentage of total employment that is in the nonbasic, or service, sector. This percentage rose gradually from 32 percent in 1920 to 77 percent in 1978. The increase has been influenced by rising per capita incomes in the basic sector in the South attributable, at least in part, to:

- increased productivity throughout the basic sector;
- a rising ratio of manufacturing employment to agricultural employment in the basic sector; and
- a rising ratio of high wage to low wage industries within the manufacturing sector.

The ability of the South to attract manufacturing has been central to its economic growth over the past 60 years. As the previous analysis indicates, the recent acceleration of economic growth is not a result of recent change in the growth rate of manufacturing. Nor has it been caused by the migration of plants to the South. Actual plant or firm migration has generated very little employment change in either the North or the South (Garn and Ledebur 1982). Rather, the significant shifts in employment have resulted from a lower percentage of plant closures and a higher percentage of starts in the South than in either the Northeast or the Northcentral regions. Although such statistics understate the more subtle forms by which firms shift capital between regions (Bluestone and Harrison 1982), they do indicate the inaccuracy of characterizing southern industrial expansion as simple migration. The problem of evaluating the causes of recent economic growth in the South, and the likelihood of its continuing, therefore becomes a problem of determining why the South has been attracting new manufacturing capacity throughout this century and the probability that these reasons will continue to exist. The following discussion focuses on the growth of the South as a whole, evaluating the relative importance of: (1) resource and labor cost and availability; (2) the development of transportation, markets, and agglomeration economies; and (3) governmental policies.

Resource Cost and Availability

The availability and cost of resources are important considerations in the location of most manufacturing activities. The South possesses advantages in the provision of several important resources, including labor, energy, and raw materials.

Labor Cost and Availability

Lower labor costs are widely considered to be one of the most, if not the most, important reason for the continued expansion of manufacturing in the South, especially when labor costs are considered as a combination of wage rates, the strength and activity of unions, and the availability and productivity of labor. The importance of this variable stems from the fact that labor is the single most costly input into manufacturing; about 50 percent of the value added in manufacturing is spent on payroll, two-thirds of which goes to production workers (Vaughan 1979).

In the South*, wages for comparable skill levels have been significantly below U.S. averages. Median wage income in the South* in 1969 typically ranged between 80 and 90 percent of U.S. values for comparable occupations; nonfarm laborers were at 77 percent of the U.S. average, while professionals were at 94 percent (U.S. Department of Commerce, Bureau of the Census 1973). In given industries or occupations the differences were even greater. In 1973, for example, average employee compensation per hour in the South in the cotton textile industry was 63 percent of that in the Northeast (McKenzie 1979).

The South is maintaining its low wage position relative to other regions, although differentials are decreasing and in several highly skilled occupations wages are as high as in the North (Birch 1980; Browne 1978; Advisory Commission on Intergovernmental Relations 1980). Wage rates for most occupations, particularly blue collar and unskilled occupations, are still below national averages and are projected to remain below these values for a number of years to come. Rising incomes are more a result of a shift toward higher wage industries and an increasing employment-to-population ratio than a result of rising wages. Workman's compensation, unemployment insurance, and benefit levels are also lower in the South, and these help create lower total labor costs (Hekman and Smith 1982).

In many cases, the extent of unionization and labor-management conflict — work stoppages, rigid work rules, absenteeism — can be more important to overall labor costs than wage rates (Schmenner 1982). The oblique and euphemistic language used by industrial developers underlines the importance of this factor (Cobb 1982, pp. 99-100):

> When Governor Fielding Wright of Mississippi courted the Whirlpool Corporation, he assured executives, "The particular area you have in mind has an abundance of intelligent native labor and is entirely free of those conditions that tend to impair employer-employee relations." With this cryptic description of the nonunion climate in Mississippi came the implicit promise that no conditions that were likely to "impair employer-employee relations" would be allowed to develop. . . . The executive director of Tennessee's Department of Commerce and Industry explained to a Louisiana counterpart that one of the factors that brought Goodyear Tire and Rubber Company to Union City, Tennessee, was the fact that Union City was a "prime farming area." It seemed to him that Goodyear felt that "farm acclimated" labor could do the best job in its new plant, and he failed to mention that "farm acclimated" labor was likely to prove amenable to lower wages and resistant to the entreaties of union organizers.

These differences in labor-management relationships were actively supported by business, civic, and legislative leaders, who perceived a cheap disciplined labor force to be one of the few competitive advantages the South had to offer.

A number of indicators confirms the general perception that low levels of labor-management conflict in the South continue to be favorable to industry. Labor union membership as a percentage of total employment is much lower in most southern states than in the nation (U.S. Department of Commerce, Bureau of the Census 1980). Membership in all southern states is below the U.S. value of 24 percent. Only Kentucky (23 percent), Tennessee (18 percent), and Alabama (19 percent) approach the U.S. value, and two states — North Carolina and South Carolina — have only 7 percent of their work force unionized. Right-to-work laws in all southern states except Kentucky, Oklahoma, and New Mexico make it more difficult for unions to grow; very few of the northern and Pacific industrialized states have such laws. Days idled due to work stoppages in most southern states are also well below U.S. averages, particularly in Florida, Georgia, North Carolina, and South Carolina (Table 1-1). Unions are making a few inroads in the South, especially through the migration of union members and unionized industries, but clear differences between the South and the rest of the nation remain.

Research evidence supporting the continuing importance of labor costs in the growth of manufacturing in the South comes from a variety of sources. Both econometric analyses that are able to control for other variables and surveys of corporate executives find that labor costs are important to the location decision (Carlton

TABLE 1-1
DAYS IDLED DUE TO WORK STOPPAGES PER NONAGRICULTURAL
EMPLOYEE, 1978

State	Days Idled per Employee
Alabama	0.80
Arkansas	0.17
Florida	0.07
Georgia	0.10
Kentucky	1.73
Louisiana	0.16
Mississippi	0.25
New Mexico	0.50
North Carolina	0.05
Oklahoma	0.26
South Carolina	0.06
Tennessee	0.43
Texas	0.12
U.S. Average	0.43

SOURCE: U.S. Department of Commerce, Bureau of the Census 1980, pp. 412, 431.

1979; Moriarty 1980). Anecdotal evidence indicates labor costs may be even more important than survey evidence indicates. A South Carolina study found that, "off-the-record," low wages and the absence of significant union activity were at the top of most executive's lists (Watkins 1980, p. 6). An executive of Fantus Corporation, a plant location consulting firm, stated that "nine out of ten times you can hang it on labor costs and unionization" (Watkins 1980, p. 6).

The most convincing evidence for the importance of labor costs relies upon studies of the manufacturing product cycle (Malecki 1981; Rees 1979a; Hekman 1980; Hansen forthcoming; Cromley and Leinbach 1981). The location of new product development tends to be concentrated in the largest industrialized urban centers where interindustry linkages are strong, research and educational facilities are concentrated, and information networks meet. The growth stage of a product is characterized by the introduction of mass production. As a product passes through this stage, the input of technical, managerial, and professional skills decreases and production labor costs become increasingly significant. During the mature stage there is little innovation, with production characterized by long, routine runs. Wages and the availability of relatively unskilled workers become a primary locational consideration. The manufacture of products in this stage tends to gravitate toward low wage areas, both foreign and domestic, and frequently takes place in branch plants of larger firms that maintain their corporate headquarters and innovative capacity in other areas.

Much of the early growth in southern manufacturing consisted of mature industries, where labor costs dominated other locational considerations. Textiles, apparel, and shoe manufacture, among the first industries to reach the mature stage, moved much of their domestic capacity to the South in the first half of the twentieth century in order to compete with low wage foreign production. Since then, furniture and leather have also established much of their capacity in this region. These industries are still growing slowly in the South at a time when total production in the nation is declining. The southern growth of manufacturing capacity in other more innovative industrial sectors, such as consumer electronics and the specialty chemicals/metals group, is largely a result of the attraction of low wages for established, mature products within these industries (Schmenner 1982). This view is supported by studies characterizing the types of plants that actually locate in the South (Cromley and Leinbach 1981; Malecki 1981; Hekman 1980; Schmenner 1982). Such plants, particularly in nonmetropolitan areas, tend to be branch plants specializing in the mass production of standard products; corporate management and research and development in innovative industries continue to be concentrated in the Northeast or California.

In sum, the ability of lower wages and a labor-management environment favorable to industry to attract production capacity for established products is a major, if not the most important, reason behind the continuing expansion of manufacturing capacity in the South. If southern wages approach national levels and if regional differences in labor activism diminish, the ability of the South to attract as large a percentage of national growth in manufacturing as it has in recent years may decrease. There is as yet, however, little indication that the labor cost advantage of the South with respect to the North is disappearing, or that the importance of labor costs to U.S. manufacturing as a whole will decrease. The greater danger, to the North as well as the South, is competition from cheap foreign labor, particularly in consumer electronics, scientific instruments, shoes, and apparel (Schmenner 1982).

Energy Cost and Availability

The South has been a region of abundant, low-cost energy. In 1981, Texas and Louisiana produced almost 44 percent of the nation's crude oil and 69 percent of the natural gas. Oklahoma produced another 5 percent of the crude, and Oklahoma and New Mexico together produced another 15 percent of the gas (calculated from U.S. Department of Energy, Energy Information Administration, Office of Oil and Gas 1982). Kentucky produced almost 18 percent of the nation's coal in 1980 (calculated from U.S. Department of Energy, Energy Information Administration, Office of Coal, Nuclear, Electric and Alternate Energy Fuels 1982). In 1974 these five states were large net exporters of energy, large enough to make the South as a whole a net exporter in spite of net imports by the other eight states in the study area (Boercker et al. 1977). In addition, the area possessed 35 percent of the electrical generating capacity, 45 percent of the crude oil refining capacity, 77 percent of the natural gas processing plants, and a good to very good pipeline distribution system (Brunson and Bever 1977).

TABLE 1-2
AVERAGE RETAIL PRICE OF ENERGY TO INDUSTRIAL USERS, 1980

| | *Dollars Per Million Btu's* | | | | |
Region	*Electricity*	*Natural Gas*	*Distillate*	*Residual Fuel Oil*	*Coal*
Southeast	8.15	1.62	3.62	2.44	1.39
Southwest	7.23	1.18	3.65	2.24	1.74
New York and New Jersey	10.53	2.77	3.77	2.50	1.48
United States	8.34	1.56	3.60	2.49	1.34

SOURCE: U.S. Department of Energy, Energy Information Administration, 1980.

As Table 1-2 indicates, the South also possesses price advantages in most fuels. In 1980, average retail prices to industrial users for electricity, natural gas, and residual fuel oil were well below national averages in the Southwest, although prices in the Southeast more closely approximated national values. Compared to the industrialized Northeast, however, prices in the South overall were very favorable; in both southern regions prices for all fuels except coal were well below those for New York and New Jersey, for example.

Energy prices and availability will continue to be favorable relative to other regions. Although southern production as a percentage of U.S. production is expected to decline, the South will continue to offer relatively abundant and secure energy supplies because it possesses a significant proportion of the nation's proved reserves — 43 percent of the crude oil, 64 percent of the natural gas, 78 percent of the gas liquids, and 10 percent of the coal (Science and Public Policy Program 1982). The general pattern of relative prices is projected to continue, although regional differentials will tend to diminish with electricity prices in the Southwest and distillate prices in the Southeast experiencing particular gains (U.S. Department of Energy, Energy Information Administration 1980).

Energy production can contribute to regional economic growth in two ways. Extraction activities themselves are a basic industry.

In general, the impact of these industries on growth in the South as a whole is less substantial than the total value of output would indicate because wages are a small proportion of value added (Hoch 1980; Pagoulatos and Anschel 1981). Energy extraction activities, corporate headquarters, and services, however, have contributed very significantly to the economic base of certain limited areas such as eastern Kentucky; Houston and Dallas, Texas; the Mississippi delta region of Louisiana; and Tulsa, Oklahoma. Even though recent and projected future increases in extractive activities will continue to support economic growth and even boom conditions in certain areas of the South, most of these reserves have finite lifetimes. Depletion of fossil fuel reserves, a more cyclical response of the oil and gas industry to national economic conditions, and response to variation in world energy prices may create serious dislocations in the economies of localized areas in the near future (Federal Reserve Bank of Dallas 1982; Pagoulatos and Anschel 1981).

Energy extraction can also contribute to regional economic growth if its availability or low price attracts manufacturing. There is considerable disagreement over the role abundant supplies and low prices in the South have had on manufacturing location. Miernyk (1977), for instance, believes southern energy advantages in both price and reliability of supply may have been important to only a few very energy-intensive industries such as chemicals, primary metals, and stone/clay/glass. Hoch (1980) and Carlton (1979), however, believe energy prices are more important in a wider range of industries than energy costs per dollar of value added indicate. Since the supply disruptions of the 1970s, the availability of a secure and dependable supply has become for many industries more important than price.

Differentials in energy prices and availability are likely to become more important to industrial location in the future, but regional differences in prices are expected to decline (Rostow 1977; Hoch 1980; and Miernyk 1977). The net effect of these trends is difficult to predict. Energy availability, and perhaps price, will continue to favor the location of energy intensive industries in the South for a number of years (Hoch 1980), but the uncertainty surrounding future energy sources is so great even medium range projections have little meaning.

Other Raw Materials and Resources

The South possesses a number of raw material resources that have attracted manufacturing. Manufacturing sectors with strong raw material locational orientations include food processing, lumber products, pulp and paper, petroleum refining, petrochemicals, and primary metals (Miernyk 1977). Some of these sectors, particularly chemicals, petroleum refining, and primary metals, presently have more locational flexibility than others but are sensitive to energy prices and to the attraction of established agglomerations of related industries, many of which reflect a raw material orientation. The South possesses resources essential to most of these industries, including favorable soils, slopes, and climate for a variety of agricultural products requiring food processing; extensive forest resources managed primarily for pulp production; petrochemical feedstocks; and copper and zinc mines, plus access to the Caribbean bauxite deposits.

In the past, the South has had a greater proportion of raw material oriented industries than has the United States as a whole, reflecting the resources available and the South's past difficulty with attracting many industries not tied to immobile resources. Although today raw material oriented industries as a whole are not more important in the South than in the total United States, southern supplies of certain raw materials are very important to some industries and regions within the South (Table 1-3). Growth rates of these

TABLE 1-3
GROWTH OF RAW MATERIAL ORIENTED INDUSTRIES

Industry	Percent of U.S. Earnings	Percent Change 1969-1978	
		South	United States
Food Processing	23	3	12
Pulp and Paper	26	46	24
Chemicals	29	47	23
Petroleum Refining	36	54	41
Primary Metals	13	59	23

SOURCE: U.S. Department of Commerce, Bureau of Economic Analysis, 1980.

industries indicate that raw material resources will probably continue to contribute to manufacturing growth in the South. Domestic resources used by the chemicals, petroleum refining, and primary metals industries are subject to depletion, but the current concentrations of these industries in areas with access to water transportation and pipelines may allow them to maintain growth using foreign raw materials. The success of the Gulf Coast aluminum refining industry based on Caribbean bauxite is a case in point.

Transportation

Although transportation costs are less important than they once were because of the decline in transportation costs relative to other inputs, they are still a major factor in the locational decisions of many industries, particularly those with bulky or low value inputs or products (Smith 1971; Moriarty 1980). Poor rail and highway transportation networks along with discriminatory rate structures have been widely cited as one of the hindrances to southern industrialization prior to World War II (Watkins and Perry 1977; Serow 1981).

Since World War II, however, improvements in transportation networks, often financed with federal funds, have increased the accessibility of the South. Studies of firms locating in the South today indicate that availability of transportation is a major criterion in their choice of state or region (Moriarty 1980). Federal highway construction since 1950, combined with the shift of most freight to the highways from the railroads, opened many areas of the South, especially nonmetropolitan areas, to manufacturing. For example, a study of industrial location in nonmetropolitan Kentucky found the presence of a limited access highway increased the probability of attracting a branch plant (Cromley and Leinbach 1981).

Extensive port development, particularly along the Gulf Coast, has allowed cargo tonnage handled by these ports to increase dramatically. Waterborne imports and exports handled by Gulf ports increased by almost 600 percent between 1960 and 1979 in contrast to only 177 percent for the nation as a whole (U.S. Department of Commerce, Bureau of the Census 1980). New Orleans, Houston, and Baton Rouge were the second, third, and fourth largest U.S. ports by tonnage handled in 1976 (Greene et al. 1978). Airport construction has proceeded at a rapid pace in the South, adding to the attraction of several cities for corporate headquarters, research and development activity, and service sectors for regional or national markets. Atlanta and Dallas/Fort Worth have developed into major regional air hubs with excellent connections to the rest of the nation; Houston, New Orleans, Tampa, and Miami are also major centers. Finally, the Texas/Louisiana/Oklahoma area remains the focus of the United States petroleum and natural gas pipeline distribution system, providing many southern states with good access to oil and gas for both fuel and raw material use.

Development of Regional Markets, Agglomeration Economies, and Innovative Capacity

Southern economic and population growth are being facilitated by conditions which have been historically restricted to the Northeast and other highly industrialized areas. Among these conditions are the development of: (1) a strong internal regional market; (2) agglomeration economies; and (3) an increasing industrial innovative capacity.

Manufacturing location has become increasingly market oriented during the twentieth century; sustained economic growth of a region therefore often depends on the development of large internal markets (Pluta 1980; Moriarty 1980). As the South's regional population and economy become the largest in the nation, the national market for basic industries is increasingly located inside the region. The region thus becomes more attractive to industry because transportation and other communication costs to markets are reduced. The region becomes less dependent on exports to other regions and less susceptible to competition from other regions in the effort to attract basic industry. As a result, regional growth becomes more self-sustaining, generating growth internally rather than capturing it at the expense of other regions. The importance of this factor increases as the size of the regional market increases and as other advantages diminish.

The importance of the market as a factor in industrial location in general, and to present and future growth of the South in particular, is emphasized by many studies of both national and southern industrial location decisions that have found access to markets to be an important determinant of such decisions (Moriarty 1980). Proximity to market has been identified as particularly important for such industries as food processing, plastics fabrication, paper converting, the heavy chemicals/oil/rubber/glass complex, and others (Schmenner 1982).

The geographic concentration, or agglomeration, of manufacturing plants can bring economic benefits that cannot be obtained in more isolated locations and that contribute to a self-sustaining momentum. As more firms relocate in an area, they create additional agglomeration economies that attract additional firms. Agglomerations play an important role in maintaining a southern attractiveness to industry and become increasingly influential as other advantages, such as labor costs, diminish. Development of agglomeration economies is one of the prime determinants of regional growth in general and the growth of the South in particular (Richardson 1980; Schmenner 1982; Carlton 1979; von Boventer 1975).

Agglomeration economies include economies derived from linkages between firms and plants in the same or related industries, including flows of information and intermediate products and common reliance on the same trained labor pool and specialized services. Such economies attracted the textile machinery industry to the South on the heels of the textile industry and are responsible for the concentration of the petroleum exploration equipment manufacturing industry in the region. They also provide a continuing incentive to locate plants in the petroleum-refining/chemicals/plastics/synthetic/textiles complex in the South, when other incentives responsible for historical location decisions have disappeared.

Agglomeration economies related to the availability of a large-city infrastructure, including transportation facilities, educational facilities, urban services, and electrical utilities, have probably been more important to the overall growth of the South than have economies related to industrial linkages. Extensive infrastructure improvements in the South since World War II, largely through federal programs, have been vital to its development. Increases in population size, per capita income, and economic bases of southern cities and states have allowed them increasingly to participate in the provision of these services. The development of an adequate infrastructural base is both time consuming and expensive, but it is also cumulative and has contributed significantly to the development of the South and its ability to sustain growth.

At some point, industrial cities and regions can reach sizes where costs of concentration exceed further agglomeration economies, after which such regions lose much of their attractiveness to further development. Concentration costs include congestion, higher land and labor prices, increasing labor organization and militancy, and eventual decreasing returns to scale in the provision of infrastructure. A contributing factor to the northern decline in manufacturing in the face of rapid southern growth is a difference between the two regions in the ratio of agglomeration economies to concentration costs, as well as the costs of replacing aging infrastructure and industrial plants (Mills 1980). In several areas of the South, agglomeration economies have grown to the point where they are substantial and concentration costs are still low, creating a relatively favorable environment for growth, although cities like Houston may be regarded as having surpassed a favorable agglomeration economy to concentration cost ratio. It is probable that the ratio of agglomeration economies to concentration costs in the South generally will remain favorable for some time in the future, thereby encouraging growth. The length of this period will depend to some extent on the rate of investment in, and repair of, infrastructure and on the success of the South in managing growth.

Growth in standardized production capacity for products developed elsewhere is not associated with the same security and permanence as growth with a better balance of both innovative capacity and production capacity (Malecki 1982). Growth based on innovation is less susceptible to external control and to competition from other low cost production regions, including foreign countries. Although most of the manufacturing growth in the South has been in standardized production capacity, the innovative capacity of the South may become a more important determinant of growth as some of its resource and labor cost advantages diminish.

At the present time, research and development continues to be highly concentrated in the large metropolitan areas of the North and California (Hekman 1980; Rees 1979a; Cohen 1977; Malecki 1980). Norton and Rees (1979), Sale (1977), and Watkins and Perry (1977) are reasonably optimistic about the ability of the South to develop an innovative sector that could compete with these existing concentrations. They point to the rapid growth in the South of high technology industries and to an increase in research and development activities located in the South, hypothesizing that spinoffs from federally funded R&D and from concentrations of branch production plants can generate an innovative capability through the migration of technical personnel and entrepreneurs and the buildup of agglomeration economies. Rees (1979b) notes that the largest southern metropolitan areas — Dallas/Fort Worth and Houston — have managed to increase their innovative capacity, as suggested by the facts that most new manufacturing plants are new firms rather than branch plants and that most new branches are established by in-state firms.

The ability of the South to develop a substantial innovative capacity in the near future is questioned by others. Malecki (1980) and Cohen (1977) assert that recent growth in the Sunbelt in the high technology industries is primarily production capacity, with innovative functions still largely located elsewhere. Malecki notes that industrial R&D, the type most closely correlated with the development of new products, is also very closely correlated with the largest metropolitan areas, most of which are located in the North and California. In the southern metropolitan areas identified as having R&D concentrations in 1976,[3] Malecki (1981) found that federally funded research and development tends to dominate, with the exception of Houston, Dallas/Fort Worth, and Tulsa. Only in Huntsville, Austin, and Raleigh/Durham have federal facilities and universities attracted industrial research. According to Schmenner (1982), typical Sunbelt[4] manufacturing plants display very little or no innovation and fairly narrow production responsibilities. Thus, generation of a substantial innovative capacity in the South will be very slow in coming and will depend on the extent to which southern metropolitan areas achieve premier rank within the nation in population, access to information, and quality educational institutions.

Governmental Policies

Popular accounts of southern growth and northern stagnation have highlighted the role of governmental policies. Imbalances in the ratio of federal expenditures to federal revenues have become a source of interregional conflict, leading to characterizations such as the "Second War Between the States" (*Business Week* 1976). State and local tax policies and incentive programs are also widely perceived as having helped create a "favorable business climate" that has lured industry to southern states.

For a considerable time, the federal government has spent more money in the South and West than it has collected in tax revenue; the opposite has been the case for the Northeast and Midwest. In 1979, for example, these imbalances created an inflow of 16 billion dollars to the South and an outflow of 34 billion dollars in the Northeast and Midwest. Within the South, most states had a net inflow of federal funds (Havemann and Stanfield 1981). Alabama, Arkansas, Mississippi, Tennessee, and New Mexico had especially high spending to taxes ratios; only North Carolina and Texas experienced a net outflow.

The inequity of these imbalances has been overemphasized, however, particularly for the recent past. Geographic disparities in the flow of federal funds have been generally declining over the past 30 years. For example, while in 1979 the spending-to-tax ratio was 1.1 in the South, in 1952 the ratio was approximately 1.5 for the South as a whole and over 2.0 for selected states (Labovitz 1978). The favorable position of the South is, in part, a function of the fact that the federal income tax is progressive (Jusenius and Ledebur 1977). Southerners have lower per capita incomes and therefore pay lower per capita taxes. In 1979, federal tax receipts per capita ranged from 63 percent of the national average in Mississippi to 101 percent in Texas (Havemann and Stanfield 1981). Federal spending per capita, however, also tended to be low. It was above the national average of $2,101 in only three states (Florida, New Mexico, and Tennessee), but was less than 90 percent of the national per capita average in five southern states (Arkansas, Kentucky, Louisiana, North Carolina, and South Carolina).

Federal spending per capita in the South has been high in only a few categories (Peterson and Muller 1980). Per capita defense salary expenditures and aerospace expenditures have been high because of the large number of military bases and space program facilities in the South, but defense contracts as a whole have tended to favor the Northeast and West. Competitive bidding for goods purchased by the federal government has tended to favor the South in industries for which the South has production cost advantages. Grants-in-aid to state and local governments for public works and employment favored the South prior to the middle 1970s, but, after complaints by the North, formulas were changed to increase emphasis on the unemployment rate, largely redressing the imbalance. Despite high per capita payments for retirement programs to Florida and high per capita welfare payments to the East South-central states, per capita transfer payments for the South as a whole are very near national averages.

An inflow of federal funds can operate to stimulate regional economic development in several ways. Federal purchases from southern manufacturers increase the demand for these goods. The development of major aerospace facilities in the South has encouraged the development of high technology industry and has been a major stimulus to an increased southern innovative capacity. Salaries of federal employees and transfer payments add purchasing power to the southern market and, in fact, serve the same function as basic industry. Grants-in-aid for public works have been vital to the development of an infrastructure attractive to industry, and direct federal construction of transportation facilities such as highways and inland waterways has contributed significantly to the ability of the South to attract transport oriented industry.

Although this net inflow of federal funds has been important to the economic base of the South, observers differ over the magnitude of the effect and its importance to the South's growth. Richardson (1979), Sale (1977), and Watkins and Perry (1977) ascribe major importance to the effect of federal spending. However, Peterson and Muller (1980) and Oakland (1979) are more cautious, emphasizing the divergence between locale of spending and locale of impact within a national economy unhampered by trade barriers. The effect of the projected declines in regional disparities in dollar flows as incomes rise in the South and spending formulas change will depend on the extent to which southern development has become self-sustaining.

Many states and localities believe that economic growth may bring substantial benefits and have developed programs to attract industry. These programs are widely perceived by both the public and public leaders to contribute to the favorable business climate of many areas of the country, including the South (Boren 1980; Padda 1981). State and local taxes on industry in the South are generally below national averages and well below those in the Northeast. In 1976, state corporate income taxes on income over $25,000 in the South ranged from zero percent in Texas to 6 percent in Arkansas, Georgia, and the Carolinas (Moriarty 1980). In contrast, most other states had rates of 7 percent or above, with New York, Connecticut, Minnesota, and Arizona having rates of 10 percent or above. Unemployment insurance rates in 1979 were an average 2.7 percent of payroll in the United States, but all southern states except Alabama and Louisiana had rates under 2.2 percent (U.S. Department of Commerce, Bureau of the Census, 1980). State and local property taxes show similar regional differences. In addition to lower overall tax rates, most southern states and many localities offer additional tax incentives for new and expanding businesses, including income, property, excise, and sales tax exemptions and investment tax credits (Vaughan 1979). Although these incentives are an important element in the package of public assistance offered to firms contemplating location in the South, the initiation of such programs has invoked similar programs by competing states in the North and elsewhere. Because of the variety of programs and because a tax incentive package is often individually negotiated, the overall impact of these incentives on taxes paid remains uncertain.

In spite of the public perception that low taxes and tax incentives attract industry, the general consensus among researchers is that such business tax advantages have not by themselves played a significant role in industrial location in general or the growth of the South in particular, although they may have had a small effect on the growth of given states or localities within the South (Vaughan 1979; Pluta 1980; Kieschnick 1981; Harrison and Kanter 1978; Boren 1980; and Moriarty 1980). State and local taxes are a very small percentage of output value, and geographical variation in the amount of taxes paid is a small percentage — less than 5 to 10 percent — of locationally variable costs. Labor costs, access to markets, raw material prices, transportation costs, amenities, and infrastructure all are more important to the firm and vary more between regions, indicating choice of region is more likely to be determined by variation in these costs. Within a state or region, labor, transportation, and raw material costs are more uniform, with the result that state and local variations in taxes may be more significant; tax rates may be the deciding factor in decisions between otherwise equivalent sites (Schmenner 1982).

States and localities often offer two other types of incentives: financing assistance and labor force training. Many state and local programs, some financed in part with federal money, have been designed to increase the availability or decrease the cost of capital to firms agreeing to locate in the state or locality. Various programs make grants or loans, guarantee commercial loans, and build facilities that are then leased or sold on favorable terms (Moriarty 1980). Such incentives are available throughout the nation, although certain southern states — Alabama, Mississippi, Texas, and Oklahoma — have particularly active programs (Padda 1981). Several southern states, including Florida, North Carolina, and Kentucky, offer extensive labor force development programs outstanding in their responsiveness to industry (Schmenner 1982; Clarke and Dodson 1979).

The impact of these incentive and assistance programs on the location of industry is uncertain and has attracted little research. Such services are useful to firms, but it is unclear whether these programs actually influence locational or expansion decisions, or whether they simply provide a valued subsidy to industry without any reciprocal benefits accruing to the public. Financing is generally not a problem for branch plants of established firms because they have access to national capital markets and equity funds. However, small, independent, and high risk firms often do not have access to capital and may benefit from financial incentives. Skills levels have been lower in southern populations so that some form of training has been important to the growth of manufacturing, but many firms are willing to provide training themselves in exchange for a work force with other desirable characteristics.

In conclusion, however, it would be premature to completely discount the role of tax differentials and publically provided incentives on industrial location. Although "business climate" and many of the business-related policies and activities of government are very difficult to measure, definite perceptions about business climate exist; the perceptions themselves may be quite important to locational decisions. What may be more important than actual incentives in the formation of these favorable perceptions are the attitudes of state and local officials, as well as the local population, and their willingness to cooperate with industry in solving problems (Cobb 1982; Stafford 1982). Even though they are not by themselves important, the tax and incentive provisions included in the industrial development programs of southern states probably contribute to perceptions of a favorable business climate and therefore to industrial growth. Fisher and Hanink (1982), for example, developed a business climate index utilizing variables reflecting governmental policy, labor, and quality of life conditions. They found that states ranking in the higher quartiles were generally in the South and West, which supports the possibility of a strong role played by business climate in the growth of the South.

ATTRACTING PEOPLE

The ability of a region to attract industry is not the sole determinant of regional economic and population growth. The amenities and quality of life in a region encourage population and economic growth in three ways: by attracting the retired; by attracting labor force migrants who then create a ready supply of labor for industry; and by directly attracting firms.

The Amenities of the South

The South in general, and certain localities in particular, possess a number of amenities attractive to people. One of the major amenity-related reasons given for migration in recent years is a growing preference for smaller cities or even rural environments. The majority of Americans prefer small town living, although the proportion drops dramatically if the small town is far from a metropolitan center or if such a move involves a decrease in income (Carpenter 1980; Zuiches and Fuguitt 1976). The South, even with the largest total population, is the least metropolitanized of any region in the United States and has traditionally had a reputation for a slower, more relaxed pace of life.

Amenities related to climate, recreational opportunities, and landscape increase the attractiveness of a region and have become more important as leisure and incomes have increased. Mild winter temperatures (now that air conditioning is widely available for the muggy heat of summer) are persistently cited as a major reason for the South's growth (e.g., Graves 1976; Cebula and Vedder 1973; Jones 1975). Even the term "Sunbelt" attests to the widespread perception of the importance of climate. The mountains of northwest New Mexico, the Appalachians, the Ozarks, the Florida peninsula, and the many man-made lakes present excellent recreation opportunities and attractive landscapes. The rapid growth of these areas has been attributed at least in part to these features (Rose-man 1977).

Financial, as well as environmental, amenities may also attract people. Regional differences in personal taxes and the cost of living can be substantial. Surveys have documented the importance of these variables to many migrants, especially the retired, and employers are finding it increasingly hard to attract high salaried employees to the high income tax states of the North (Weinstein and Firestine 1978; Stevens 1980; Williams and McMillen 1980; Marfin 1981). The South continues to possess definite advantages on both counts. Even though cost of living is increasing most rapidly in southern cities (Weinstein 1981), budgets for an intermediate standard of living for a four-person family in the metropolitan South* are $1,000 to $3,000 below the U.S. metropolitan average and even below the U.S. nonmetropolitan average in most cases (U.S. Department of Commerce, Bureau of the Census 1979, p. 488). Total state and local taxes per capita in the South were in all cases lower than the national average in 1980, although they also are rising to cover new investment in infrastructure and public services (U.S. Department of Commerce, Bureau of the Census 1981).

The unique amenities that distinguish the South, however, are perhaps less important to its new, positive image than the ways in which the South has come to resemble other industrialized U.S. regions (Cobb 1982). With rising incomes, the growth of cities and metropolitan areas, and the decreased cultural differentiation from other regions brought by migration and the communications media, the South is increasingly able to offer the cultural, com-mercial, and entertainment amenities traditionally associated with the richer, more metropolitan areas of the country. In the past, officially supported racial segregation, poor educational systems, inferior public services and facilities, and unattractive, if not dilapi-dated, municipal landscapes all contributed to an image of back-wardness and poverty that deterred many potential migrants and industries. Although these problems and the old image have not entirely disappeared, concerted efforts and increased public budgets have done much to eliminate disparities between the South and other regions. Significant progress toward eliminating segregation and improving education and other public services came as business, civic, and legislative leaders, who for almost a century after the Civil War had supported a stable social hierarchy and low tax rates as the only major competitive advantages the South could offer, came to realize that racial conflict and inadequate public services were hurting continued economic growth more than they were helping (Cobb 1982).

Metropolitan, social, cultural, and public service amenities are especially important to migration decisions of scientific, professional, and managerial employees. They are not insignificant to other types of employees and to decision-makers concerned with corporate image. The importance of these factors has been underlined by Cobb (1982). He notes, for example, that Little Rock, Arkansas, which had attracted eight new plants in 1957, the year Governor Orval Faubus used National Guardsmen to block school integration, failed to capture a single new industry in the next four years. He cites a South Carolina state development staffer who "was horrified when a local official admitted to a prospective investor that much of his city's revenue came from fines on misbehaving Negroes" and a General Electric community-relations expert who asked "Where do you think the thoughts of your copywriter will be if his young-ster is one of forty-five in an overcrowded classroom presided over by some crank of a teacher who should have been retired a long time ago?"

Attracting the Retired, the Labor Force, and Industry

Although they are the least mobile of all demographic subpopu-lations, the retired are in many respects most free to respond to quality of life considerations in their choice of residence, and often are influenced by communications with friends and relatives. The influence of amenity considerations — especially climate, landscape, recreational opportunities, and a more rural environment — on migra-tion decisions of the retired to the South is apparent both from surveys of migrating retirees and from the high migration rates of this group to Florida, to the mountains of North Carolina, northern New Mexico, and northwest Arkansas, and to the warm dry regions of southern Texas and New Mexico (Plaut 1981a; Roseman 1977). Retirees often bring exogenous sources of income to a region, in the form of pensions, federal social security payments, or savings, which stimulate the economy of a region by serving as a regional economic base.

Considerable recent evidence suggests that wage earners often enter the labor force in a region for reasons primarily related to amenities rather than economic opportunities (Zuiches 1980; Plaut 1981b; Williams and McMillen 1980). Labor force migration for amenity-related reasons creates in the destination area an available supply of employees often willing to accept wages below those in less desirable areas (Wheaton 1979a). Such a labor force may strongly attract certain industrial employers.

Considerable disagreement exists on the importance of this mechanism to industrial location, particularly in the South (Plaut 1981b; Muth 1971; Graves 1976; Cebula and Vedder 1973). Much of the disagreement centers around the issue of whether, in general, people follow jobs or jobs follow people (Muth 1971; Plaut 1981b; Steinnes 1978; Greenwood 1975; Olvey 1972). Wheaton (1979b) presents evidence suggesting that there may be two subpopulations of rapidly growing cities; one in which amenities are attracting migrants who then attract industry, and another where traditional determinants of industrial location such as lower wages are attracting industry which then attracts migrants. With a few exceptions, such as Miami, San Antonio, Albuquerque, Wheaton finds that most rapidly growing southern cities fall in the category in which employment growth, rather than amenities, is driving expansion. This would be consistent with the view that the lure of jobs and the reduced social, cultural, and metropolitan disparities between the South and the rest of the nation have been more important to the migration of the work force than the pull of amenities.

Many industries, and certain functions such as management or research and development within industries, are increasingly free of locational constraints, permitting them to consider the amenities of potential sites and their attractiveness to employees. Amenities, particularly of the type found in large metropolitan areas, are most important to the ability of a firm or plant to attract and retain professional and managerial employees. Although evidence about the overall impact of amenities on industrial location decisions is not extensive, growing evidence indicates that amenity considerations are important to small entrepreneurs choosing a location for their firm, to facilities with a high proportion of professional and managerial employees, to corporations sensitive to their public image, and even to locational decisions for branch plants where cost considerations still predominate (Jones 1975; McElyea 1974; Moriarty

1980). For example, in a study of intercity moves of corporate headquarters showing a net movement to the South and the West, Burns
and Pang (1977) found such moves were more sensitive to the availability of community amenities than to costs or other business
factors.

SUMMARY

The recent rapid growth of the South is attributable to the
ability of the region to attract both people and manufacturing
capacity at a time of slow national growth in manufacturing. No
single reason, however, can be separated out as the primary cause
of the South's growth. Rather, the Sunbelt phenomenon is a result
of the convergence of a few primary, and a host of contributing,
forces – all favoring the South. The inability to isolate a few clear
causes is a result of the size of the South and its internal variation;
causes vary greatly between industries, states, and localities within
states. Although in broad perspective the details of such variation
may seem unimportant, an understanding of the complex variation
of forces within a spatial framework becomes increasingly important
as the problems of growth are identified and solutions sought. Policy,
particularly at the state and local level, is often more effective with
fewer political costs and unintended consequences if it is based on
a better understanding than that provided by averages and aggre-
gations. Although identifying the most important factors at work
for specific states or subregions within the South is impossible at
the scale of analysis of this chapter, generalizations about conditions
in the South as a whole can be made, from which analysis at local
and state levels can begin.

The continuing, steady ability of the South to attract manufacturing over the past 30 years has been the most clearly identifiable
explanation of recent growth; the recent phenomenon of a newly
resurgent South has in some respects been an artifact of sluggish
economic growth in the Northeast and the eventual absorption of
displaced agricultural labor in other sectors or regions. Although
considerable controversy exists over the reasons why the South has
attracted and continues to attract growth in manufacturing, the most
important reasons certainly include:

- lower labor costs because of lower wages for comparable skills, a plentiful labor supply, and low levels of union and labor activism;
- the development of a large regional market; and
- the growth of southern cities and the southern manufacturing sector to the point where the available infrastructure, specialized support services, pool of trained labor, and interindustry linkages attract additional industry.

Of less but still major importance, especially in localized areas, have been:

- plentiful, low cost energy supplies;
- federal spending, especially on retirement benefits, defense salaries, aerospace industries, and infrastructure such as highways;
- improved transportation networks, particularly the interstate highways; and
- abundant supplies of certain raw materials, such as agricultural and forest products and petroleum.

State and local tax rates and tax or other economic incentives are generally thought to be of minor importance to the location of industry in the region, although they do influence the selection of a site within the region and do contribute to an elusive, but important, perception of "good business climate." In sum, what is perhaps most important to the strong growth of manufacturing in the South is the gradual combination of a number of locational advantages for a set of industries with changing locational requirements.

The growing attractiveness of the South to people has been associated as much with the removal of social, cultural, and public service disparities between the South and the rest of the nation as with the pull of its amenities. Although the South has many attractive natural amenities, except for warm winters and a long warm-weather outdoor recreation season combined with plentiful water-recreation opportunities these are scarcely unique or unusual. The pulling power of local amenities has been extremely important to the growth of Florida, New Mexico, the Ozarks, and other areas. But, in general, the new image of the South in the minds of potential movers is associated more with vibrant economic growth and the removal of cultural, social, and economic disparities. Only in this context have the natural features of the South become important amenities and the regional peculiarities and differences become intriguing (Cobb 1982).

Prospects for continued long-term rapid economic and population growth depend on whether the location factors important in the past persist and the extent to which new factors develop. The South continues to possess many of its traditional advantages and has developed the large internal market and significant economies of agglomeration that provide momentum for further economic expansion. Rapid growth is therefore projected to continue for the immediate future. Changes in these variables, however, could slow or reverse the recent growth trends. Wage levels are very slowly converging toward national averages and the pool of surplus agricultural labor has disappeared, although resistance to union activity remains strong in many areas. Overall regional disparities in federal spending have been declining. Regional advantages in the cost of certain energy forms are gradually disappearing. Finally, the fact that the industrial innovative capacity of the South lags considerably behind that of the North and California makes continued industrial expansion less certain if labor and other cost advantages disappear, or if foreign competition continues to make inroads based on the same competitive advantages offered by the South.

The long-term continued growth of the South, therefore, may depend on the extent to which regional growth has, or can, become self-generating. The continued growth of regional markets and metropolitan areas, investment in public and private infrastructure and educational facilities, and the continued existence of economic benefits to further industrial concentration may all become increasingly important determinants of growth in the South.

NOTES

1. For an explanation of the differentiation between South and South*, see the footnote to Figure 1-1.

2. Detailed industry employment data were first collected by the United States Census of Population in 1920.

3. Houston, Dallas/Fort Worth, and Austin, Texas; Huntsville, Alabama; Tulsa, Oklahoma; Albuquerque, New Mexico; Knoxville, Tennessee; Orlando, Florida; and Raleigh/Durham, North Carolina.

4. South Atlantic, East South Central, West South Central, and Mountain census regions.

REFERENCES

Advisory Commission on Intergovernmental Relations. 1980. *Regional Growth: Historic Perspective*. Publication Number A-74. Washington, D.C.: ACIR, June.

Birch, David L. 1980. "Regional Differences in Factor Costs: Labor, Land, Capital, and Transportation." In *Alternatives to Confrontation: A National Policy Toward Regional Change*, edited by Victor L. Arnold, pp. 125-156. Lexington, Massachusetts: Lexington Books, D. C. Heath.

Bluestone, Barry, and Bennet Harrison. 1982. *The Deindustrialization of America*. New York: Basic Books.

Boercker, F. D., and R. M. Davis, F. G. Goff, S. S. Olson, D. C. Parzyck. 1977. *Regional Characterization Report for the National Coal Utilization Assessment*. Regional Studies Program. Oak Ridge, Tennessee: Oak Ridge National Laboratory.

Boren, David L. 1980. "The Sunbelt Myth — Blessing or Curse?" *Review of Regional Economics and Business* 5(4): 18-21.

Browne, Lynn E. 1978. "How Different Are Regional Wages?" *New England Economic Review* January/February: 33-43.

Brunson, E. Evan, and Thomas D. Bever. 1977. *Southern Growth Trends, 1970-1976*, prepared for The White House Conference on Balanced National Growth and Economic Development. Research Triangle Park, North Carolina: Southern Growth Policies Board.

Burns, Leland S., and Wing Ning Pang. 1977. "Big Business in the Big City: Corporate Headquarters in the CBD." *Urban Affairs Quarterly* 12: 533-44.

Business Week. 1976. "Special Report: The Second War Between the States," unpaged reprint. May 17.

Carlton, Dennis W. 1979. "Why Do New Firms Locate Where They Do: An Economic Model." In *Interregional Movements and Regional Growth*, edited by William C. Wheaton, COUPE Papers on Public Economics, 13-50. Washington, D.C.: The Urban Institute.

Carpenter, Edwin H. 1980. "Retention of Metropolitan-to-Nonmetropolitan Labor-Force Migrants." In *New Directions in Urban-Rural Migration: The Population Turnaround in Rural America*, edited by David L. Brown and John M. Wardwell, pp. 213-32. New York: Academic Press.

Cebula, Richard J., and Richard K. Vedder. 1973. "A Note on Migration, Economic Opportunity, and the Quality of Life." *Journal of Regional Science* 13: 205-11.

Clarke, Susan E., and Mary L. Dodson. 1979. "Growth Management Innovation: Regional Distinctions." *The Environmental Professional* 1: 101-109.

Clay, James W., and Alfred W. Stuart. 1982. "Uneven Growth: Southern Population Change at the County Level." *Economic Review* 67(6): 42-49.

Cobb, James C. 1982. *The Selling of the South*. Baton Rouge: Louisiana State University Press.

Cohen, Robert B. 1977. "Multinational Corporations, International Finance, and the Sunbelt." In *The Rise of the Sunbelt Cities*, edited by David C. Perry and Alfred J. Watkins, Urban Affairs Annual Reviews, Vol. 14, pp. 211-26. Beverly Hills: Sage.

Cromley, Robert G., and Thomas R. Leinbach. 1981. "The Pattern and Impact of the Filter Down Process in Nonmetropolitan Kentucky." *Economic Geography* 57: 208-23.

Federal Reserve Bank of Dallas. 1982. "Business Cycle Hits the Oil and Gas Industry." *DallasFed*. July.

Fisher, James, and Dean M. Hanink. 1982. "Business Climate: Behind the Geographic Shift of American Manufacturing." *Economic Review* 67(6): 20-31.

Garn, Harvey A., and Larry C. Ledebur. 1982. "Congruencies and Conflicts in Regional and Industrial Policies." In *Regional Dimensions of Industrial Policy*, edited by Michael E. Bell and Paul S. Lande, pp. 47-80. Lexington, Massachusetts: Lexington Books.

Graves, Philip E. 1976. "A Reexamination of Migration, Economic Opportunity, and the Quality of Life." *Journal of Regional Science* 16: 107-12.

Greene, D. L., T. P. O'Connor, P. D. Patterson, A. B. Rose, and D. B. Shonka. 1978. *Regional Transportation Energy Conservation Data Book*. Edition 1. Oak Ridge, Tennessee: Oak Ridge National Laboratory.

Greenwood, M. J. 1975. "A Simultaneous-Equation Model of Urban Growth and Migration." *Journal of the American Statistical Association* 70: 797-810.

Hansen, Niles. Forthcoming. "The New International Division of Labor and Manufacturing Decentralization in the United States." *Review of Regional Studies*.

Harrison, Bennett, and Sandra Kanter. 1978. "The Political Economy of State 'Job Creation' Business Incentives." In *Revitalizing the Northeast: Prelude to an Agenda*, edited by George Sternlieb and J. W. Hughes, pp. 247-78. New Brunswick, New Jersey: Center for Urban Policy Research.

Havemann, Joel, and Rochelle L. Stanfield. 1981. "'Neutral' Federal Policies are Reducing Frostbelt-Sunbelt Spending Imbalances." *National Journal* 13 (February 7): 233-36.

Hekman, John S. 1980. "The Future of High Technology Industry in New England: A Case Study of Computers." *New England Economic Review* January/February: 5-17.

Hekman, John S., and Alan Smith. 1982. "Survey of Location Decisions in the South." *Economic Review* Federal Reserve Bank of Atlanta. 67 (June): 6-19.

Hoch, Irving. 1980. "Role of Energy in the Regional Distribution of Economic Activity." In *Alternatives to Confrontation: A National Policy toward Regional Change*, edited by Victor L. Arnold, pp. 227-326. Lexington, Massachusetts: Lexington Books, D. C. Heath.

Jones, Robert R. 1975. "Sites for Scientists." *Industrial Research* 17(7): 57-60.

Jusenius, C. L., and L. C. Ledebur. 1977. "A Myth in the Making: The Southern Economic Challenge and Northern Economic Decline." In *The Economics of Southern Growth*, edited by E. Blaine Liner and Lawrence K. Lynch, pp. 131-73. Research Triangle Park, North Carolina: Southern Growth Policies Board.

Kieschnick, Michael. 1981. *Taxes and Growth: Business Incentives and Economic Development*. Washington, D.C.: Council of State Planning Agencies.

Labovitz, I. M. 1978. As cited in Advisory Commission on Intergovernmental Relations, 1980. *Regional Growth: Historic Perspective*, pp. 68-69. Washington, D.C.: Advisory Commission on Intergovernmental Relations.

Malecki, Edward J. 1980. "Dimensions of R&D Location in the United States." *Research Policy* 9: 2-22.

_____. 1981. "Product Cycles, Innovation Cycles, and Regional Economic Change." *Technological Forecasting and Social Change* 19: 291-306.

_____. 1982. "Towards a Model of Regional Economic Change and Technical Change." Paper prepared for presentation at the meetings of the Mid-Continent Regional Science Association, Vail, Colorado, June.

Marfin, Gary C. 1981. "State-Local Tax Differentials and Economic Development in the South." In *Report of the Task Force on The Southern Economy*, Appendix B, pp. B-1 to B-7. Research Triangle Park, North Carolina: Southern Growth Policies Board.

McElyea, J. Richard. 1974. "Setting Your Sights on R & D Sites." *Industrial Research* 16(May): 46-48.

McKenzie, Richard B. 1979. *Restrictions on Business Mobility: A Study in Political Rhetoric and Economic Reality*. Washington, D.C.: American Enterprise Institute for Public Policy Research.

Miernyk, William H. 1977. "Rising Energy Prices and Regional Economic Development." *Growth and Change* 8: 2-7.

Mills, Edwin S. 1980. "Population Redistribution and the Use of Land and Energy Resources." In *Population Redistribution and Public Policy*, edited by Brian J. L. Berry and Lester P. Silverman, pp. 50-69. Washington, D.C.: National Academy of Sciences, National Research Council.

Moriarty, Barry M., ed., 1980. *Industrial Location and Community Development*. Chapel Hill: University of North Carolina Press.

Muth, Richard F. 1971. "Migration: Chicken or Egg?" *Southern Economic Journal* 37: 295-306.

Norton, R. D., and J. Rees. 1979. "The Product Cycle and the Spatial Decentralization of American Manufacturing." *Regional Studies* 13: 141-51.

Oakland, William H. 1979. "Alternative Models for Assessing Regional Public Policy Impacts." In *Interregional Movements and Regional Growth*, edited by William C. Wheaton, COUPE Papers on Public Economics, pp. 109-56. Washington, D.C.: The Urban Institute.

Olvey, L. D. 1972. "Regional Growth and Interregional Migration – Their Pattern of Interaction." *Review of Regional Studies* Winter: 139-63.

Padda, Kuldarshan. 1981. "Report Card on the States." *Inc.* October: 90-98.

Pagoulatos, Angelos, and Kurt R. Anschel. 1981. "An I-O Study of the Economic Structure of Appalachian Kentucky." *Growth and Change* 12(10): 2-8.

Peterson, George E., and Thomas Muller. 1980. "Regional Impact of Federal Tax and Spending Policies." In *Alternatives to Confrontation: A National Policy toward Regional Change*, edited by Victor L. Arnold, pp. 207-24.

Lexington, Massachusetts.: Lexington Books, D. C. Heath.

Plaut, Thomas R. 1981a. "Migration Trends of the Elderly in the United States and the Southwest." *Texas Business Review* May-June: 105-108.

———. 1981b. *Economic Base, Labor Force Migration and Regional Employment Growth in the United States.* Publication Number BP-81-8. Austin: University of Texas, Bureau of Business Research.

Pluta, Joseph E. 1980. "Taxes and Industrial Location." *Texas Business Review* January/February: 1-6.

Rees, John. 1979a. "Technological Change and Regional Shifts in American Manufacturing." *Professional Geographer* 31: 45-54.

———. 1979b. "Regional Industrial Shifts in the U.S. and the Internal Generation of Manufacturing in Growth Centers of the Southwest." In *Interregional Movements and Regional Growth*, edited by William C. Wheaton, COUPE Papers on Public Economics, pp. 51-74. Washington, D.C.: The Urban Institute.

Richardson, Harry W. 1979. *Regional Economics.* Urbana: University of Illinois Press.

———. 1980. "Polarization Reversal in Developing Countries." *Papers of the Regional Science Association* 45: 67-85.

Roseman, Curtis C. 1977. *Changing Migration Patterns Within the United States.* Resource Papers for College Geography No. 77-2. Washington, D.C.: Association of American Geographers.

Rostow, Walt W. 1977. "Regional Change in the Fifth Kondratieff Upswing." In *The Rise of the Sunbelt Cities*, edited by David C. Perry and Alfred J. Watkins, Urban Affairs Annual Reviews, Vol. 14, pp. 83-103. Beverly Hills: Sage.

Sale, Kirkpatrick. 1977. "Six Pillars of the Southern Rim." In *The Fiscal Crisis of American Cities*, edited by R. E. Alcaly and D. Mirmelstein, pp. 165-80. New York: Vintage.

Schmenner, Roger W. 1982. *Making Business Location Decisions.* Englewood Cliffs, New Jersey: Prentice-Hall.

Science and Public Policy Program. 1982. *Southern Regional Environmental Assessment: Environmental Status Report.* Washington, D.C.: Environmental Protection Agency, Office of Exploratory Research.

Serow, William J. 1981. "An Economic Approach to Population Change in the South." In *The Population of the South: Structure and Change in Social Demographic Context*, edited by Dudley L. Poston, Jr. and Robert H. Weller, pp. 198-226. Austin: University of Texas Press.

Smith, David M. 1971. *Industrial Location.* New York: John Wiley and Sons.

Stafford, Howard A. 1982. "The Effects of Environmental Regulations on Industrial Location in the United States." Paper presented at the Association of American Geographers/International Geographical Union Symposium on Industrial Systems, San Antonio, April 1982.

Steinnes, Donald N. 1978. "Causality and Migration: A Statistical Resolution of the 'Chicken or Egg Fowl-up.'" *Southern Economic Journal* 45: 218-26.

Stevens, Joe B. 1980. "The Demand for Public Goods as a Factor in the Non-metropolitan Migration Turnaround." In *New Directions in Urban-Rural*

Migration: The Population Turnaround in Rural America, edited by David L. Brown and John M. Wardwell, pp. 115-36. New York: Academic Press.

U.S. Department of Commerce, Bureau of Economic Analysis. 1980. *Regional Economic Projections*. Washington, D.C.: Bureau of Economic Analysis.

U.S. Department of Commerce, Bureau of the Census. 1923. *1920 Census of Population, Composition and Characteristics by State*. Washington, D.C.: Government Printing Office.

———. 1933. *1930 Census of Population, Composition and Characteristics by State*. Washington, D.C.: Government Printing Office.

———. 1943. *1940 Census of Population: Characteristics of the Population*. Washington, D.C.: Government Printing Office.

———. 1952. *1950 Census of Population: Characteristics of the Population*. Washington, D.C.: Government Printing Office.

———. 1963. *1960 Census of Population: Characteristics of the Population*. Washington, D.C.: Government Printing Office.

———. 1973. *1970 Census of Population: Characteristics of the Population*. Washington, D.C.: Government Printing Office.

———. 1975. *Historical Statistics of the United States, Colonial Times to 1970*. Part 1. Washington, D.C.: Government Printing Office.

———. 1979. *Statistical Abstract of the United States: 1979*. Washington, D.C.: Government Printing Office.

———. 1980. *Statistical Abstract of the United States: 1980*. Washington, D.C.: Government Printing Office.

———. 1981. *Statistical Abstract of the United States: 1981*. Washington, D.C.: Government Printing Office.

U.S. Department of Energy, Energy Information Administration. 1980. "Series B Mid-Range Mid-World Oil Price Projections." Unpublished data.

U.S. Department of Energy, Energy Information Administration, Office of Coal, Nuclear, Electric, and Alternate Fuels. 1982. *Coal Production – 1980*. Washington, D.C.: Government Printing Office.

U.S. Department of Energy, Energy Information Administration, Office of Oil and Gas. 1982. *U.S. Crude Oil, Natural Gas, and Natural Gas Liquids Reserves: 1981 Annual Report*. Washington, D.C.: Government Printing Office.

Vaughan, Roger J. 1979. *State Taxation and Economic Development*. Washington, D.C.: Council of State Planning Agencies.

von Boventer, Edwin. 1975. "Regional Growth Theory." *Urban Studies* 12: 1-29.

Watkins, Alfred J. 1980. "From a Colony for Northern Industry to a Battleground in an Economic War." *The Texas Observer* October 3: 3-9, 22.

Watkins, Alfred J., and David C. Perry. 1977. "Regional Change and the Impact of Uneven Urban Development." In *The Rise of the Sunbelt Cities*, edited by David C. Perry and Alfred J. Watkins, Urban Affairs Annual Reviews, Vol. 14, pp. 19-54. Beverly Hills: Sage.

Weinstein, Bernard L. 1981. "The Southern Economy in the 1980s: A Likely Scenario." In *Report of the Task Force on The Southern Economy*.

Appendix B, pp. 12-13. Research Triangle Park, North Carolina: Southern Growth Policies Board.

Weinstein, Bernard L., and Robert E. Firestine. 1978. *Regional Growth and Decline in the United States: The Rise of the Sunbelt and the Decline of the Northeast.* New York: Praeger.

Wheaton, William C. 1979a. "Introduction." In *Interregional Movements and Regional Growth,* edited by William C. Wheaton, COUPE Papers on Public Economics, pp. 1-12. Washington, D.C.: The Urban Institute.

———. 1979b. "Metropolitan Growth, Unemployment, and Interregional Factor Mobility." In *Interregional Movements and Regional Growth,* edited by William C. Wheaton, COUPE Papers on Public Economics, pp. 237-52. Washington, D.C.: The Urban Institute.

Williams, James D., and David Byron McMillen. 1980. "Migration Decision Making among Nonmetropolitan-Bound Migrants." In *New Directions in Urban-Rural Migration: The Population Turnaround in Rural America,* edited by David L. Brown and John M. Wardwell, pp. 189-212. New York: Academic Press.

Zuiches, James J. 1980. "Residential Preferences in Migration Theory." In *New Directions in Urban-Rural Migration: The Population Turnaround in Rural America,* edited by David L. Brown and John M. Wardwell, pp. 163-88. New York: Academic Press.

Zuiches, James J., and Glenn V. Fuguitt. 1976. "Residential Preferences and Mobility Expectations." Paper presented at the Annual Meetings, American Sociological Association, New York, August.

2   *Anticipating Future*
Growth in the Sunbelt
Thomas E. James, Jr.

INTRODUCTION

In the past decade, a major shift has taken place in the distribution of population, centers of industrial development, and income in the United States. Prior to the 1970s, the Northeast region had the greatest concentration of population and was the location of most industrial activity. However, this is no longer the case. The southern tier of states commonly known as the Sunbelt now claims that distinction.[1]

As discussed in Chapter 1 (Roberts and Butler 1983), controversy continues to characterize the discussion as to why this phenomenal growth in the Sunbelt is taking place and whether or not it is likely to continue in the future. Explanations for this growth include: (1) low labor costs, plentiful labor supply, and few unions; (2) the development of a large regional market; (3) ample, low cost energy; (4) availability of raw materials; (5) high levels of federal

The Sunbelt has been the focus of an Integrated Environmental Assessment conducted by the Science and Public Policy Program of the University of Oklahoma over the past two years. The author wishes to acknowledge the contribution of other members of the research team to the development of this chapter: Michael D. Devine (Project Director), Basil G. Achilladelis, Steven C. Ballard, Michael A. Chartock, Elizabeth M. Gunn, Richard L. Johnson, Karen J. Selland, and particularly, Rebecca S. Roberts who was responsible for much of the original analysis.

spending; (6) low taxes and cheap land; (7) climate; and (8) positive perceptions about the amenities and the quality of life in the South.

The rate of future growth and development in the South depends, in large part, on the degree to which the factors discussed in the previous chapter continue to operate in the Sunbelt. Current projections indicate that the rapid growth and development of this region of the country is expected to continue:

- the South is projected[2] to add about 20 million people to its population over the next 30 years, representing 42 percent of the total national increase;
- the growth of employment opportunities in the South is expected to parallel population growth. Between 1978 and 2010, real dollar earnings[3] and employment are projected to rise 214 and 53 percent respectively, compared to 167 and 37 percent for the nation. By 2010 the South will account for 28 percent of total U.S. earnings and provide 30 percent of the jobs in the country; and
- the growth of employment opportunities, particularly jobs in higher wage industries, is projected to increase the economic well-being of southerners. Per capita incomes traditionally have lagged behind national averages. However, they are expected to increase about 100 percent by 2010 and reach 95 percent of the U.S. average.

If these projections are accurate, the states in the Sunbelt face increasing requirements to manage this growth and development in ways that will maximize positive impacts on the quality of life while minimizing negative consequences, such as environmental degradation, and inadequate social services. This chapter describes the historical and projected trends in population, employment, industrial development, and income in the Sunbelt. Information about these trends is necessary in order to anticipate potential future problems and develop growth management strategies to successfully alleviate these problems. The remaining chapters discuss some of the issues related to growth management in the Sunbelt.

POPULATION

Overall Growth of the Sunbelt

As indicated by the data presented in Table 2-1, the Sunbelt has been growing very rapidly in recent years; population increased 22 percent between 1970 and 1980 — a period during which the

TABLE 2-1

REGIONAL DISTRIBUTION OF POPULATION 1960-2000

(thousands)

Region[a]	1960	1970	1980	1990	2000	2010	Absolute Change 1970-1980	Percent Change 1970-1980	Absolute Change 1980-2010	Percent Change 1980-2010
Southeast	27,884	31,856	38,860	42,307	46,636	50,621	7,004	22	11,761	30
Southwest	17,902	20,336	25,043	27,563	30,639	33,288	4,707	23	8,245	33
Sunbelt	45,786	52,192	63,903	69,870	77,275	83,909	11,711	22	20,006	31
Northeast	54,815	60,660	61,882	63,667	64,929	66,151	1,222	4	4,270	7
Northcentral	50,306	55,289	57,508	61,047	63,707	65,904	2,219	4	8,396	15
West	28,415	35,071	43,209	48,395	53,935	58,838	8,138	23	15,629	36
U.S.	179,323	203,212	226,505	232,979	259,846	274,803	23,293	11	48,298	21

[a]For a list of the states included in each region, see Appendix.

SOURCE: Compiled from U.S. Department of Commerce, Bureau of the Census 1981, pp. 10-11; U.S. Department of Commerce, Bureau of Economic Analysis 1980.

39

nation as a whole grew only 11 percent. Only the West grew at a slightly faster rate of 23 percent. On the other hand, the North-eastern and Northcentral regions grew at a rate of only about 4 percent. This pattern of relative regional growth is expected to continue in the future, although annual growth is projected to decline slightly. Between 1980 and 2010, the Sunbelt is expected to continue to grow more rapidly (31 percent) than any region except the West (36 percent).

In absolute terms, the South is growing faster than any other region. From 1970 to 1980, the South added 11.7 million people — 1.4 times more people than the West, 5 times more people than the Northcentral region and almost 10 times more people than the Northeast. The increase in the South represents 50 percent of total U.S. population growth during this time. As a result of these trends, the South has moved in rank from the third largest of the four regions in 1960 to the largest region in 1980 (Figure 2-1).

By 2010, 30 percent of the total U.S. population is expected to reside in the South. From 1980 to 2010, the South is expected to add just over 20 million new residents. This is 42 percent of the total national increase and 30 percent more than the West, the region

Figure 2-1: Regional Population as a Percentage of the U.S. Total

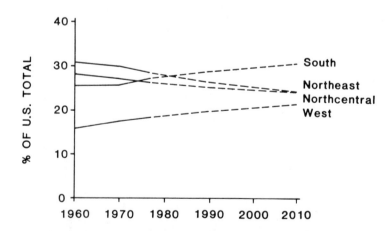

Source: Compiled from U.S. Department of Commerce, Bureau of the Census 1981, 10-11; U.S. Department of Commerce, Bureau of Economic Analysis 1980.

projected to have the next largest population increase. Although the Southwest is growing at a faster rate than the Southeast, absolute growth in the Southeast is greater because of its larger initial base.

Growth Within the Sunbelt

Individual states within the South are growing at widely varying rates, but from 1970 to 1980 all grew more rapidly than the U.S. average of 11 percent (Table 2-2). Florida's 44 percent growth rate was four times the national average; New Mexico (28 percent) and Texas (27 percent) were the next fastest growing Sunbelt states.

These trends are significant departures from previous patterns of population growth. Most of the Sunbelt had experienced very slow growth for decades prior to 1970; generally, all southern states except Florida and Texas had growth rates lower than the national average during the three decades from 1940 to 1970. Oklahoma, Arkansas, and Mississippi actually experienced population losses during some of these decades. However, beginning in the late 1960s population growth rates in the South began to increase dramatically and to surpass national averages.

In most southern states, growth rates from 1980 to 2010 are projected to continue to be greater than the national average but less than during 1970 to 1980. Florida is projected to grow at a rate of two and three times the U.S. average, and Texas and New Mexico are projected to grow at one to two times the U.S. average. Only Arkansas and Alabama are projected to grow at rates below the national average.

Over the next 30 years, Florida and Texas, the states with the highest projected growth rates, are expected also to receive most of the absolute increase in population. During this period, Florida's population is projected to increase by approximately 4.4 million people and account for 37 percent of the growth in the Southeast. Texas, with an increase of 5.7 million people, is expected to be responsible for 69 percent of the growth in the Southwest region. Georgia, North Carolina, Tennessee, and Louisiana also are expected to experience large population increases.

Two factors contribute to regional population growth — net migration and natural increase.[4] The major reason for the change in population growth rates was a reversal of migration patterns. For

TABLE 2-2
TOTAL POPULATION BY STATE FOR THE SUNBELT
(thousands)

Region/State	1960	1970	1980	1990	2000	2010	Absolute Change 1970-1980	Percent Change 1970-1980	Absolute Change 1980-2010	Percent Change 1980-2010
Southeast										
Alabama	3,267	3,444	3,890	4,056	4,251	4,483	446	13	593	15
Florida	4,952	6,789	9,740	11,114	12,683	14,142	2,951	44	4,402	45
Georgia	3,943	4,590	5,464	5,715	6,251	6,706	874	19	1,242	23
Kentucky	3,038	3,219	3,661	3,983	4,279	4,548	442	14	887	24
Mississippi	2,178	2,217	2,521	2,709	2,981	3,229	304	14	708	28
North Carolina	4,556	5,082	5,874	6,287	6,871	7,380	792	16	1,506	26
South Carolina	2,383	2,591	3,119	3,344	3,672	4,033	528	20	914	29
Tennessee	3,567	3,924	4,591	5,098	5,648	6,100	667	17	1,509	33
Total	27,885	31,856	38,860	42,307	46,636	50,621	7,004	22	11,761	30
Southwest										
Arkansas	1,786	1,923	2,286	2,361	2,514	2,680	363	19	394	17
Louisiana	3,257	3,641	4,204	4,539	4,901	5,253	563	16	1,049	25
New Mexico	951	1,016	1,300	1,422	1,537	1,627	284	28	327	25
Oklahoma	2,328	2,559	3,025	3,270	3,557	3,810	466	18	785	26
Texas	9,580	11,197	14,228	15,972	18,130	19,915	3,031	27	5,687	40
Total	17,902	20,336	25,043	27,563	30,639	33,288	4,707	23	8,245	33

SOURCE: Compiled from U.S. Department of Commerce, Bureau of the Census 1981, 10-11; U.S. Department of Commerce, Bureau of Economic Analysis 1980.

decades prior to 1955, the South was a region of net outmigration. From 1955 to 1970, significant migration into Florida and Texas resulted in the South being a region of net inmigration (Morrison 1980). To a lesser degree, Georgia and Oklahoma experienced a net inmigration during this earlier period. During the decade of the 1970s, however, all of the Sunbelt states had a net inmigration.

Inmigration is not the only source of southern population growth — the South traditionally has had high rates of natural increase. In 1979, the South had a higher birth rate and lower death rate than any other region but the West (U.S. Department of Commerce, Bureau of the Census 1981). As a result, only in Florida has inmigration been responsible for more than half of the total population increase. Although natural increases will continue to be an important component of population change, rates of natural increase rapidly are approaching national averages. Age adjusted fertility and mortality rates already are similar to, or lower than, the U.S. average (Poston, Serow, and Weller 1981).

Metropolitan and Nonmetropolitan Growth

One of the characteristics of the population changes that took place prior to 1970 was the dominating pattern of rapid metropolitan and slow or even negative nonmetropolitan growth. This pattern held in all major U.S. regions from 1960 to 1970, with the pattern being more pronounced in the South and West. Since 1970, metropolitan growth rates have decreased and nonmetropolitan growth rates have increased in all regions. However, the reversal occurred to a much greater extent in the Northeastern, Northcentral, and Western regions than in the South (U.S. Department of Commerce, Bureau of the Census 1981).

In contrast, the South is experiencing substantial growth in both metropolitan and nonmetropolitan counties, with metropolitan areas having the highest rates and receiving the greatest numbers of new residents. Suburban counties within metropolitan areas are receiving the preponderance of metropolitan growth. Within the nonmetropolitan class of counties, most growth in absolute terms is occurring around urban centers with populations of 2,500 to 25,000 (Berry and Dahmann 1980). Growth also tends to be localized in nonmetropolitan counties surrounding metropolitan areas.

Not all Sunbelt states follow the pattern typical of the South as a whole. Kentucky, on the border of the northern manufacturing belt, follows the metropolitan outmigration and nonmetropolitan inmigration typical of the North (Morrill 1979). The delta states of Mississippi and Louisiana exhibit the metropolitan inmigration and nonmetropolitan outmigration typical of the pre-1970 South.

The continued high growth rates in metropolitan areas can result in a variety of impacts, including: increased demands for social services; requirements for expanded transportation systems; increased demand for resources such as raw materials for construction and industrial use, water for drinking, parks and recreational areas; air pollution due to increased automobile use; and the need for expanded waste treatment capacity, including solid waste disposal sites and sewage treatment facilities. The nonmetropolitan areas are also continuing to grow and will experience the same types of impacts, although to a lesser degree. However, nonmetropolitan areas may not have a well-developed institutional capacity to deal with these impacts. Thus, both metropolitan and nonmetropolitan areas in the Sunbelt could face serious growth management issues in the future.

EMPLOYMENT

Total Employment

Employment trends are very similar to population trends, and employment in the Sunbelt contrasts sharply with the pattern for the Northeast and Northcentral regions, and with the nation as a whole (Table 2-3). The growth rate of southern employment from 1969 to 1978 was 29 percent as compared to 18 percent for the nation, 13 percent for the Northcentral region, and 7 percent for the Northeast. Only the West had a growth rate (32 percent) greater than the South. However, the South increased its total number of jobs to over six million, the largest absolute increase of any region. As a result, the South has moved from third among the four regions in 1969 to second in 1978; it is projected to surpass the Northeast by 1985. Employment grew most rapidly in Florida, Texas, and New Meixco; Florida and Texas together received 45 percent of the increase in jobs. With the exception of Florida,

TABLE 2-3

EMPLOYMENT BY REGION AND STATE, 1969-2010

(thousands)

Region/State[a]	1969	1978	1990	2000	2010	Absolute Change 1969-1978	Percent Change 1969-1978	Absolute Change 1978-2010	Percent Change 1978-2010
Southeast									
Alabama	1,304	1,584	1,918	2,073	2,193	280	22	609	38
Florida	2,642	3,808	4,982	5,673	6,207	1,166	44	2,399	63
Georgia	1,984	2,429	2,912	3,171	3,374	445	22	945	39
Kentucky	1,213	1,484	1,916	2,112	2,252	271	22	768	52
Mississippi	812	1,008	1,269	1,445	1,589	196	24	581	58
North Carolina	2,288	2,749	3,312	3,620	3,837	461	20	1,088	40
South Carolina	1,094	1,338	1,694	1,898	2,062	244	22	724	54
Tennessee	1,618	2,029	2,643	2,909	3,121	411	25	1,092	54
Total	12,956	16,467	20,644	22,900	24,634	3,511	27	8,167	50
Southwest									
Arkansas	725	931	1,128	1,237	1,323	206	28	392	42
Louisiana	1,346	1,699	2,176	2,428	2,637	353	26	938	55
New Mexico	370	521	660	730	784	151	41	263	51
Oklahoma	998	1,268	1,574	1,726	1,850	270	27	582	46
Texas	4,620	6,235	8,140	9,252	10,146	1,615	35	3,911	63
Total	8,059	10,654	13,678	15,372	16,740	2,595	32	6,086	57

continued

45

TABLE 2-3, Continued

Region/State[a]	1969	1978	1990	2000	2010	Absolute Change 1969-1978	Percent Change 1969-1978	Absolute Change 1978-2010	Percent Change 1978-2010
Sunbelt	21,105	27,121	34,322	38,272	41,374	6,016	29	14,253	53
Northeast	26,210	27,970	31,644	32,338	32,905	1,760	7	4,935	18
Northcentral	23,424	26,545	31,088	32,505	33,613	3,121	13	7,068	27
West	14,767	19,492	24,932	27,828	30,103	4,725	32	10,611	54
Total U.S.	85,416	101,928	121,986	130,943	137,995	15,712	18	36,867	37

[a]For a list of the states included in each region, see Appendix.

SOURCE: Calculated from U.S. Department of Commerce, Bureau of Economic Analysis 1980.

46

employment grew more slowly in the Southeast than it did in the Southwest.

These general trends are expected to continue through 2010. The South is projected to continue to have the second highest employment growth rate in the nation and to add the greatest absolute number of jobs (14.3 million). This would represent 39 percent of the increase in U.S. employment. Employment growth within the Sunbelt states is projected to continue to occur at a rate greater than that for the United States. Texas and Florida are expected to grow most rapidly and to add the most jobs. In addition, the states of the Southeast are expected to reverse this pattern of low growth rates; several of these states — Kentucky, Mississippi, South Carolina, and Tennessee — are expected to increase employment levels and experience the more rapid growth typical of the South as a whole.

Manufacturing Employment

The primary impetus for the rapid growth in total employment in the South is manufacturing employment. In the nation, growth of manufacturing employment has been slow; only 2 percent between 1969 and 1978 (U.S. Department of Commerce, Bureau of Economic Analysis 1980). However, the shifts in manufacturing employment among regions have been dramatic. Between 1969 and 1978, manufacturing employment in the Northeast declined by 12 percent, while in the South it increased by 16 percent. These trends are expected to continue.

Over the next 30 years, manufacturing employment in the Sunbelt is expected to increase by 59 percent compared to a 26 percent increase for the United States and a 5 percent decrease for the Northeast (Table 2-4). The South is projected to move from third in manufacturing in 1978 to first in 2010, with 32 percent of all U.S. manufacturing employment. Clearly, the traditional stereotypes of an industrial Northeast and rural South do not reflect current and future realities.

All the Sunbelt states are projected to increase manufacturing employment more rapidly than the United States as a whole, with increases of more than 80 percent expected in Louisiana, New Mexico, Oklahoma, and Texas. Absolute increases will be highest

TABLE 2-4
CHANGE IN MANUFACTURING EMPLOYMENT, 1978-2010
(thousands)

Region/State[a]	Employment		Absolute Change	Percent Change
	1978	2010	1978-2010	
Southeast				
Alabama	375	521	146	39
Florida	431	699	268	62
Georgia	523	667	144	28
Kentucky	298	442	144	48
Mississippi	241	428	187	78
North Carolina	814	1,091	277	34
South Carolina	395	588	193	49
Tennessee	532	799	267	50
Total	3,609	5,235	1,626	45
Southwest				
Arkansas	222	312	90	41
Louisiana	213	422	209	98
New Mexico	35	64	29	83
Oklahoma	177	334	157	89
Texas	978	1,932	954	98
Total	1,624	3,065	1,441	89
Sunbelt	5,233	8,300	3,067	59
Northeast	6,507	5,801	− 256	− 4
Northcentral	6,582	7,478	896	14
West	3,024	4,701	1,677	56
Total U.S.	20,896	26,280	5,381	26

[a]For a list of states included in each region, see Appendix.

SOURCE: Calculated from U.S. Department of Commerce, Bureau of Economic Analysis 1980.

in Texas, North Carolina, Tennessee, Florida, and Louisiana. Together, these five states are projected to receive over one-third of the total increase in U.S. manufacturing employment with Texas alone accounting for almost 20 percent.

INDUSTRIAL DEVELOPMENTS[5]

General Trends

Industrial earnings in real dollars are projected to grow more rapidly between 1978 and 2010 in the Sunbelt (214 percent) than in the United States as a whole (167 percent) or any other major U.S. region (U.S. Department of Commerce, Bureau of Economic Analysis 1980). In absolute terms, earnings in the Sunbelt are projected to grow from 211 billion dollars to 661 billion, a change equal to about one-half the total earnings of the United States in 1978. Trends in the two Sunbelt regions are similar. Earnings in the Southeast are projected to grow from 123 billion to 381 billion dollars (209 percent) and in the Southwest from 87 to 280 billion dollars (221 percent).

When changes in industrial earnings are broken down by major industrial sectors, it is apparent that almost all sectors are projected to grow more rapidly in the South than in the United States (Tables 2-5 and 2-6). Among the three sectors of manufacturing, mining, and agriculture – the "basic" sectors supplying the impetus for growth in the remaining "service" sectors – earnings in manufacturing in both regions and in mining in the Southeast are growing more rapidly than in the total United States. Agriculture in both regions is projected to grow at a similar rate and mining in the Southwest is projected to grow at a slower rate than the corresponding U.S. sectors. Thus, it appears that growth in manufacturing is the primary force behind the projected high growth rate of total Sunbelt earnings relative to total U.S. earnings.

Core Manufacturing Industries

Explanations for the expected growth in manufacturing earnings can be found by examining projections for industries representing

TABLE 2-5
SOUTHEAST SECTOR EARNINGS
(millions of 1972 dollars)

Sector	1969	1978	1990	2000	2010	Percent Change 1978-2010 Southeast	U.S.
All Industry	86,137	123,318	205,565	285,002	380,641	209	167
Agriculture, Forestry, Fisheries	3,708	4,260	4,763	5,539	6,522	53	59
Mining	625	1,562	3,523	4,815	6,206	298	171
Construction	5,823	7,743	13,162	18,080	24,030	210	172
Manufacturing	23,169	31,077	51,518	71,437	95,310	207	121
Transportation, Communication, Public Utilities	5,689	9,446	16,427	23,278	31,548	234	177
Wholesale Trade	5,121	8,054	13,333	18,158	23,913	197	151
Retail Trade	9,465	13,030	21,447	29,564	39,265	201	154
Finance, Insurance, and Real Estate	4,174	6,523	11,934	17,249	23,687	263	204
All Service	12,306	18,725	35,201	51,896	72,289	286	237
All Government	15,674	22,311	33,337	43,780	56,314	152	128

SOURCE: U.S. Department of Commerce, Bureau of Economic Analysis 1980.

TABLE 2-6
SOUTHWEST SECTOR EARNINGS
(millions of 1972 dollars)

Sector	1969	1978	1990	2000	2010	Percent Change 1978-2010 Southwest	Percent Change 1978-2010 U.S.
All Industry	56,310	87,408	148,831	207,878	280,152	221	167
Agriculture, Forestry, Fisheries	2,114	2,200	2,802	3,142	3,609	64	59
Mining	2,445	5,253	6,852	7,137	7,643	45	171
Construction	4,155	7,288	10,878	14,282	18,545	154	172
Manufacturing	11,226	16,746	32,549	48,373	67,352	302	121
Transportation, Communication, Public Utilities	4,367	7,372	12,704	17,861	24,140	227	177
Wholesale Trade	3,744	6,565	11,054	15,134	20,032	208	151
Retail Trade	6,416	9,407	15,309	20,991	27,948	197	154
Finance, Insurance, and Real Estate	2,870	4,747	8,825	12,792	17,691	273	204
All Service	8,301	13,283	25,611	38,246	53,945	306	237
All Government	10,455	14,168	21,616	29,058	38,103	169	128

SOURCE: U.S. Department of Commerce, Bureau of Economic Analysis 1980.

51

the traditional core of a manufacturing economy — machinery, fabricated metals, primary metals, and transportation equipment.

For example, in terms of earnings, machinery is the dominant manufacturing industry in the Sunbelt and is projected to become even more dominant in the future. In 1978, the industry was the largest source of manufacturing earnings in the Sunbelt and generated 4.7 and 3.5 billion dollars of earnings in the Southeast and Southwest respectively. The rate of earnings growth between 1978 and 2010 is projected to be the most rapid of any manufacturing sector in the Southwest (455 percent) and the fourth most rapid in the Southeast (326 percent). This growth represents a third of the total projected U.S. growth in machinery earnings and would bring the Sunbelt share of U.S. machinery earnings to 27 percent. Texas is expected to produce a third of all machinery earnings in the Sunbelt in 2010.

In 1978, the fabricated metals industry produced earnings of 1.8 billion dollars in the Southeast and 1.5 billion dollars in the Southwest. By 2010, the industry is projected to have grown by 273 percent and 386 percent in the Southeast and Southwest, respectively. These increases will result in the Sunbelt's share of the U.S. industry earnings increasing from 17 to 27 percent. The production of fabricated metals is widely distributed throughout metropolitan areas in the South. This pattern is expected to continue with Texas remaining the largest producer and Florida and Tennessee accounting for substantial shares.

The primary metals industry also is projected to experience substantial growth over the next 30 years. By 2010, earnings in the Southeast are expected to have increased by 220 percent over their 1978 level of 1.6 billion dollars. The Southwest is projected to increase 1978 earnings of .9 billion dollars by 381 percent. Consequently, the South's share of the total earnings of the U.S. primary metals industry will increase to 20 percent. At that time, the industry is expected to be concentrated in Alabama and Texas with secondary concentrations in Georgia, Kentucky, Tennessee, and Louisiana.

Transportation equipment is another industry that is important to the growth of the manufacturing sector in the Sunbelt. In 1978, this industry was the fifth largest source of manufacturing earnings in both regions of the South — 2.2 billion dollars in the Southeast and 1.5 billion dollars in the Southwest. At that time, the South accounted for 12 percent of U.S. transportation equipment earnings. Projected growth rates (233 percent for the Southeast and 226 percent for the Southwest) are similar to the overall manufacturing earnings growth for the Sunbelt and will bring the Sunbelt's share of U.S. earnings to 16 percent. Texas is projected to have the greatest share of earnings with Florida, Georgia, Kentucky, Tennessee, and Louisiana also having large shares.

Structure of Sunbelt Economy

The structure of the Sunbelt economy, or the relative importance of individual sectors to total Sunbelt earnings, also is projected to change. Some of these changes reflect trends in the U.S. economy as a whole:

- services and finance, insurance, and real estate are increasing their shares;
- agriculture and government are decreasing their shares; and
- wholesale trade, retail trade, transportation, and construction are maintaining their shares.

Other structural changes in the Sunbelt are in contrast to U.S. patterns. Nationally, the share of total earnings derived from manufacturing is projected to decline from 26 percent to 22 percent between 1978 and 2010. In the Sunbelt, manufacturing in the Southeast is projected to maintain its share of total earnings at about 25 percent and in the Southwest to increase its share from 19 percent to 24 percent. At the national level, mining is expected to maintain its 1.6 percent share of total earnings. Although mining in the Southeast is expected to increase slightly and reach the national average, in the Southwest, where mining has contributed 6 percent of the total earnings, its share is projected to decrease to slightly less than 3 percent. Even with this percentage decrease, absolute earnings will increase. These trends emphasize the growing importance of the Sunbelt as one of the nation's leading manufacturing regions. Although agriculture and mining are still important sectors in the Sunbelt, their contribution to the overall industrial base is expected to decline.

INCOME

Per Capita Income

For decades, the South has been a relatively impoverished region. Although increases in per capita income have taken place, many southerners continue to remain significantly below the average U.S. per capita income (Table 2-7). In 1978, the average per capita income for the South was 88 percent of the U.S. average. Among individual states, only Florida and Texas were near the U.S. average, and Mississippi and Arkansas fell below 80 percent of the U.S. average. Even when per capita income figures are adjusted for cost of living differentials, the South still lags (Jusenius and Ledebur 1977). These income differentials have provided strong incentives for southern communities and states to encourage economic growth.

Due to the expected trends in increased employment and industrial development, improvements in per capita income in all Sunbelt states are projected to continue. Per capita income in constant 1972 dollars in the South is expected to increase from $4,630 in 1978 to $10,494 in 2010, an increase in purchasing power of over 100 percent. Per capita income in the South as a whole is projected to increase from 88 to 95 percent of the U.S. average.

The geographical distribution of gains in per capita income is an important element when considering the benefits of economic growth in the South. Florida, Kentucky, Louisiana, and Texas are the only states projected to be within three percentage points of the U.S. average in 2010. Many states are projected to continue to lag behind with per capita incomes in Mississippi, South Carolina, and Arkansas expected to still be below 90 percent of the U.S. average. Nevertheless, many of the states in the South are expected to make impressive increases in average per capita income during the 40 years prior to 2010. For example, in 1969 the average per capita income in Mississippi was only 63 percent of the U.S. average; by 2010 Mississippi's per capita income is expected to be about 84 percent of the U.S. average. While the per capita income still will be low compared to the U.S. average, the increase is substantial. Alabama, Georgia, and Louisiana also are projected to experience large increases.

Historically, per capita income has been significantly higher in metropolitan areas than in nonmetropolitan areas. Although this trend is continuing, significant gains in per capita income have

TABLE 2-7
PER CAPITA INCOME
(thousands)

Region/State[a]	Per Capita Income (1972 dollars)			Percent of U.S. Per Capita Income		
	1969	1978	2010	1969	1978	2010
Southeast						
Alabama	3,046	4,217	10,204	73	81	93
Florida	3,883	5,052	10,856	94	97	98
Georgia	3,499	4,519	10,203	84	86	93
Kentucky	3,240	4,403	10,741	78	84	97
Mississippi	2,630	3,721	9,287	63	71	84
North Carolina	3,383	4,426	10,108	82	85	92
South Carolina	3,105	4,195	9,817	75	80	89
Tennessee	3,250	4,374	9,924	78	84	90
Total	3,367	4,489	10,322	81	86	94
Southwest						
Arkansas	2,903	4,081	9,481	70	78	86
Louisiana	3,208	4,492	10,700	77	86	97
New Mexico	3,187	4,399	10,028	77	84	91
Oklahoma	3,470	4,751	10,445	84	91	95
Texas	3,700	5,164	11,065	89	99	100
Total	3,503	4,848	10,754	84	93	97
South	3,419	4,630	10,494	82	88	95
Northeast	4,526	5,389	11,169	109	103	101
Northcentral	4,267	5,376	11,334	103	103	103
West	4,424	5,681	11,332	106	109	103
Total U.S.	4,154	5,233	11,037	100	100	100

[a]For a list of states included in each region, see Appendix.

SOURCE: Calculated from U.S. Department of Commerce, Bureau of Economic Analysis 1980.

been extremely widespread, indicating the benefits of growth are reaching most areas within the Sunbelt (U.S. Department of Commerce, Bureau of the Census 1977). In general, nonmetropolitan counties are experiencing the highest percentage gains in per capita income while metropolitan counties receive larger absolute gains.

Wage Rates

Per capita income increases are produced by the combination of increase in the employment to population ratios and increases in wage rates. Historically, the South has had the lowest wage rates in the country as well as low employment to population ratios.[6] For example, earnings per employee, a measure of wage rates, were only 90 percent of the U.S. average in 1978 (Table 2-8). Only Kentucky, Louisiana, New Mexico, and Texas had average earnings per employee that were above 90 percent of the U.S. average. In North Carolina, South Carolina, and Arkansas, these earnings were 85 percent or less of the U.S. average.

One of the reasons for these low values is the fact that the South has had a disproportionate share of employment in the low wage lumber, furniture, textile, apparel, and leather goods industries (U.S. Department of Commerce, Bureau of the Census 1981). The relatively low per capita incomes in the Carolinas, despite high employment to population ratios, can be explained by the concentrations in these states of low wage industries.

The projections indicate wages will increase substantially. Earnings per employee in the South are expected to rise from $7,781 in 1978 to $15,950 in 2010 in real 1972 dollars, an increase of over 100 percent. Although the absolute increase is large, it represents an increase from 90 to only 93 percent of the U.S. average; the South is projected to continue to lag behind other regions. While all southern states are projected to see improvements in absolute earnings per employee, only Kentucky, Louisiana, and Texas are expected to reach or come close to the U.S. average. Mississippi, the Carolinas, Tennessee, and Arkansas are projected to continue to fall below 90 percent of the U.S. average earnings per employee. The variations among individual southern states in earnings per employee are largely a function of employment patterns in high and low wage industries.

TABLE 2-8
EARNINGS PER EMPLOYEE
(thousands)

Region/State[a]	Earnings per Employee (1972 dollars)			Percent of U.S. (average)		
	1969	1978	2010	1969	1978	2010
Southeast						
Alabama	6,671	7,772	16,224	84	89	95
Florida	7,361	7,660	15,161	93	88	94
Georgia	6,728	7,675	15,678	85	88	92
Kentucky	6,525	7,939	16,881	82	91	99
Mississippi	5,979	6,879	14,459	75	79	84
North Carolina	6,290	7,342	15,210	79	85	89
South Carolina	6,197	6,998	14,570	78	81	85
Tennessee	6,620	7,557	15,299	83	87	89
Total	6,647	7,484	15,416	84	86	90
Southwest						
Arkansas	6,166	7,399	14,550	78	85	85
Louisiana	6,671	8,250	17,407	84	95	102
New Mexico	6,511	8,184	15,613	82	94	91
Oklahoma	6,858	7,688	15,703	86	89	92
Texas	7,215	8,485	17,135	91	98	100
Total	6,952	8,243	16,740	87	95	98
South	6,764	7,781	15,950	85	90	93
Northeast	8,353	8,928	17,775	105	103	104
Northcentral	8,268	9,082	17,800	104	105	104
West	8,452	9,051	17,271	106	104	101
Total U.S.	7,954	8,687	17,119	100	100	100

[a]For a list of states included in each region, see Appendix.

SOURCE: Calculated from U.S. Department of Commerce, Bureau of Economic Analysis 1980.

SUMMARY

This chapter has described trends in population, employment, industrial development, and income for the Sunbelt as a region and for its individual states. The general pattern is one of growth over the past decade and expectations that this growth will continue. The Sunbelt, already the most populous region in the U.S., is expected to grow by 31 percent over the next 30 years, receiving 42 percent of the U.S. population increase. Although Florida and Texas are expected to account for about half of this increase, all of the Sunbelt states except Alabama and Arkansas are projected to grow more rapidly than the national average. If future trends resemble the trends of the past few years, growth will be widely distributed throughout the region.

Employment in the South is growing more rapidly in absolute terms than any other region, and at a rate second only to that for the West. Employment growth is projected to continue to be concentrated in Florida and Texas, although growth rates in all Sunbelt states are expected to be greater than for the United States as a whole.

Growth in manufacturing employment provides the major thrust for overall employment growth in the South. At a time when manufacturing employment is growing slowly in the United States and even declining in the Northeast, manufacturing employment is projected to grow by 59 percent in the South over the next 30 years. This growth represents three out of every five new U.S. manufacturing jobs.

The Sunbelt is expected to experience substantial growth in all industrial sectors over the next 30 years. Growth rates in almost all sectors are projected to be significantly above the U.S. averages, and absolute increases are expected to be above increases in most other regions of the country. In contrast to the nation as a whole, where manufacturing is projected to decrease in relative importance, manufacturing in the Sunbelt is projected to continue to grow rapidly and to maintain its share of the regional economy.

The industrial growth taking place in the South will bring important benefits to the region. Increases in the employment to population ratio and wage rates over the next 30 years are projected to continue to increase the economic well-being of the South. Employment to population ratios are projected to rise to near the national average throughout most of the South. Wage ratios are expected to double in constant dollars and rise to 93 percent of the U.S. average. As a result, per capita incomes are projected to more than double and to reach 95 percent of the U.S. average. These income increases are expected to be widely distributed throughout the South. Per capita incomes in all Sunbelt states are growing more rapidly than the U.S. average. Although metropolitan areas have the highest incomes at present, incomes in many nonmetropolitan areas are growing as fast or faster than in metropolitan areas. Although the South as a whole and certain states in particular are projected to continue to lag behind U.S. averages, the absolute and relative gains are expected to be significant.

Thus, the demographic and economic changes described in this chapter indicate that:

- the Sunbelt as a region is growing rapidly. Although Florida and Texas frequently lead the way, growth in population, employment, industrial development, and income is taking place throughout the region and generally at rates faster than the U.S. as a whole;
- the growth of the Sunbelt does not appear to be a short-term phenomenon. This rapid growth began in the late 1960s and is projected to continue for at least the next 30 years; and
- the development of the Sunbelt has brought and is expected to continue to bring significant benefits to the region, including increased employment and rising per capita incomes.

In order to continue to reap the benefits of growth and development while at the same time avoiding the potential negative impacts, serious attention must be given to the problems and issues associated with managing this growth. The following chapters address some of these issues.

NOTES

1. In this chapter, the terms "Sunbelt" and "South" refer to the 13 states in Federal Region 4 — Alabama, Florida, Georgia, Kentucky, Mississippi, North and South Carolina, and Tennessee — and Federal Region 6 — Arkansas, Louisiana, New Mexico, Oklahoma, and Texas. These two regions are very close

to the most frequently used classifications of the Sunbelt (Browning and Gesler 1979). Other states often mentioned as part of the Sunbelt are Arizona and California, while Kentucky is often excluded.

2. The projections of population, employment, industrial development, and income used in this chapter are the Regional Projections developed by the Bureau of Economic Analysis (BEA), Regional Economic Division, of the United States Department of Commerce.

3. As used by the Bureau of Economic Analysis, earnings refers to labor and proprietor's income.

4. Net migration is the difference between the number of inmigrants and outmigrants; natural increase is the number of births minus the number of deaths.

5. The discussion of industrial trends is based on the Bureau of Economic Analysis (BEA) projections of earnings by state by industry. Change in earnings is usually a more accurate indicator of output than is change in employment because changes in output per employee typically are reflected in earnings but not in employment changes. All earning figures are expressed in terms of constant 1972 dollars.

6. With more rapid growth in employment than in population over the next 30 years, employment to population ratios in the South are expected to converge on the U.S. average. Only Florida (87 percent) and New Mexico (96 percent) are not expected to reach at least 98 percent of the U.S. average. The continued low index for Florida is a function of the high proportion of retirees in the state.

REFERENCES

Berry, Brian J. L., and Donald C. Dahmann. 1980. "Population Redistribution in the United States." In *Population Redistribution and Public Policy*, edited by Brian J. L. Berry and Lester P. Silverman, pp. 8-49. Washington, D.C.: National Academy of Sciences.

Browning, Clyde, and Wil Gesler. 1979. "The Sunbelt — Snowbelt: A Case of Sloppy Regionalizing." *Professional Geographer* 31(1): 66-74.

Jusenius, C. L., and L. C. Ledebur. 1977. "A Myth in the Making: The Southern Economic Challenge and Northern Economic Decline." In *The Economics of Southern Growth*, edited by E. Blaine Liner and Lawrence K. Lynch, pp. 131-73. Research Triangle Park, North Carolina: Southern Growth Policies Board.

Morrill, Richard L. 1979. "Stages in Patterns of Population Concentration and Dispersion." *Professional Geographer* 31: 55-65.

Morrison, Peter A. 1980. "Current Demographic Change in Regions of the United States." In *Alternatives to Confrontation: A National Policy toward Regional Change*, edited by Victor L. Arnold, pp. 63-94. Lexington, Massachusetts: D. C. Heath, Lexington Books.

Poston, Dudley L., Jr., William J. Serow, and Robert H. Weller. 1981. "Demographic Change in the South." In *The Population of the South: Structure and Change in Social Demographic Context*, edited by Dudley L. Poston and Robert H. Weller, pp. 3-22. Austin: University of Texas Press.

Roberts, Rebecca S., and Lisa M. Butler. 1983. "The Sunbelt Phenomenon: An Overview of the Causes of Growth." In *The Future of the Sunbelt: Issues in Managing Growth and Change*, edited by Steven C. Ballard and Thomas E. James, Jr. New York: Praeger.

U.S. Department of Commerce, Bureau of the Census. 1977. *County and City Data Book 1977: A Statistical Abstract Supplement*. Washington, D.C.: Government Printing Office.

_____. 1981. *Statistical Abstract of the United States 1981*. Washington, D.C.: Government Printing Office.

U.S. Department of Commerce, Bureau of Economic Analysis (BEA). 1980. *Regional Economic Projections*. Washington, D.C.: Bureau of Economic Analysis.

APPENDIX

States of Federal Regions

SOUTHEAST*
(Federal Region 4)

Alabama
Florida
Georgia
Kentucky
Mississippi
North Carolina
South Carolina
Tennessee

SOUTHWEST*
(Federal Region 6)

Arkansas
Louisiana
New Mexico
Oklahoma
Texas

NORTHEAST
(Federal Regions 1, 2, 3)

Connecticut
Delaware
Maine
Maryland
Massachusetts
New Hampshire
New Jersey
New York
Pennsylvania
Rhode Island
Vermont
Virginia
West Virginia

WEST
(Federal Regions 8, 9, 10)

Alaska
Arizona
California
Colorado
Hawaii
Idaho
Montana
Nevada
North Dakota
Oregon
South Dakota
Utah
Washington
Wyoming

NORTHCENTRAL
(Federal Regions 5, 7)

Illinois
Indiana
Iowa
Kansas
Michigan
Minnesota
Missouri
Nebraska
Ohio
Wisconsin

---

*Federal regions 4 and 6 are South/Sunbelt.

Capital Flight: Anticipating Sunbelt Problems
Daniel J. McGovern

INTRODUCTION

The economic renaissance sweeping across the South and South-western United States over the past decade brought dramatic increases in capital investment and new jobs. Manufacturing employment expanded by more than 21 percent between 1970 and 1979 — fully 64 percent of the total U.S. manufacturing growth (Southern Growth Policies Board 1981b, p. 14). This burst of activity in manufacturing served as the cornerstone for broad-based growth in whole-sale and retail trade, services, and government employment. It also inspired a new sense of confidence about the future of the Sunbelt.

This optimism contrasts sharply with the atmosphere of depression which hangs over many states in the Frostbelt. Factory shut-downs and capital transfers have reached epidemic proportions in the Great Lakes and Northeast regions of the country. Between 1977 and 1980 more than 77 large scale factories (of 100,000 square feet or more) closed their doors, throwing 51,649 workers permanently out of their jobs (Hoffman Associates Inc. 1981). The pace of job destruction actually quickened in 1981; Wisconsin alone recorded

The author would like to express his appreciation to Teresa Peck for her invaluable advice and support and to Mark Hagen for his excellent research assistance.

34 total plant closings with a loss of 2,976 jobs. (Wisconsin Department of Development 1982b, pp. 4, 18).

While the Great Lakes and Mid-Atlantic states have been hit hardest by factory closings, the wave of shutdowns has not left the Sunbelt untouched. Alabama, Florida, Kentucky, Louisiana, and North Carolina all registered higher than average job losses due to factory closings (Hoffman Associates Inc. 1981; Schmenner 1982, pp. 180-183). California experienced the most large-scale shutdowns among the 50 states (Hoffman Associates Inc. 1981). And one recent study showed that newly opened plants in the South were *twice as likely to close* as comparable plants in the North (Bluestone and Harrison 1980, p. 33).[1] Clearly, the Sunbelt's enthusiasm over its recent growth must be tempered by an awareness of its dependence on fluctuating trends in capital investment. The very real possibility exists that the economic boom in the Sunbelt could collapse under the pressure of large-scale capital transfers from the region.

Some scholars argue that plant closings and capital shifts are a sign of economic vitality; they are temporary adjustments in a dynamic economy which enable entrepreneurs to more efficiently employ money and resources (McKenzie 1979). If this is the case, the Sunbelt should have no concerns over capital movements into and out of the region.

However, two decades of research on factory closings demonstrate that shutdowns are neither temporary nor insignificant phenomena. The personal and social costs of a plant closing are enormous. Individual loss of employment often leads to a sharp rise in alcoholism, wife battery, child abuse, homicide, and suicide (Brenner 1977; Ferman 1978; Shostak 1980). For the community, factory closings often result in sharp increases in crime, social service costs, declining tax revenues, and a general decline in community volunteerism and well-being (Bluestone and Harrison 1980, pp. 67-71). From this perspective, Sunbelt states should be as concerned about maintaining existing employment as they are about attracting new capital investment. In fact, as we shall see later, the form of new capital investment may be one of the greatest threats to existing employment in the Sunbelt.

A key premise to this research is that, although manufacturing employment and capital investment have grown in the Sunbelt, the causes of this growth are not understood. Community developers and government officials seem quite unfamiliar with those factors which affect business expansion and location decisions. Sunbelt states need to recognize which forces determine the flow of capital, both new investment and disinvestment, if they hope to grow while avoiding the ravages of capital flight and plant shutdowns.

Three major theoretical views on the movement of capital are set forth in this chapter. Each theory is explained briefly along with its implications for the Sunbelt. Then Wisconsin is used as a case study to empirically test the competing theories. Relating these findings back to the character and conditions of the Sunbelt, this chapter analyzes the future prospects for capital expansion into and capital flight from the Sunbelt.

In the conclusion, a set of recommendations are provided for planners and government officials on how to induce new capital investment into the Sunbelt while maintaining existing employment. The answers are neither simple nor obvious. Over the past decade Frostbelt states have pursued a variety of strategies including tax abatements, job training, regulatory holidays, and state subsidies for new investors — yet the factories continue to close. The findings presented here indicate that conventional solutions may be among the most critical factors speeding the decline of the Frostbelt region, a fact which underscores the need for a very careful reconsideration of our public policies on economic development.

EXPLAINING CAPITAL MOVEMENTS

The recent drive to attract investment capital and jobs to the Sunbelt often pits states in this region against ones from the Frostbelt which are struggling to preserve existing factories and employment — a battle once labeled the "second war between the states" (Goodman 1971, pp. xiv-xv). Government officials and community leaders try to second-guess the decision-making processes of businesses, hoping to identify factors which can be used to entice new companies to locate in a region or convince existing firms to remain. One consequence of this competition has been a bizarre bidding contest between states to see who can offer the most attractive combination of tax exemptions, job training programs, technical assistance, and social amenities (Goodman 1971; *New York Times* October 10, 1982b, p. Y35). Ironically, despite the many billions of dollars in tax abatements and special benefits at stake, most government officials operate with inadequate information about factors which affect business location decisions.

Scholars studying this question over the past three decades have outlined three models or perspectives which attempt to explain the phenomenon of capital movement. This section presents a brief overview of the three perspectives and notes the implications of each for Frostbelt and Sunbelt states. The subsequent section will test the relative strength of each model in explaining capital expansions and contractions.

Geographic Constraints

Classic location theory is based on the assumption that enterprises adapt to the most intractable elements of the production process: land, transportation, labor, energy, and capital. At early stages of the development of manufacturing, land availability and access to raw materials and markets play the most significant role in determining plant location (Isard 1956; Greenhut 1956; Beckman 1968). Subsequent improvements in transportation, and technological innovations reduce the necessity for locating facilities near resources, support services, or consumers, and called into question the geographic constraints approach. Recent empirical work, however, tends to support the continuing importance of geographical constraints (Minneapolis Metropolitan Council 1979; Schmenner 1982).

Historically, the Sunbelt has enjoyed certain geographic advantages over the Frostbelt including abundant land at lower cost, a large pool of available workers, lower-cost energy, and a warm climate. Advances in technology and transportation also made the Sunbelt more accessible to national markets and multistage production processes. Recently some of these "natural" advantages have turned into liabilities. Nationwide increases in energy costs hit particularly hard land-intensive manufacturing plants and cities with widely dispersed factories and employees (e.g., Los Angeles). Southern workers often tend to be more poorly educated and consequently less productive than their counterparts in the North. Finally, the infrastructure required by an industrial community is less well developed in the Sunbelt, especially truck, rail, and water transportation. (Southern Growth Policies Board 1981a; 1981b).

If these factors are important considerations in making location decisions, Sunbelt states could be facing sharp limitations on their future economic growth.

Regional Cost Differences

The regional cost differences approach assumes that modern corporations have much greater mobility and greater willingness to move. To these companies, intrastate or interstate differences in wages, energy costs, taxes, and levels of unionization may offer sufficient inducements to close down existing facilities and transfer them elsewhere, or to open new facilities in a lower-cost region (McKenzie 1979; Bluestone and Harrison 1980; Schmenner 1982).

From this perspective Sunbelt states enjoy clear advantages over the Frostbelt because of lower rates of taxation, wages, and unionization (McKenzie 1979; Southern Growth Policies Board 1981b). In recent years hourly wages, tax rates, and consumer prices have climbed in the Sunbelt reducing to some extent this regional advantage (Southern Growth Policies Board 1981b). The real challenge comes from international business; corporations large enough to shift capital from the industrial Northeast to the Southwestern United States may almost as easily transfer facilities to Mexico, the Philippines, or Taiwan. With wage differentials between Texas and neighboring Mexico reaching as high as 13 to 1 (Stepan 1979, p. 666), businesses calculating interstate differences in production costs may decide to go the additional distance and locate outside the United States where taxes and wages are appreciably lower than in the Sunbelt (*Business Week* July 9, 1979, pp. 50-54; International Labour Office 1973; Barnet and Mueller 1974). Whether firms can or will shift production and jobs to take advantage of these regional and national differences may depend in large measure on the character of the economic enterprise.

Individual Firm Characteristics

A number of firm-specific characteristics seem to affect a company's decision to transfer capital or to shut down existing facilities. Absolute size and the scale of operations interact with regional characteristics to form a matrix of decisional outcomes. Large, nationally-based firms evidence greater concern for regional variations in wages, taxes, and energy costs. Locally-oriented, smaller scale firms seem to shift production facilities more quickly, but in response to the need for more space, perceived sales advantages in metropolitan areas, and personal convenience considerations of executives (Wheeler 1981; Schmenner 1980a; 1982).

Corporate ownership patterns may play the greatest role in explaining the decision to close down plants and shift capital out of communities. Conglomerates and out-of-state firms do not view the company as an integral part of the community, established to provide products, services, and employment for the citizens of the local area. Rather, these types of businesses find it easier to exclude social and personal considerations from the economic calculation; they will shift production to maximize corporate profit, especially short-term profit even at the expense of long-term institutional well-being (Marchetti 1980; *Washington Post* October 10, 1980, p. D3). While this may coincide with the economic efficiency criteria of capitalism, it devastates the community and often is unnecessary for the economic stability and performance of the corporation. However, the scale and ownership patterns of corporations may make it inevitable. As discussed below, this is possibly the most serious source of concern for Sunbelt communities.

From these three streams of literature on industrial location – the geographic constraints approach, the regional cost differences thesis, and the individual firm perspective – a multidimensional explanation for plant openings or shutdowns can be generated. Certainly all three sets of factors will have an impact on the decisions to close down older plants and to open new ones. But these two acts are not necessarily interconnected. Often a plant shutdown will occur at a time and place far removed from new capital expansion. While the two events are linked by similar national and global economic forces, intuitively one would expect certain variables to have greater explanatory power for patterns of new plant construction and other variables to account better for plant closings and permanent job loss.

New plants may take advantage of current technologies and structures which overcome past limits of land, labor and transportation. Where early U.S. manufacturing was limited to those regions where raw materials and water transportation were readily available (e.g. the Great Lakes, the Ohio River Valley, and the Atlantic Coast), contemporary manufacturers enjoy the benefits of an extensive interstate highway system, compartmentalized production processes, and technology intensive rather than raw material intensive products. Hence the geographic constraints perspective will be of lesser importance in explaining new plant location.

New investment decisions may also arise from different forms of corporate structure. The emergence of large conglomerates and the concentration of production and market shares into a relatively small number of firms allows for much greater flexibility in corporate decision making. A conglomerate based in Houston may choose to expand an existing facility in Wisconsin, open a more modern one in Kansas, or take the capital out of that industry and funnel it into an entirely new line of business. Consequently, new plant construction will probably reflect more clearly regional cost considerations and be greatly influenced by the national or global orientation of its corporate owners.

Older plants tend to be tied to communities. They were established in a particular era to serve specific local or regional markets and have adapted over time to the geographic constraints of land, labor availability, and transportation. While some of these geographic advantages may deteriorate over time and new geographic constraints emerge (e.g. traffic congestion, air pollution, etc.), older plants will still reflect the original geographic considerations.

Regional cost differences may be irrelevant to an established plant insofar as it has adjusted its business calculations to the prevailing wage and tax rates. Aggressive price competition from producers in other low cost regions may drive an established firm out of the market. But unless the older factory is one of several production units operated by a multistate or multinational corporation, the individual plant cannot respond to regional cost differences short of going out of business.

Obviously, the key variable underlying both shutdowns and new plant construction is the organization and ownership of the parent firm. Single unit and privately owned companies will probably open in communities most familiar to them; conglomerates will more readily shift capital to maximize national or global profit opportunities. Final termination of production and employment will probably be most affected by the location or residence of the factory owners. Local owners living in the community where their production facilities operate must answer to the employees and townspeople. Consequently, one would expect locally owned businesses to hold out longer in a difficult market and stay despite the relative cost disadvantages of a particular community. Out of state or conglomerate firms lack this social bond and may find it easier to shift jobs from the region (Logue 1980; Bluestone and Harrison 1980).

The central argument, then, is that several factors are important in explaining the incidence of plant shutdowns and new plant openings in a given geographic area. Accordingly, the following sets of competing hypotheses can be presented:

Hypothesis 1: New plants will open in regions with greater land area, labor availability, and better transportation systems.

Hypothesis 2: Established plants will not be affected appreciably by the availability of land, labor, or good transportation.

Hypothesis 3: New plants will be located in areas with lower wages, smaller tax levies, and less union influence.

Hypothesis 4: Plant shutdowns will occur equally often across areas of high or low wages, taxes, and unionization.

Hypothesis 5: New plant openings will not vary directly by ownership type; equal numbers of in-state and out-of-state owned plants should open in a given community.

Hypothesis 6: Plant shutdowns will occur much more often among firms owned and headquartered out of state.

Empirical tests of these hypotheses will permit a comparative evaluation of the geographic location and the regional cost differences approaches. It will demonstrate whether the same dynamics affect plant shutdowns as determine plant opening decisions. Finally, the analysis will explore the relative impact of firm ownership on plant and capital movements. Based on this analysis, general conclusions about capital movements are drawn and projections about the future of the Sunbelt are made.

RESEARCH DESIGN

In order to tap both the regional differences and the character-istics of individual plants, the scope of this study is limited to the total reported plant closings and new factories constructed in Wis-consin between January 1, 1970 and December 31, 1980. Analysis was performed at two levels: first, capital activity at the county level was explored, then the individual cases of factory openings or closings were examined.

At the county level, data were collected on all cases of total closings or new plant construction, reported by the Wisconsin Department of Development. This explicitly excludes cases of partial shutdown or plant expansions.[2] The total numbers of shutdowns and jobs lost were aggregated for each of the 72 counties over the 11 years of the study. Similar aggregate figures were generated for plant openings and new jobs created. Comparisons of capital invest-ment and disinvestment could thus be made across the 72 counties.

Wisconsin counties differed significantly in their geographic and economic profiles. County data were gathered on: (1) population; (2) land area; (3) miles of state highways; (4) average unemployment rates; (5) average wage rates; and (6) adjusted property tax rates (see Appendix). These measures will permit the testing of Hypoth-eses 1-4.

At a different level of analysis, each discrete instance of a factory opening or closing was evaluated to determine the number of jobs created or lost and the ownership type — whether it was Wisconsin or out-of-state owned. The annual editions of the *Classified Direc-tory of Wisconsin Manufacturers* from 1970 through 1980 served as the source for this information. Lack of available data precluded analysis of industry type, conglomerate versus single firm units, or other key company level data. Notwithstanding this limitation, the findings on ownership add much to our understanding of capital movement.

PLANT CLOSINGS AND NEW PLANT EXPANSION: EVIDENCE FROM WISCONSIN

Over the 11 year period, 269 Wisconsin factories closed their doors. Excluding 53 for which exact employment figures are not available, this amounted to more than 25,600 jobs. The number of shutdowns varied greatly across the 72 counties, with several encountering no shutdowns while one county suffered 34 closings. This county, Milwaukee, lost at least 7,760 jobs due to total shutdowns.

From 1970 to 1980, a total of 878 new plants or branch facilities opened in the state, creating 27,752 new jobs. On a county by county basis the distribution of new plants ranged from zero to 52. The new jobs were also not distributed equally; 2,156 new jobs were concentrated in one county, Waukesha — not the same county which lost 7,760 jobs. Indeed, Milwaukee suffered a net loss of more than 5,000 jobs.

Clearly there is great variation in the ebb and flow of capital and employment in this state, which ranks sixth in the nation in percent of workers employed in industry and twelfth in agriculture (*Wisconsin Blue Book 1981-1982* 1981, pp. 670-671). This cross-county variation in shutdowns and new plant openings provides an ideal opportunity to test the relative strengths of competing theories of capital movement.

Geographic Constraints versus Regional Cost Differences

To test the geographic constraints and regional cost difference approaches, four measures of capital disposition — new plants, new jobs, plant shutdowns, and jobs lost — were correlated with eight measures of the geographic, economic, and political environment. Table 3-1 shows the results of these tests.

As predicted by classical location theory, demographic and transportation variables correlated most strongly with all measures of capital disposition. The greater number, and largest, shutdowns occurred in the most populous counties. (The correlation between population density and shutdowns is .8345, the correlation between density and job loss is .9220.) This stands to reason as many Wisconsin cities were founded around industry, and more populous areas generally would have larger numbers of manufacturing establishments. New plants also tended to gravitate toward larger communities, although the connection is much less strong (r = .4033). In fact, the region with the greatest number of new plants is the largest suburban county of Milwaukee, the state's largest city. Sheer availability of land had no apparent effect on new plant construction.

TABLE 3-1
GEOGRAPHIC, ECONOMIC, AND POLITICAL EXPLANATIONS OF PLANT CLOSINGS
(Zero Order Correlations)

	County Population	County Land Area	Highway Miles	Highways Per Mile	Population Density	Average Wage Rate	Average Unemployment	Tax Rate
Plant Shutdowns	.8698 (.001)	−.2214 *	.4545 (.001)	.8210 (.001)	.8345 (.001)	.1609 *	−.2756 *	.2429 *
Jobs Lost	.9089 (.001)	−.1984 *	.3388 (.002)	.7932 (.001)	.9220 (.001)	.1723 *	−.1480 *	.3038 *
New Plants	.5887 (.001)	−.0239 *	.6222 (.001)	.5326 (.001)	.4033 (.001)	.1049 *	−.2281 (.027)	.0788 *
New Jobs	.6829 (.001)	.0174 *	.6437 (.001)	.5648 (.001)	.5013 (.001)	.1350 *	−.1988 *	.1535 *

*Indicates not significant at the .01 level.

SOURCE: Data from *Wisconsin: New Industries and Plant Expansions reported in Wisconsin* (Madison: Wisconsin Department of Development). Annual, 1970-1982.

Highway access seems to play a major role in setting capital location. Contrary to expectation, the older plants closed in the most densely trafficked areas (r = .8210), but these may also be the declining core cities. Good road systems are a significant consideration in new plant construction (r = .622 for the correlation between the highway miles in a county and new plants in that county). Slight differences in absolute miles of highway and highway density point to the same urban/suburban split on new plant construction; this trend will be more evident in the partial correlations presented later. Hypothesis 2 needs to be reconsidered as plant closures do seem to be linked to geographic factors. The exact ties will be described in a later section.

Regional cost theory is not supported by the analysis. Differences in the average wage rates among counties failed to explain either the decision to close plants or the locational commitment when new plants opened. Cross-county differences in the availability of labor (measured indirectly as the average unemployment rate) did little to explain numbers of jobs lost or created. Taken together the differences in wage rates and differences in employment may indicate the relative strength of unions in a county. When wages are low and unemployment high, unions probably enjoy little clout. Yet, this combination of factors still failed to explain a statistically significant portion of the variation in capital movement.

Perhaps the most widely discussed cause of capital relocation and the prescription most often used to entice new business is the rate of taxation in a region. As indicated in the Minneapolis Metropolitan Council study (1979) and by the data presented here, a higher tax burden does not drive new business away. Nor do businesses gravitate toward those regions which enjoy the lowest taxes (r = .0788). Higher tax levies may speed plant closings among the very largest firms, as indicated by the .3038 correlation between tax rates and numbers of jobs lost.

These findings are crucial for Sunbelt states and cities, as the impetus to offer tax breaks to new businesses fits with the ethos of contemporary national and local politics. Yet, while damaging the tax base, burdening middle class citizens, and reducing the ability of cities to finance basic services, these tax breaks do virtually nothing to create new investment and jobs according to these data.

From the simple correlations one emerges with a sense that traditional location theory is vindicated and regional cost differences account for little of the capital transfer in the United States. This is confirmed by multivariate analysis — only population, land, and highway characteristics consistently show up as significant (see Table 3-2). However, two important caveats must be considered. The high coincidence of plant closings and openings in the most populous areas suggests that city and county size are masking the true impact of the other variables. Also, the apparent interregional cost differences *within* Wisconsin may be significantly smaller than *interstate* cost differences. While such considerations may affect a smaller, instate firm only marginally, larger national level operations may stand to gain much more over a period of time from a shift of several facilities and many jobs to a low wage, low tax area. Each of these problems will be considered in turn.

TABLE 3-2

COMBINED EFFECTS OF GEOGRAPHIC, ECONOMIC, AND POLITICAL
VARIABLE ON PLANT CLOSINGS AND OPENINGS
(Multiple Regressions)

		R^2 Change	Beta
Plant	Population	.75648	.32549
Shutdowns	Highways per		
	Square Mile	.01881	.33489
		.77529	
Jobs	Population	.82611	.86438
Lost	Unemployment	.00178	.06414
		.82789	
New	Population	.34657	.27913
Plants	Highways per		
	Square Mile	.02277	.42978
	Tax Rate	.01953	−.09392
	Land Area	.00906	.31518
		.40680	
New	Population	.46629	.52056
Jobs	Land Area	.02699	.31562
		.49328	

SOURCE: Data from *Wisconsin: New Industries and Plant Expansions reported in Wisconsin* (Madison: Wisconsin Department of Development). Annual, 1970-1982.

In order to reduce the excessive influence population size had on the analysis of shutdowns and new openings, partial correlations were performed on the measures of capital investment and the six contextual variables while controlling for population. Table 3-3 displays these results.

Once again classical location theory wins out over the regional cost approach. Transportation systems seem to be the single most important determinant of capital disposition, with land availability weakly correlated with the number of new jobs created. Plant openings and new jobs occur most often where there are good highway systems, but *not* where highway density is greatest. An examination of individual counties reveals something of the underlying process. Companies are locating along the interstate highway system but away from the central cities. This may be explained by the greater mobility of the contemporary workforce, and the national market orientation of many newer businesses (Black 1980).

Shutdowns followed the opposite pattern. They strike most in areas where the road system is most dense; more jobs are lost in the densely populated areas, the central cities. This reinforces data from national studies which indicate a flight of manufacturing from central cities to the suburbs and smaller outlying cities (Black 1980; Schmenner 1980a). This trend applies as strongly to Sunbelt cities as it does to Frostbelt cities, and may become even more critical unless Sunbelt communities solve growing transportation problems (Black 1980; Southern Growth Policies Board 1981b, pp. 26-28).

These results lead to a reformulation of Hypotheses 1 and 2. Businesses continue to be constrained by transportation systems and proximity to markets, but the trend seems clearly to shift plants from center cities to the suburbs — an important consideration in the future growth planning of Sunbelt cities. Regional cost differences disappear as influencing factors once the size of the population is controlled. Apparently companies find the cross-county wage and tax differences insufficient to warrant shifting production and employment. This tends to cast doubt on Hypotheses 3 and 4, and refutes claims made by business that high wages and taxes discourage investment.

Recall, however, the second caveat set forth above: this conclusion may be spurious due to the homogeneity of the sample. Cross-county wage and tax differences may not reflect the contrast between Frostbelt and Sunbelt states. According to McKenzie

TABLE 3-3

EXPLANATIONS OF PLANT CLOSINGS AND NEW PLANT OPENINGS CONTROLLING FOR POPULATION

(Partial Correlations)

	County Land Area	Highway Miles	Highways Per Mile	Population Density	Average Wage Rate	Average Unemployed	Tax Rate
Plant Shutdowns	-.0614 *	.1415 *	.2779 (.009)	.0594 *	-.0229 *	-.1585 *	-.1442 *
Jobs Lost	.0051 *	-.1909 *	.0345 *	.4526 (.000)	-.0182 *	.1012 *	-.0501 *
New Plants	.1344 *	.4945 (.000)	.0580 *	-.6082 (.000)	-.0145 *	-.1334 *	-.1729 *
New Jobs	.2357 *	.5149 (.000)	-.0701 *	-.6354 (.000)	-.0000 *	-.0792 *	-.1310 *

*Indicates not significant at the .01 level.

SOURCE: Data from *Wisconsin: New Industries and Plant Expansions reported in Wisconsin* (Madison: Wisconsin Department of Development). Annual, 1970-1982.

(1979, p. 44) Frostbelt employers tend to pay manufacturing workers from 16.7 percent to 31.8 percent more than Sunbelt employers pay. Per capita taxes in the Frostbelt run from 1.6 percent less than Mountain states to 27 percent more than West South Central states (including Oklahoma, Texas, and Louisiana) (McKenzie 1979, pp. 49-50). Obviously some interregional cost differences do exist. Yet, the average wage differed by more than 130 percent across Wisconsin counties and the average county tax rate varied by more than 55 percent (*Wisconsin Statistical Abstract* 1979; *Wisconsin Blue Book 1981-1982* 1981). Apparently interregional cost differences are much less important in capital location decisions than current advocates suggest. A more compelling explanation lies in the character of individual firms, as the data in the following section clearly indicate.

Company-specific Characteristics and Capital Movement

A variety of company level variables obviously must influence the individual company's decision to open or close a plant. On the other hand, certain types of enterprises may follow common and somewhat predictable patterns of capital expansion or contraction. Hypotheses 5 and 6 state that the impacts of firms which are headquartered outside the state will be quite different from the impact or behaviors of those owned and operated by natives of the state. The data clearly support this.

A total of 269 factories closed in Wisconsin between 1970 and 1980. Of the 216 plant shutdowns for which employment data are available, 108 listed their head offices as "out-of-state". These shutdowns accounted for 15,504 jobs destroyed, or *more than 60 percent of the total jobs eliminated* in an 11 year period of time (see Table 3-4). The average shutdown engineered by an out-of-state firm cost 50 more jobs than an in-state closing. While one might argue that this stems from greater investment and job creation at an earlier time by out-of-state firms, the plant opening data deny this.

Over the 11 year period, out-of-state firms created 167 branch plants while Wisconsin companies opened 152 (see Table 3-5). However, for the 298 cases where data are available on employment levels, out-of-state firms created almost exactly the same number of jobs per plant.

Plant relocations tell a slightly different story. Wisconsin firms transferred or relocated more than four times the number of facilities than out-of-state firms shifted, with a net gain of 2,313 jobs. The new plants were relatively small (13-14 workers on average), suggesting that smaller enterprises play a large role in job creation. Indeed, for all Wisconsin firms branching out or relocating, the average new facility employed 28.6 workers.

TABLE 3-4

PLANT CLOSINGS BY OWNERSHIP TYPE 1970-1980

	Out-of-State	*Wisconsin*	*Total*
Plants Closed	108	108	217
Jobs Lost	15,504	10,117	25,621
Average Jobs/Plant	143.6	93.7	118.6

SOURCE: Compiled from *Classified Directory of Wisconsin Manufacturers.* Annual, 1970-1980; *Wisconsin Department of Development.* Annual, 1970-1982.

TABLE 3-5

BRANCH PLANTS AND RELOCATED PLANTS BY OWNERSHIP TYPE
1970-1980

	Out-of-State	*Wisconsin*	*Total*	*Out-of-State as % Total*
Branch Plants Opened	167 (162)	152 (136)	319 (298)	
New Jobs Created	8,099	6,445	14,544	55.68%
Average Jobs/Plant	49.99	47.39	48.81	
Plants Relocated	47 (45)	197 (170)	244 (215)	
New Jobs Created	1,320	2,313	3,633	36.33%
Average Jobs/Plant	29.33	13.61	16.90	
Total Plants	214 (207)	349 (306)	563 (513)	
Total Jobs	9,419	8,758	18,177	51.82%
Average Jobs/Plant	45.5	28.62	35.44	

SOURCE: Compiled from *Wisconsin Department of Development.* Annual, 1970-1982.

While most communities would prefer large scale production facilities employing hundreds or thousands of workers, in reality smaller firms produce the bulk of employment in Wisconsin and the United States as a whole (*Wisconsin Department of Development* 1982a, p. 8; Beal 1981). Moreover, community reliance on a single employer often leads to acute hardship should that company close. This fear holds especially for communities where the major employer is headquartered outside the region. A brief comparison of shutdown and plant expansion data for out-of-state firms underscores this concern. While these companies built 217 new facilities in Wisconsin and added 9,419 jobs, they closed at least 108 plants destroying 15,504 jobs — 60 percent of the total jobs lost in shutdowns.[3]

Why would a firm want to eliminate more jobs than it creates? This question assumes that the same actors who destroy jobs are the ones who created them, or have created other jobs in the state. In fact, a growing number of firms based outside Wisconsin have purchased firms only to liquidate the company, seize the assets, and eliminate jobs. Over the past five years this state has witnessed nearly $8 billion worth of financial takeovers of Wisconsin businesses by out-of-state firms. In the largest of these the net job loss numbers in the thousands (Anderson-Roethle 1977-1982; Marchetti 1980; McGovern 1982). This trend not only underscores the different forces behind plant closings and openings, but also serves as a serious omen to Sunbelt states. One must examine very carefully the type of capital expansion that is occurring in the Sunbelt, for the consequences are not necessarily positive.

The Nature of Capital Expansion in the Sunbelt

Most studies of regional economic growth point to a rapid expansion of new industry and employment in the South and Southwestern United States. From 30 to 50 percent of the national job growth from 1970-1976 has occurred in these regions (Black 1980, p. 89). Manufacturing employment in the Sunbelt has expanded at five times the national rate, and now claims 22.4 percent of all nonagricultural jobs in that region (Southern Growth Policies Board 1981b, pp. 12-14). However, the form of this economic expansion contains grounds for serious concern.

According to a survey by Roger Schmenner (1982) of 410 large multiplant firms, corporate acquisition of smaller companies represents one of the greatest changes in Sunbelt employment over the past decade. In the East Southcentral, West Southcentral, and Mountain states, large firms opened 537 new plants while they took over management control of 727 existing plants (Schmenner 1982, p. 177). They increased employment by 14.4 percent at existing plants and added 15.5 percent more jobs by constructing new factories. But more than one-fifth (20.9 percent) of the increases in employment among these 410 firms came from acquisitions of smaller firms. This places 181,518 already-existing jobs under the control of Fortune 500 companies (Schmenner 1982, p. 178). The jobs were not newly created — merely the "ownership" of the jobs was transferred.

Sheer economic size, conglomerate structure, and out-of-state ownership do not necessarily mean that a corporate actor will act arbitrarily and contrary to the best interests of the community. But once capital investment reaches a certain scale and takes on a certain form, it loses the conventional ties which bind it to a community. Externally owned firms tend to transfer facilities more readily and with much greater impact than locally owned firms. The evidence from Wisconsin and from national studies (Bluestone and Harrison 1980; Schmenner 1982) confirms this pattern; the trends in the Sunbelt today portend a similar dilemma in the not too distant future. Hypotheses 5 and 6 are thus supported, raising serious concerns about the economic stability of recent Sunbelt growth.

To briefly summarize the findings on capital movements in Wisconsin, traditional geographic factors seem to play an important role in locational decisions while regional cost differences were relatively unimportant. Established plants closed and jobs were eliminated in the more densely populated, heavily built-up areas — primarily central cities. Newer plants and jobs emerged in suburban communities, not far from major cities and along interstate highways. Cross-county differences in wages, taxes, and availability of workers (and apparently levels of unionization) had little or no effect on the decision either to close a plant or open a new one. These generalizations must be tempered, however, by an awareness of the crucial role of corporate size and ownership.

Wisconsin based firms added more plants and virtually as many jobs as out-of-state firms. Most of these facilities were small, reinforcing the conventional wisdom that smaller entrepreneurs create much of the employment in the United States. However, out-of-state firms were responsible for more than 60 percent of the jobs lost to plant closings. These closings were much larger in scale compared to new factory openings and point to a net outflow of jobs over time. With the rate of corporate mergers and acquisitions accelerating in Wisconsin (and in the Sunbelt) the future of stable manufacturing employment is not bright.

RECOMMENDATIONS FOR THE SUNBELT

Findings regarding capital movements in the Frostbelt may or may not be transferable to the Sunbelt, a region different in many ways from the Great Lakes region. Yet, certain trends and problems are endemic to the U.S. economy as a whole, and hard lessons learned in the older industrial centers may save currently expanding regions from substantial difficulties later on. If Sunbelt communities are to effectively encourage growth and regulate capital movements, special attention must be paid to five major issues: taxes, public services, capital investment policies, high technology, and government regulations.

Taxes and Tax-Incentives to Attract Investment

State and local governments react to the prospect of new factory expansions with almost spontaneous offers for tax incentives, tax credits, or even cash grants (Goodman 1971). The data presented here demonstrate that tax differences play no appreciable role in management's location decisions. This may stem from the fact that taxes represent a relatively small portion of business production costs (Bluestone and Harrison 1980, pp. 177-180), and that taxes imposed by one level of government are credited against the tax liability at another level (Southern Growth Policies Board 1981b, p. B-1). Yet, many communities become pitted against one another in a tax cutting contest which does little to attract new investment or halt capital transfers out of the community. Sharp reductions in taxes do, however, diminish government's ability to provide key public services — factors which very much affect managements' decisions to open and close factories.

Public Services

Governments perform a variety of services which aid and benefit businesses, including police and fire protection, road construction, education, land use planning, and regulation of banking, finance, and commerce. One of their most important functions is construction and maintenance of an inter- and intracity highway system. Data from this study demonstrate that companies seriously consider the road systems when locating plant facilities. Older plants are closing in densely populated, metropolitan areas while new factories are going up in suburban areas well serviced by major highway networks. This finding should be of considerable importance to Sunbelt communities where they are still completing parts of the interstate highway system (Southern Growth Policies Board 1981b), and where weak public transit systems have been cited as the key factor in the economic stagnation of Birmingham and possibly other major cities (*Wall Street Journal* March 10, 1981, p. 2:25).

Other vital public services such as education require major infusions of money. Although this study did not explore the direct impact of an educated workforce on plant openings or closings, other studies on Wisconsin development report that it is a crucial component of economic growth (Wisconsin Department of Development 1982a; Strang 1982). A number of Sunbelt states suffer acute deficiencies in both basic and vocational education. Southern states spend only 73 percent of the money per pupil that non-Southern states provide. Many Sunbelt states have extremely high dropout rates; for example in Florida, Georgia, Mississippi, North Carolina, and Texas more than one-fourth of all students drop out before completing high school (Southern Growth Policies Board 1981b, pp. 15-22). Improved educational opportunities must be a priority commitment of Sunbelt states, and one which cannot be attained without a strong and stable tax base.

Capital Investment Policies

Recent research suggests that the Sunbelt may soon run short of investment capital (Southern Growth Policies Board 1981b, pp. 5-7). To remedy this the Southern Growth Policies Board recommended:

The growth of manufacturing employment should continue in the South through the expansion of existing industry, the location of new branch plants of national and multinational corporations, and the location of foreign owned manufacturing facilities (1981a, p. 19).

Any of the three investment sources would potentially supply the needed capital for economic growth in the South. However, the three channels of capital flow carry significantly different ramifications for the regional economy. This study shows that small production units, particularly locally owned ones, are the key source of new manufacturing jobs in Wisconsin; other studies confirm this for the nation as a whole. Externally based corporations, both national and multinational, offer expanded employment opportunities. But many of the jobs "created" are simply acquisitions of already existing jobs. Moreover, the rate of job destruction engineered by externally controlled firms far exceeds that of local companies. The cumulative effect of mergers, acquisitions, and large scale plant transfers could over time present a significant net loss of employment.

States could follow a two-fold strategy to expand capital investment while limiting the hazards of capital flight. First, states might limit the acquisition of locally owned firms by externally based conglomerates. Such legislation would not necessarily preclude mergers or takeovers; instead, the states could require corporations to maintain a social account or ledger, reporting the net changes in jobs, the location and amounts of new capital investment, and any retraining or relocation services provided for disemployed workers. This requirement would enable communities to keep track of the economic and social impact of corporations.

Coupled with this, states should enact plant closing legislation which would at a minimum require companies to provide advance notification of employment shifts. This would give government agencies time to step in and either try to ameliorate those conditions which encourage shutdowns or facilitate the shift of employees to training programs and/or other employment. A more comprehensive program, already operating in Sweden and West Germany, would require employers to report on measures taken to help workers adjust to the dislocation before the plant could be closed (*Economic Dislocation* 1979, pp. 9-26). General Motors and the United Auto Workers have already initiated a similar program in the United States with federal and state government support. These organizations have established a $10 million fund to retrain 8,400 workers displaced by two plant closings in California (Mueller 1982; *New York Times* September 25, 1982a, p. 10). A mandatory program of this sort, requiring all companies who shut down production facilities to retrain and aid in relocating their former employees, stands little chance of being enacted in the state legislatures due to the current competition for a "favorable business environment." Yet, in the long run the real winners would be the state taxpayers who shoulder the billions of dollars in social service costs associated with factory closings and economic dislocation.

In the absence of such comprehensive measures to regulate capital flow, states should follow a path of selective development, encouraging expansion by local firms and recruiting from out-of-state only those firms which will supply sorely needed types of employment or which offer long-term stable and dependable growth.

High Technology Investment

Virtually every state has developed a program to attract high technology companies. With the recent stress on productivity and computerization of production processes, this seems to be a reasonable plan for future economic growth. But the strategy is fundamentally flawed and unlikely to serve as the cornerstone for sustained economic growth.

A high technology firm by its very definition employs a greater percentage of highly skilled technicians, engineers, and scientists (Tomaskovic-Dewey and Miller 1982, pp. 33-34). Certainly as new jobs these are a boon to the community; however, they cannot begin to substitute for the loss in blue collar and semiskilled employment resulting from capital disinvestment. Furthermore, the job-creation capacity of high technology firms falls far below the national average for all industries. From 1969 to 1979, employment in high technology enterprises grew at a rate of between 2 to 5 percent, adding at most 169,000 jobs; overall national employment grew at a rate of 27.6 percent during the same period, producing 19 million jobs (Tomaskovic-Dewey and Miller 1982, pp. 34-35). Obviously, the answer to high structural unemployment will not be found in these industries.

Some argue that new occupations and industries will emerge to service high technology enterprises, or that mass production of technology intensive products will generate blue collar employment. Yet, the statistics from the past decade belie this. Many of the established high technology industries (plastics, electrical distribution equipment, radios and televisions, aircraft, household appliances, and scientific and engineering equipment) witnessed a *net loss* of employment between 1969 and 1979 – as much as 140,000 jobs across 24 industrial groups (Tomaskovic-Dewey and Miller 1982, p. 36). Ironically, it was often the application of productivity related technology which produced this job loss.

If new semiskilled employment does occur in these areas often the jobs are narrowly defined, routinized, and tedious tasks performed for relatively low wages (Mueller 1979; Norton and Rees 1979; International Labour Office 1973). Where state and local governments subsidize this new employment, they have helped create two classes of employment – a small number of highly paid white collar professionals, and a larger group of poorly paid, white collar (or white smock), semiskilled jobs.

The net gain to the community is not clear as the public sector picks up the cost of job related training, tax credits to the companies, or subsidies to cover research and development costs plus the free use of state universities and research centers. The companies provide some employment in the short run. But, these jobs are the ones most easily performed by less skilled, low wage workers outside the United States. Given sufficient international wage differentials these same factories can readily move to Singapore, Taiwan, Mexico, or the Philippines, if they are of sufficient size and corporate structure.

If the benefit/cost ratio in government investments for these jobs is so poor, why do so many states compete for this type of employment? The answer seems to be two-fold: white collar positions associated with "high technology" are glamorous, adding prestige to the state's occupational profile; and, "everyone else is doing it." With a lack of any identifiable alternative sources of employment growth in the near future, states succumb to a new bidding war for high technology companies. Just as in the case of external capital investment, states should think very carefully about offering any special inducements to high technology firms until the policymakers have explored all of the ramifications of this strategy.

Government Regulations

One factor commonly cited as a determinant of business location decisions is the state and local application of government regulations. The administration of regulations, rather than individual rules and laws are the problem, according to manufacturers. With the proliferation of public agencies sharing authority over location decisions (e.g., environmental protection agencies, zoning boards, parking and transit authorities, land use planning bodies, etc.), many companies complain that government jurisdictional overlap, duplication of reporting, and general inaction slows the planning and construction of new plants and the creation of new jobs.

Certainly many regulations are vital to community well-being. On the other hand, businesses stymied with long lead-times due to multiple regulations may face increased construction costs, additional production expenses, and potentially lost sales and revenue. The recent creation of an ombudsman in some states to speed the processing of new business permits, and to coordinate and centralize the regulatory process seems to greatly facilitate economic growth (Schmenner 1980b, pp. 459-460, 462). A recent example graphically illustrates this point.

The Province of Ontario, Canada appointed just such an official who obtained in less than one month all of the permits required for a paint manufacturing company to open a new facility. The same company, headquartered in Wisconsin, waited for more than one year to receive comparable permits in its home state (Hassett 1982).

While not a panacea for regulatory problems nor an escape hatch to avoid legitimate restrictions, the ombudsman can educate, aid, and direct a plant location team through the tangled regulatory thicket, and thereby speed the process of capital expansion. Small businesses — key generators of new jobs — are the ones most in need of this service. For the state, it would greatly facilitate the development of locally owned and financed jobs, a vital element in stable long-term economic development.

CONCLUSION

This study identifies several key lessons and challenges for the Sunbelt. First, many companies, particularly the smaller entrepreneurial firms which create most of the employment in the United States, respond to constraints of geography and transportation. They generally do *not* respond to wage differentials or tax incentives. Case studies have demonstrated that companies who take tax breaks and then establish plants in a community would very likely have done so anyway. In effect the company gets a bonus for doing what it had planned all along, and the city or state gets a sizable long-term tax loss with no guarantee that the company will not move after five or ten years.

Second, larger companies may respond to regional cost differences (lower wages, taxes, etc.), but this does not necessarily bode well for the South or Southwestern regions of the United States. Companies of sufficient size to take advantage of transcontinental shifts in plants, equipment, and communication may as easily transfer their capital to Latin America or Asia.

Finally, the sudden new boom in capital investment among the Sunbelt states may be a transient gain. Frostbelt experience suggests that out-of-state investment may quickly turn into job flight beyond the borders with potentially a *net loss* of jobs. Large-scale firms or mass-production units which provide much of the new employment in the Sunbelt are ones who recently pulled up stakes and moved out of the Frostbelt. One must look critically at the nature of new investment, and not accept it enthusiastically because it appears to bring economic growth.

Future growth in the Sunbelt ultimately depends upon a commitment to community well-being. Capital investment should be encouraged, but investment should be channeled into the smaller, faster growing enterprises which generate long-term, stable employment and revenues for the community. Governments should not rush to give tax incentives and reductions to prospective business developers; rather, it should focus on the traditional role it performs best – to maintain high quality schools, transportation systems, and community services. When capital investment, employment, production, sales, and services reinforce one another in a well-integrated system, communities in the Sunbelt will enjoy a much more stable and prosperous future.

NOTES

1. This may be due to an "accelerating velocity of capital turnover" in the South and in newer firms, (Bluestone and Harrison 1980, p. 50).

2. The former category is quite significant as job loss from partial closings may be three to six times greater than total shutdowns; unfortunately, these data are not recorded systematically in any state in the United States. No federal agency systematically collects any data on plant shutdowns (Joyce 1982).

3. The same comparison cannot be made for in-state firms as a separate reporting category (new plant construction — comprised primarily by in-state firms) could not be included in the analysis. By excluding that category a plant to plant comparison of in-state/out-of-state firms can be made, but this precludes comparisons of aggregate figures on out-of-state versus in-state creation of new jobs.

REFERENCES

Anderson-Roethle, Inc. 1977-1982. *Wisconsin Merger and Acquisition Report.* Milwaukee, Wisconsin: Anderson-Roethle.

Barnet, Richard J., and Ronald Mueller. 1974. *Global Reach.* New York: Simon and Schuster.

Beal, David. 1981. Economics and business editor of the *Milwaukee Journal* speaking before the Social Science Roundtable at the University of Wisconsin-Parkside.

Beckman, Martin. 1968. *Location Theory.* New York: Random House.

Black, J. Thomas. 1980. "The Changing Economic Role of Central Cities and Suburbs." In *The Prospective City*, edited by Arthur P. Solomon, 80-123. Cambridge, Massachusetts: MIT Press.

Bluestone, Barry, and Bennett Harrison. 1980. *Capital and Communities.* Washington, D.C.: Progressive Alliance.

Brenner, M. Harvey. 1977. "Personal Stability and Economic Security." *Social Policy*, May/June, pp. 2-4.

Business Week. 1979. "Neo-Merchantilism in the 1980's: The Worldwide Scramble to Shift Capital." July 9, pp. 50-54.

Classified Directory of Wisconsin Manufacturers. Annual, 1970-1980. Milwaukee: Wisconsin Manufacturers Association.

Economic Dislocation: Plant Closings, Plant Relocations and Plant Conversion. 1979. Joint Report of Labor Union Study Team Participants. United Auto Workers; United Steelworks of America: International Association of Machinists and Aerospace Workers.

Ferman, Louis, ed. 1978. *Mental Health and the Economy.* Kalamazoo, Michigan: W. E. Upjohn Institute.

Goodman, Robert. 1971. *The Last Entrepreneurs: America's Regional Wars for Jobs and Dollars.* New York: Simon and Schuster.

Gordus, Jeanne Prial, Paul Jarley, and Louis A. Ferman. 1981. *Plant Closings and Economic Dislocation.* Kalamazoo, Michigan: W. E. Upjohn Institute.

Greenhut, Melvin L. 1956. *Plant Location in Theory and Practice*. Chapel Hill: University of North Carolina Press.

Hassett, Paul. 1982. President, Wisconsin Association of Manufacturers and Commerce. Testimony before the Wisconsin Legislative Council. Madison, Wisconsin. August 27.

Hoffman Associates Inc. 1981. *The Hoffman Index*. New York: Howard P. Hoffman Associates.

Illinois Advisory Committee to the U.S. Civil Rights Commission. 1981. *Shutdown: Economic Dislocation and Equal Opportunity*. Chicago: Illinois Advisory Committee to the U.S. Civil Rights Commission.

International Labour Office. 1973. *Multinational Corporations and Social Policy*. Geneva: International Labour Office.

Isard, Walter. 1956. *Location and Space-Economy*. Cambridge, Massachusetts: MIT Press.

Joyce, Thomas. 1982. Project Monitor, Employment and Training Administration, U.S. Department of Labor. Personal conversation. February 9.

Logue, John. 1980. "When They Close the Factory Gates: How Big Steel Scrapped a Community." *Progressive*, August, pp. 16-29.

Marchetti, Peter. 1980. "Runaway and Takeovers: Their Effect on Milwaukee's Economy." *Urbanism: Past and Present* 5: 1-11.

Mason, Colin M. 1980. "Industrial Decline in Greater Manchester, 1960-1975." *Urban Studies* 17: 173-184.

McGovern, Daniel. 1982. Comments prepared for the Economic Policy Committee Democratic Caucus of the U.S. House of Representatives, Public Hearing in Racine, Wisconsin, February 16.

McKenzie, Richard B. 1979. *Restrictions on Business Mobility*. Washington: American Enterprise Institute.

Minneapolis Metropolitan Council. 1979. *Industrial Migration Trends in the Twin Cities Metropolitan Area, 1960-1977*. Minneapolis/St. Paul, Minnesota: Metro Council.

Mueller, John. 1982. Director, Corporate Public Relations Department, General Motors. Personal conversation. October 12.

Mueller, Ronald. 1979. "Poverty is the Product." In *Transnational Corporations and World Order*, edited by George Modelski, pp. 245-61. San Francisco: W. H. Freeman.

New York Times. 1982a. "Retraining Accord Reached on Coast." September 25, p. 10.

———. 1982b. "Harvester Move Hailed as Ohio City Wins Plant." October 10, p. Y35.

Norton, R. D., and J. Rees. 1979. "The Product Cycle and the Spatial Decentralization of American Manufacturing." *Regional Studies* 13: 141-52.

Schmenner, Roger W. 1980a. "Choosing New Industrial Capacity." *Quarterly Journal of Economics* 45: 103-20.

———. 1980b. "Industrial Location and Urban Public Management." In *The Prospective City*. edited by Arthur P. Solomon, pp. 446-68. Cambridge, Massachusetts: MIT Press.

_____. 1982. *Making Business Location Decisions*. Englewood Cliffs, New Jersey: Prentice-Hall.
Shostak, Arthur. 1980. "The Human Cost of Plant Closings." *American Federationist*, August.
Southern Growth Policies Board. 1981a. *Final Report: 1980 Commission on the Future of the South*. Research Triangle Park, North Carolina: Southern Growth Policies Board.
_____. 1981b. *Report of the Task Force on the Southern Economy*. Research Triangle Park, North Carolina: Southern Growth Policies Board.
Stepan, Alfred. 1979. "U.S.-Latin American Relations." In *America and the World, 1979*, edited by William P. Bundy, pp. 659-92. New York: Pergamon Press.
Strang, William. 1982. "Expectations for Wisconsin's Economy and the Means to Realize Them." In *Wisconsin's Economy in 1990*, pp. 133-48. Madison: University of Wisconsin Bureau of Business Research.
Tomaskovic-Dewey, Donald, and S. M. Miller. 1982. "Recapitalization: The Basic U.S. Urban Policy of the 1980s." In *Urban Policy Under Capitalism*, edited by Norman I. Fainstein and Susan S. Fainstein, pp. 231-42. Urban Affairs Annual Reviews, vol. 22. Beverly Hills: Sage.
Vernon, Raymond. 1971. *Sovereignty at Bay*. New York: Basic Books.
Wall Street Journal. 1981. "Ailing Birmingham Struggles to Join Sunbelt Euphoria." March 10, sec. 2, p. 25.
Washington Post. 1980. "Report Blames Mergers for Some Economic Woes." October 10, p. D3.
Wheeler, James O. 1981. "Effects of Geographic Scale on Location Decisions in Manufacturing." *Economic Geography* 57: 134-45.
Wisconsin Blue Book 1981-1982. 1981. Madison: Wisconsin Legislative Research Bureau.
Wisconsin Department of Development. Annual, 1970-1982. *Wisconsin: New Industries and Plant Expansions Reported in Wisconsin*. Madison: Wisconsin. Department of Development.
_____. 1982a. *Wisconsin Manufacturing: Charting a Course for Renewed Vitality*. Madison: Wisconsin Department of Development.
_____. 1982b. *Wisconsin: New Industries and Plant Expansions Reported in Wisconsin, 1981*. Madison: Wisconsin Department of Development.
Wisconsin Statistical Abstract, 1979. Madison: Wisconsin Department of Industry, Labor and Human Relations.

APPENDIX

Measures for Testing Geographic, Economic, and Political Variables

Concept	*Measure*	*Data Source*
LAND AREA	County Size in Square Miles	*Wisconsin Blue Book 1981-1982*, 1981, 718
POPULATION	County Population	*Wisconsin Blue Book 1981-1982*, 1981, 718
POPULATION DENSITY	Population/Land Area	
HIGHWAY MILES	State Trunk Highway Miles	*Wisconsin Blue Book 1981-1982*, 1981, 814
HIGHWAYS PER MILE	Highway Miles - Land Area	
UNEMPLOYMENT	Average Rate of Unemployment by County, 1972	*Wisconsin Statistical Abstract*, 1979, I-10
WAGE RATE	Average Wage Rate, Hourly Pay by County, 1972	*Wisconsin Statistical Abstract*, 1979, J-15
TAX RATE	Effective Full Value Rate After Tax Relief, General Property Taxes by County, 1979	*Wisconsin Blue Book 1981-1982*, 1981, 790-791

4 Urban Health Care Delivery in the Sunbelt

Mary G. Almore and
Frances Richardson

INTRODUCTION

The Omnibus Budget Reconciliation Act (OBRA) of 1981 and some of the provisions of the continuing budget resolutions under which the government continues to operate have significant implications for urban health care delivery. It is difficult to chronicle all these implications, just as it would be with respect to any "quality of life" indicator. Our concern shall be primarily with "discretionary" programs which are more vulnerable to manipulation than are the Entitlement Programs. In particular, we will focus on programs for which no appropriations have been included after fiscal 1983, which have been included in block grants, and/or which represent real dollar decreases in funding rather than merely a slowing of the rate of growth. Consideration will be given to general implications for health care delivery proposals, particularly for the Sunbelt.

BACKGROUND

The Reagan administration achieved a rather high level of success in getting budget recommendations passed in the summer and fall of 1981, culminating in the 1981 OBRA. Administration success has come with a bit more difficulty in the summer and fall of 1982. However, health care delivery again has been impacted negatively in terms of proposed allocations. President Reagan initially proposed a 25 percent across the board cut in social programs, excluding Entitlement Programs but including nonentitlement health care, along with consolidation of many programs into block grants. Had Congress followed these initial recommendations, Sugarman (1981) has pointed out that, taking predicted levels of inflation into account, real dollar decline would have exceeded 55 to 60 percent by 1984 as measured against 1980. The president's proposals were not followed in all cases. Still, funding was held constant through 1984 in several instances related to health care delivery, while in other instances, no funds were appropriated beyond 1982 or 1983.

Along with calling for further cutbacks in social programs and combining more programs into block grants, President Reagan formalized his concept of "new federalism" in his State of the Union message on January 26, 1982. The new federalism proposal already has been revised and continues to be the subject of debate at various levels of government. A major component of this debate is the issue of whether programs designed at the grass roots level are more effective and responsive to people's needs. While it seems clear that cuts in social programs will not come as easily in 1984 as in 1981, especially vis-à-vis defense spending, the president does retain considerable personal popularity as shown, for example, by the public opinion polls. Alternatives are now being more widely discussed, but the administration shows limited inclination to consider them viable unless they impact negatively on social programs rather than defense expenditures.

Whatever legislation ultimately is passed, it is clear that: (1) states will have more control and financial responsibility for social programs, including many of those related to health care; (2) programs already consolidated into block grants will not be broken out into categorical programs; and (3) appropriations for at least most social programs will not be restored or increased. Entitlement Programs are no longer as sacrosanct as they were and, while it is still claimed that the truly needy will not suffer, the safety net appears to be getting smaller and, for many, uncomfortably close to the ground. These forces will create planning and management problems of varying degrees throughout the nation. But, as we review some of the areas in which health care related reductions have been made or proposed, we find some particular implications for the Sunbelt. Before proceeding with that review, however, we would like to discuss migration, a major factor contributing to Sunbelt social service delivery problems.

SUNBELT MIGRATION AND URBAN
HEALTH CARE DEMANDS

Migration to the Sunbelt is certainly not a new phenomenon. Although a moderate amount of emigration from the South has take place, rapid population increases of the past two decades have brought in not only many more people, but also quite diverse groups.[1] Central and southern Florida especially have been popular areas for retirees. Many of these people are on fixed incomes and suffer some degree of the chronic illnesses often associated with older people. Thus, they are likely recipients of services provided by social health care programs.

The Reagan administration's proposal for new federalism has generated many criticisms, including those related to the inability of states to provide adequate social services. In response to these criticisms, the president indicated that people who were not satisfied with what was available in one state could "vote with their feet" and migrate as did their forefathers. Large numbers of people are doing just that and abandoning the depressed economy of the Frost-belt for the assumed opportunities to be found in the South. Their efforts to find new employment are not always successful — steel-making skills are not in great demand in Birmingham; automobile workers have a difficult time finding similar jobs in an area where the relatively few automobile assembly plants have already been operating at less than full capacity for several years. The more people continue to move to the Sunbelt because they perceive it as an area of opportunity, yet are not able to find jobs, the greater the demand for social services and the greater the stress placed on agencies and institutions that provide the services.

There also has been a large influx of Cubans, Haitians, and Southeast Asians, many of whom place significant demands (at least in the aggregate) on social services, including health care. Among the Sunbelt states, Texas in particular has a large number of illegal aliens from Mexico and an increasing number from Central American countries. Although some believe that illegal aliens don't make many demands for social services because they are fearful of being identified and deported, others express the fear that there will be a dramatic increase in such demands if any type of amnesty program is instituted. To the degree that any of the above groups require health care or other services, they are among the most vulnerable to cutbacks in support for social programs.

As noted in Chapter 2, the Sunbelt has become the most populous region of the country and is expected to continue to grow at a faster rate than any region except the West. Thus, the need for social services is likely to be greater in the South than other areas of the country because of the sheer number of people and the large number of at-risk groups. At the same time, state and local service providers may not be as well equipped to meet these needs due to cutbacks in federal support. The next section will focus on some of the health care programs that have been negatively affected by the Reagan budget proposals and the potential implications for the Sunbelt.

PROFESSIONAL HEALTH EDUCATION AND RESEARCH PROGRAMS

The potential for a critical shortage of nurses and allied health professionals in this country has been frequently discussed. Yet funds for Health Professions and Nurse's Training were budgeted to decrease over 56 percent from 1981 and 1982. Under the 1981 OBRA some increases were recommended for 1983 and 1984 but, at their maximum, they would still have been more than 25 percent below the 1981 allocations (Sugarman 1981). For 1983 and beyond, no capitation funding will be available for Allied Health Professions. Capitation funds were formula funds (i.e., amount per full-time or part-time student) made available to programs showing an increase in enrollment and/or providing education for special disadvantaged groups. Their use was largely discretionary (for example, faculty development, purchase of relevant soft- and/or hardware, student scholarships) so long as program improvement was the basic goal. Also beginning in 1983, support for nurses will be lost for capitation funding, loans, traineeships, fellowships, research grants, and special projects for nurse training/education (*The Nation's Health* 1982). Nevertheless, medical treatment and technology is becoming increasingly complex and sophisticated and a nurse who has been out of the field for as little as a year should have at least two months refresher training to become current. These technical and other medical advances are of limited value without a sufficient number of skilled personnel.

Thus, at a time when increases in Sunbelt population can be expected to create demands for even more skilled nurses and allied health professionals, budget cutbacks will make it more difficult for prospective and current students to complete their educations. Also, the Sunbelt has several schools of nursing that have achieved national recognition for their programs. This helps to attract students from other geographical areas, at least some of whom remain in the area after graduation. Cutbacks will make attracting these students more difficult if financial assistance is not available. If they cannot attend these schools and must go elsewhere instead, there is little in terms of competitive salaries to attract them to the Sunbelt to work in contrast to such areas as California and the east coast.

Beginning in 1983, modest increases have been proposed in research funds for the National Institute of Alcohol Abuse and Alcoholism and for the National Institute of Drug Abuse. However, in both cases funds for clinical training have been eliminated (Research Report Network 1982). While the federal program based in Miami and designed to reduce drug trafficking has apparently met with quite a bit of success in intercepting illegal drugs, one negative effect has been to spread the importation of such drugs throughout the Gulf Coast, leading to plans to establish another major program of this type in Houston. Since no such program is entirely successful, one possible outcome of these efforts may be to make illicit drugs even more accessible in at least parts of the Sunbelt. It seems incongruous to simultaneously reduce the number of available treatment personnel by eliminating funds for clinical training in these areas.

The 1983 budget proposal for the National Institute of Mental Health calls for a decrease of 74.2 million dollars from 1981; again, all funds for clinical training have been eliminated. The National Institutes of Health budget appears to be surviving essentially intact; in fact the 1983 proposed allocation calls for 179 million dollars more than the 1980 allocation. Indications point to this reflecting the Institutes' focus on pure research, which the current administration reportedly favors over applied research. Still, the proposed increase is less than 3 percent, well below recent inflation rates. According to representatives of the Institutes, this will result in a 14 percent decrease in new and competing research grants and an 8 percent decrease in the number of research trainees (*The Nation's Health* 1982). Whether this will impact more on the Sunbelt than on other geographical areas cannot be determined until the funds are actually allocated and specific grants awarded.

MENTAL HEALTH

Although separating mental health from other health care considerations is a rather arbitrary exercise, it is done for budgetary purposes. Aside from research considerations, already briefly mentioned, mental health programs have been a popular target for actual and/or proposed budget reductions. Turkington (1982) suggests that one reason for this appears to be a lack of perceived cost-effectiveness. In the same article she also reported on testimony given by psychiatrists, psychologists, social workers, and congressmen before the House Post Office and Civil Service Subcommittee on Compensation and Employee Benefits. The witnesses pointed to a number of documented studies which demonstrated ". . . that successful treatment of mental illness actually reduces the demand for medical and surgical care and cuts out needless in-patient hospitalization for illnesses that are not organically based" (Turkington 1982, p. 36).

Several examples of actual or proposed cutbacks may be noted. The Health Care Reform Act (H. R. 850), as passed by the House in 1981, specifically excludes mental health benefits from mandated health care benefits (*Advance* 1981; Welch 1981). Effective January 1, 1982, the Federal Employees Health Benefits Program (which then affected 9.2 million federal employees) increased the cost of insured mental health benefits by an average of 31 percent while reducing benefits by about 12.6 percent (*Advance* 1982; Turkington 1982). Congress also cut 7.4 million dollars from funds already budgeted for demonstration programs for the chronically mentally ill and another 6.2 million from the 68 million dollars already allocated for various other mental health services. In addition, it cut the entire 25 million dollars that had been set aside for new community mental health services. Some existing community mental health programs may receive support under the Title XIX block grant scheduled to go into effect in 1983 (Armstrong 1981).

There is no reason to assume a decrease in psychological difficulties in the near future, ranging from the ordinary problems of living which we all experience from time to time through serious mental illness, with the implications that that has for physical health as well. What can be assumed is a diminution of intervention strategies, at least at the community level. Yet, Brenner, who specializes in monetary matters and mental health, cites increased suicide, depression, alcoholism, domestic violence, and mental illness as factors associated with economic stress. He has estimated an increase of 4,200 first admissions to state mental hospitals for every 1 percent increase in unemployment (*Newsletter* 1982).

Ahr, Gorodesky, and Chu have found a correlation between unemployment rates and out-patient records indicating that psychiatric patients return to hospitalization more frequently during times of economic adversity (*Newsletter* 1982). The Mental Health Association in Fort Worth reports that half of the 19,000 admissions to the state mental hospitals in Texas last year were readmissions, a percentage which the association attributes largely to inadequate community facilities including residential services.

MATERNAL AND CHILD HEALTH

Beginning in 1982, Maternal and Child Health Services became a block grant under the 1981 OBRA. Appropriations for this grant were scheduled to remain constant from 1982 through 1984, reflecting a rather significant real dollar reduction (Sugarman 1981). Furthermore, these recommendations represented a reduction of about 7 percent from 1980 allocations while adding yet another category of potential fund recipients (Rehabilitation Services for Disabled Children Receiving Supplementary Security Income) previously funded under another program. Proposals made in 1982, but not yet translated into allocations, call for a slight increase in the Maternal and Child Health Care block grant, but only to compensate for the federal government's abolishing the Special Supplemental Food Program for Women, Infants, and Children (WIC), allowing individual states the option to pick up the program. However, the compensatory funds requested are approximately 27 percent below current WIC operating levels. Yet, a study done at the Harvard School of Public Health found that:

WIC resulted in a marked reduction in the incidence of low birthweight infants. Low birthweight is the eighth leading cause of death in the US (sic), and is also associated with increased disabilities such as blindness,

deafness, and mental retardation. The Harvard study found that because of the reduced incidence of low birthweight, fewer infants need
extended hospitalization after birth, and that each dollar spent in the
prenatal component of WIC actually averts $3 (sic) in hospital costs
(Miller 1982, p. 8).

Although no evidence exists to support a contention that low
birthweight is a more significant problem overall in the Sunbelt
than it is in other regions, the potential for it to become a more
serious problem in the Sunbelt reflects: (1) the level of migration
to the Sunbelt combined with the fact that some of those migrating
will not find employment or the level of employment that they
anticipated; and (2) the generally lower level of expenditures for
social services in the Sunbelt. For example, one would not anticipate
that states which now rank forty-ninth and fiftieth (Texas and
Mississippi) in categorial welfare benefits and have no programs of
General Assistance will readily fund a program such as WIC.

Health care services for children have been affected through
other programs also. For example, the Center for Disease Control
and hence, the people they serve have not fared well under the
Reagan budgets. Nationwide, between 500 and 700 trained disease
investigators will be lost and between three and five million children
will go unprotected by immunization for various diseases. The 20
percent cut in funding and 30 percent increase in the costs of
vaccines since 1981 have combined to produce a real dollar loss
of five million dollars. Past experience does not augur well for states
and local communities making up for these federal cuts. From 1972
to 1976 federal spending for measles control dropped from 4 million
dollars to 2 million dollars; by 1977 the incidence of rubella had
increased 200 percent from the 1972 level. While the impact of these
cuts will not be limited to the Sunbelt, again that area's traditionally
limited expenditures for social services may well exacerbate the
problems experienced in the region. For example, it is estimated that
in North Carolina alone between 80,000 and 100,000 children will
lose fluoridation services, with a projected increase in dental cavities
of at least 35 percent among those children (Pickett 1982).

Funding for developmental disabilities also affects the health
and welfare of a number of children. Under the 1981 OBRA such
funding was scheduled to be held constant from 1982 through 1984
(Sugarman 1981) and the administration continues its efforts to have

these programs included in a block grant (Bauknecht 1982). The administration and congressional supporters sought to delete all funding under the Education for All Handicapped Children Act (PL 94-142) in 1981 and was successful in reducing funds by more than 25 percent to about $200.00 per child served. Already New Mexico has withdrawn from the programs which frees it of all federal regulations pertaining to the nature and quality of services offered — indeed, of offering any of the services at all (*Update* 1982).

SELECTED AT-RISK GROUPS: MENTAL AND PHYSICAL HEALTH CONSIDERATIONS

Several groups of people who may be considered at risk in terms of physical and/or mental health problems have been affected by Reagan budget policies. For example, beginning with the 1983 fiscal year all funding for urban health projects for Indians is scheduled to be eliminated. Certainly, this will have potential impact on several Sunbelt states including, for example, Florida, North Carolina, Oklahoma, and Texas (*The Nation's Health* 1982).

Recommended fiscal 1983 funding for special mental health programs represents a reduction of 60.3 million dollars from the 1980 appropriation for programs which focus on crime and delinquency, minorities, rape, and aging (Research Report Network 1982). Yet, according to the U.S. Department of Justice (1982), the Sunbelt holds approximately 40 percent of all prisoners in the United States and also has a significant number of minorities. Research and services programs for these groups will likely be negatively impacted by reductions of this magnitude.

Child abuse prevention and treatment programs have also suffered losses as a result of administration budget actions. Under the 1981 OBRA, funding for this category was scheduled to be reduced by over 17 percent from 1980-1981 levels effective 1982, to be held constant from 1982 through 1983, and to be completely eliminated in fiscal 1984. This was to take place in spite of the increased attention that has been focused on child abuse as a social problem with both physical and mental health implications. Although actual appropriations for 1983 and beyond remain uncertain, indications are that they will not change appreciably from previous recommendations. Yet, as with psychological problems in general,

there is no reason to assume that problems of child abuse will diminish in the near future. Indeed, increases in child abuse have been
associated with economic dislocation (e.g., Straus 1980; Horowitz
and Wolock 1981). While problems of unemployment and under-
employment have generally been more severe in the Frostbelt, the
Sunbelt has certainly not been spared economic dislocation and
may well experience an increase in children at risk. This is especially
likely if people continue to migrate to the area in search of employment and find frustration instead.

BLOCK GRANTS AND PROGRAM IMPLEMENTATION

Regardless of the ultimate outcome with respect to new federalism, the consolidation of a number of health care programs into
block grants can have significant implications for program implementation, especially in combination with curtailments in Entitlement
Programs and a generally unhealthy economy. In contrast to categorical grants, block grants tend to include a broader range of related
activities with less precise purpose and to be less subject to federal
regulations and standards. In several instances all that is necessary
for a state to refuse to fund a block grant program (or parts of a
program) under the guidelines established by the 1981 OBRA is a
finding by the state that the program, or some portion(s) of it, does
not meet performance criteria set by the state.

Concepts and practices such as block grants and new federalism
do tend to have a certain popular appeal for quite a few people.
For one thing, they appear to respond to the contention that state
and local governments are closer to the people, have a better understanding of their needs, and are, therefore, in a better position to
meet those needs than is the federal government. For another thing,
they appear — initially at least — to offer the potential of simple
solutions. As Drew (1982, p. 119), for example, has contended:
"In a political debate, the tactical advantage of making something
sound very simple is that those who oppose it are often forced to
make it sound complicated and appear to be against something
worthy . . ." But, in addition to giving states greater control and
flexibility, such concepts and practices as these also give the states
significant responsibilities. As Nichols (1982, p. 4) has pointed out,
if the states do not meet those responsibilities adequately, the results

can be ". . . monumental snarls of inequity, inefficiency and waste, contributing to neglect, suffering and death, with the vulnerable segments of our population most at risk." Already debate has begun regarding the distribution of such federal funds as will be available. Should they be distributed on the basis of a state's per capita income, which would tend to favor the Sunbelt, or on the basis of a state's real or potential tax base, which would tend to favor the Frostbelt (e.g., Weinstein 1982).

In the interim, several short-term results can be anticipated: (1) more persons will enter the ranks of the marginal, physically and/or psychologically, where their roles will be more as consumers than as producers; (2) the emergency room and county hospital clinics will become the substitute family doctor for more people, including those of the middle-class, further straining already strained facilities; (3) health care costs will increase, especially where hospitalization itself may increase as people seek to maximize their insurance benefits; (4) more people will be institutionalized as those who are currently marginal lose even more of their community support systems; and (5) the number of skilled health care professionals will be even less adequate.

There are more politically oriented implications as well, including increased competition between: (1) geographical regions; (2) states within regions; (3) various urban areas within a state; (4) urban and rural interests; and (5) programs to be funded from such monies as are available. There also will be inequities among the states, in some cases because a conscious choice will be made to basically ignore the needs of selected target groups who are not seen as meriting our concern and expenditures, in some cases because the people will not be willing to approve necessary tax increases, and in some cases because an adequate tax base will simply not be there. These results and implications will not be limited to the Sunbelt, of course, but several management issues particularly relevant to the Sunbelt can be cited.

MANAGEMENT ISSUES FOR THE SUNBELT

The question of migration to the Sunbelt and the various implications of that migration have already been noted. But we would point out again that simply coping with large increases in population and controlling growth in ways that are not damaging to the quality of life will require a degree of proactive planning which has not generally characterized the Sunbelt. Also, state legislatures which tend to be dominated by rural interests will have to become more cognizant of, and sympathetic to, urban issues – including health care – if we are going to avoid exacerbating problems and, certainly, if we are going to seek to solve problems.

The question of the available tax base is an important one. For example, a large proportion of Florida's population is comprised of the elderly living on limited incomes and/or currently receiving tax breaks such as increased homestead exemptions. Others, such as Mississippi, the Carolinas, and Alabama, traditionally have fairly low per capita incomes and some have been further hurt by reductions in the textile and steel industries. Still other Sunbelt states, such as Louisiana and Texas, could potentially broaden their tax base with revenues from oil and gas. But, even though the major oil companies are doing well financially (in part because of large investments in enterprises other than oil and gas), many smaller, independent producers have already had to curtail or shut down their operations in the face of what is currently an over-supply of these resources. Some of the more affluent states, such as Texas, will need to plan more carefully in terms of husbanding their funds than they have had to do for some years.

Sunbelt states in general have been rather reluctant to expend funds for social programs regardless of the availability of real or potential funds. As a rule, they have also been reluctant to raise taxes for such programs. Although favorable tax structures have been one factor contributing to the growth in the Sunbelt, both politicians and the public are going to have to review their priorities and preferences with respect to taxing and spending for social programs. The decision in at least some states may be to continue limited taxation and expenditures for these programs as much as possible. But the issues must be addressed. In spite of sanguine pronouncements each time an economic indicator seems to have improved, there is not a solid basis for predicting any dramatic economic turn-around in the near future. Given that and the reductions in federal funding for health care that have already occurred, it would seem both cruel and, in the long run, counterproductive to deny such care to large numbers of people on the basis of their inability, or limited ability, to afford it. Considering, and where appropriate, changing traditional approaches to taxing and/or spending for urban health care needs is an important issue to the future well-being of Sunbelt residents.

SUMMARY

Several major changes in urban health care delivery in the Sunbelt already enacted or proposed have been discussed and some of the potential implications of those changes presented. Some rather significant reductions have been made and indications are that more reductions will be forthcoming, along with more responsibility for planning and disbursement devolving to the states. Continued growth in the Sunbelt will ultimately increase demands for health care delivery for all economic classes; finding reasoned and reasonable solutions to the problems posed constitutes a significant challenge. This challenge cannot be ignored in spite of the uncertainties generated by the fact that the federal government continues to operate under ongoing budget resolutions and uncertainty about what directions new federalism might eventually take. A reactive stance rather than a proactive approach has been the norm too long; if this type of management persists it is likely to exact a heavy cost in terms of the quality of life in the Sunbelt.

NOTES

1. For a more complete discussion of the reasons behind the recent growth in the Sunbelt and information concerning current and future growth, see Chapters 1 and 2.

REFERENCES

Advance. 1981. Vol. 6, November. Washington, D.C.: Association for the Advancement of Psychology.
_____. 1982. Vol. 8, January. Washington, D.C.: Association for the Advancement of Psychology.
Armstrong, Barbara. 1981. "The Bottom Line: Reagan Wins Cuts for this Year." *APA Monitor* 12 (August/September): 5.
Bauknecht, Virginia. 1982. "Capital Commentary." *The American Nurse* January, p. 6.

Drew, Elizabeth. 1982. "A Reporter in Washington, D.C." *The New Yorker,* February 8, pp. 118-22.

Horowitz, Bernard, and Isabell Wolock. 1981. "Maternal Deprivation, Child Maltreatment, and Agency Interventions Among Poor Families." In *The Social Context of Child Abuse and Neglect,* edited by L. H. Pelton, pp. 137-84. New York: Human Sciences Press.

Miller, Arden. 1982. "WIC Block Grant Scheme Would Diminish Benefits." *The Nation's Health* March, p. 8.

Newsletter. 1982. New York: American Orthopsychiatric Association, Winter.

Nichols, Barbara. 1982. "Who Speaks for the Poor as States Slice Block Grants?" *The American Nurse* January, p. 4.

Pickett, George. 1982. "CDC Budget Gives Disease a Chance." *The Nation's Health* March, p. 12.

Research Report Network. 1982. *Status Report on the Federal Budget as It Affects Psychology, and Behavioral and Social Research, Training, and Services.* Washington, D.C.: American Psychological Association, July 1.

Straus, Murray A. 1980. "Stress and Child Abuse." In *The Battered Child* 3rd ed., edited by C. H. Kempe and R. E. Helfer, pp. 86-103. Chicago: The University of Chicago Press.

Sugarman, Jule M. 1981. *Citizen's Guide to Changes in Human Services Programs.* Washington, D.C.: Human Services Information Center.

The Nation's Health. 1982. Washington, D.C.: American Public Health Association, March.

Turkington, Carol. 1982. "Experts Criticize Cutbacks in FEHB Plan Coverage." *APA Monitor* 13 (January): 1, 36, 41.

U.S. Department of Justice. Bureau of Justice Statistics. 1982. *Prisoners at Mid-year 1982.* Washington, D.C.: Bureau of Justice Statistics.

Update. 1982. Washington, D.C.: Mental Health Law Project, January.

Weinstein, Bernard L. 1982. "Truth About Wealth, Poverty: Reader's Reply." *The Dallas Morning News* October 9, p. 27A.

Welch, Wayne. 1981. "New Health Insurance Bills Lose in 'Competition' Hearings." *APA Monitor* 12 (November): 1, 37.

5 State Government Capacity for Managing Sunbelt Growth
Steven C. Ballard and
Elizabeth M. Gunn

INTRODUCTION

Sunbelt states have been experiencing rapid growth and change over the past two decades.[1] Once viewed as poor relatives in the national partnership, southern states are now envied as growth centers for industry, energy production, agriculture, and forestry. Many benefits are derived from this growth, including increased population, capital, and jobs. However, rapid regional growth also creates pressures for environmental change through increasing demands for land and water and increasing generation of waste materials. A critical question for states in the Sunbelt is how to continue to attract the benefits of growth while developing strategies for environmental and natural resource management.

This question is occurring within a rapidly changing political and institutional context, including decreased emphasis on federal regulatory intervention and decentralization of financial responsibility. In many respects, new federalism initiatives should be attractive to the states, since federal dominance in the environmental

The Sunbelt has been the focus of an Integrated Environmental Assessment conducted by the Science and Public Policy Program over the past two years. The authors wish to acknowledge the contribution of other members of the research team to the development of this chapter: Michael D. Devine (Project Director), Basil G. Achilladelis, Michael A. Chartock, Thomas E. James, Jr., Richard L. Johnston, Rebecca S. Roberts, and Karen J. Selland.

area has been a major source of friction between the federal, state, and local governments (Hall, White, and Ballard 1978; Menzel 1981). A particularly contentious element of federal-state relationships has been the issue of whether states have the capacity or willingness to carry out various environmental mandates (Jones 1974; Lieber 1975; Hebert and Wright 1982). Previous studies comparing the adoption of growth management programs in the 50 states have found the southern states typically ranked in the lower half (Clarke and Dodson 1979; Walker 1969). Thus, with increasing state financial and programmatic responsibility, a key growth issue will be the capacity of Sunbelt states to adopt, implement, and maintain environmental policies to protect human resources, natural resources, and the attractive quality of life which have made growth possible.

This chapter discusses state government capacity to manage growth in the 1980s. Specific attention is given to managing natural resource problems. The following section briefly identifies key environmental problems likely to face state governments in the Sunbelt over the next decade. This is followed by a review and assessment of indicators of state management capacity.

KEY ENVIRONMENTAL PROBLEMS AND ISSUES

Growth in the Sunbelt is creating new pressures on states and localities to manage their human and physical resources. Even in areas where growth is not particularly rapid, better information is needed about the nature and source of pollutants in air, water, and land resources. Among the most important environmental problems facing the South are water resource management, hazardous waste management, coastal zone management, and air quality protection (Science and Public Policy Program 1982).

Water Resources

Water resources management is likely to be the most critical issue facing Sunbelt states over the next few decades. In some states — particularly New Mexico, Texas, Oklahoma, and Florida — water shortages have been a long-standing problem. However, the critical concern about water resources is that the factors that have led to water resource conflicts in the West and Southwest are now emerging in the Southeast. These factors are competition among industrial, municipal, and agricultural interests (Kyl 1982) and increasing water quality problems which limit the use of water resources. Further, the legal and regulatory systems of many Sunbelt states reflect a history of water abundance. Thus, little precedent exists for a strong state role in resolving conflicting demands; administrative arrangements are typically underdeveloped; and baseline information on ground water resources often is not available (Science and Public Policy Program 1982).

A particularly important management need will be to understand the relationships between water quality and water availability. Water quality problems include point source pollutants from industrial plants and municipal waste water treatment facilities, and nonpoint sources such as runoff from mining, construction, silvacultural and agricultural practices. The most serious threat to water quality is hazardous wastes. One source estimates that over 41 million tons of hazardous wastes are produced each year, over 40 percent of which are generated in the Sunbelt; only about 10 percent of hazardous wastes have been disposed of in a manner sufficient to protect water resources (U.S. Environmental Protection Agency 1980).

Ground water depletion is a relatively new concern for eastern states, but even states with a history of water scarcity have not developed adequate management systems. Seven states (Florida, Georgia, Kentucky, Mississippi, Oklahoma, South Carolina, and Tennessee) have enacted legislation authorizing statewide permit systems for regulating ground water withdrawals, but only Florida and Oklahoma have developed their systems into comprehensive programs. Georgia and Kentucky, for example, exempt agriculture from the permitting process. Tennessee's permitting law is essentially a registration requirement. Similarly, South Carolina's recently enacted permitting system is actually an information gathering system (Science and Public Policy Program 1983). Although seven states (Mississippi, North Carolina, South Carolina, Florida, Louisiana, New Mexico, and Texas) have authority to designate critical areas which allow the state to regulate ground water use, experiences with these areas have been mixed. For example, in South Carolina, the state may regulate such an area only after a request for help by a local governmental unit (Science and Public Policy Program 1983). North Carolina has not developed the capacity to implement and enforce a permitting system in such vital areas (Sherwani 1980; Howells 1978). Four states (Florida, New Mexico, North Carolina, and Oklahoma) have some form of conjunctive management, which recognizes the interrelationship between surface and ground water.

Sunbelt states have increasingly recognized water resource management as a primary growth concern. In his recent State of the State address, Governor Riley of South Carolina included water in his top five priorities for attention:

> Our single most essential natural resource is water. . . . This year, I will . . . take a look at our ability to deal with drought and other water use conflicts, the adequacy of the state's water quality standards, the need for automatic civil penalties for water pollution, and baseline environmental studies so that our economic growth will be compatible with the quality of our environment (Jacobs 1982, p. 4).

However, lack of funds and information may constrain capacity for action. In Oklahoma, Governor George Nigh said in 1981 that "water is the major issue of the '80's" (Bean 1981, p. 21). However, a year later, faced with a slowing economy and voter rejection of a proposed state water fund, Nigh (1982) told Oklahoma that money would not be available for development of alternative water sources.

Hazardous Wastes

The Sunbelt produces about 41 percent of the nation's hazardous wastes and has about 25 percent of the generators. Chemicals and allied products account for the major portion of these hazardous wastes; as much as 85 percent of the wastes generated in the Southeast and 81 percent of wastes generated in the Southwest. Other major sources in the Sunbelt include stone, clay and glass production, fabricated metals, petroleum and coal products, textile mill products, and primary metal production. These last five generators are localized to a few states (Science and Public Policy Program 1982).

The extent of ground water and soil contamination from inadequate waste disposal practices are a growing concern as officials continue to identify existing sites throughout the United States that could threaten human health and the environment (Maugh 1979). The South has a large proportional share of locations on the

Environmental Protection Agency's (EPA) recent list of the 115 sites needing priority attention for emergency cleanups (*EPA Journal* 1981). Hazardous waste activities were subsumed as part of the Resource Conservation and Recovery Act (RCRA) of 1976 which addressed the broader area of solid wastes. Unlike many other environmental programs for which the federal government assumed major responsibility, hazardous waste management has become largely a state responsibility. Yet few states have the capacity to deal effectively with hazardous waste management for several reasons, including:

• data gaps and regulatory and scientific uncertainties are still prevalent because of the newness of the concern;
• siting of hazardous waste facilities requires that states develop strategies for settling jurisdictional disputes based on a variety of criteria including geologic evidence of suitability, social acceptability, and economic costs;
• monitoring programs for ground water quality typically are not in place; and
• scientific, technical, and professional personnel have been difficult both to find and retain.

Land Use

Coastal zone management and land use issues will also be important as population and industrial growth increase along the coasts and energy-related port expansions and drilling occur. The Sunbelt is especially rich in coastal and riverine marshes and bottomland hardwoods, with over one-half of the nation's wetlands located in the Southeast (Science and Public Policy Program 1982).

At least four significant land use problems exist in the Sunbelt: (1) siting of new energy or industrial facilities; (2) protection of valuable coastal zone resources; (3) preservation of historic and cultural resources; and (4) protection of agricultural lands from erosion and urbanization. States are particularly concerned about the location of new energy and industrial facilities because of environmental impacts, the potential for "boom-bust" growth cycles, and deterioration of the aesthetic value of resources (Council of State Governments (1980).

The states have been the primary actors in the nation's land management control system, despite several federal laws affecting private land use decisions. Federal laws do not give categorical protection to critical resources, but they do discourage incompatible use of wetlands, prime farmland, floodplain, and unique areas. The trend has been for states to develop their own legislation to protect critical natural resources (Advisory Commission on Intergovernmental Relations 1981).

There are two major concerns in developing a state land-use policy: (1) balancing private and public interests; and (2) coordinating local interests with state responsibilities. The tension between the rights of individuals or corporations to decide how to use their land and the societal concern over ensuring that various uses do not harm the public is becoming one of the most difficult policy issues facing states. For example, the "not in my backyard" syndrome has resulted in the virtual impossibility of siting hazardous facilities in many states (O'Hare 1977).

The second issue involves the authority of one level of government over another. In the past, states essentially left land-use planning to the localities. More recently, many states have reasserted their authority to zone land for specific purposes (Florestano and Marando 1981). An important concern in this regard is the ability of states to control land uses while preserving sufficient flexibility to account for differences among local areas.

Air Quality

Growth and development in the Sunbelt have not been significantly restricted by air quality regulations. However, the possibility for future restrictions exists in many areas, particularly southern Florida, the Ohio River Basin area in Kentucky, counties in Tennessee and Alabama with large coal-fired electric generation and industrial plants, the Gulf Coast area of Texas, and port areas of Louisiana. Population growth in these areas will increase the number of people at risk as well as the local mobile source emissions problem. Increasing industrialization and energy development will affect the potential interaction of pollutants and continue to raise air quality concerns in the future (Science and Public Policy Program 1982).

State governments and many industrial interests continue to seek changes in the Clean Air Act which would increase their flexibility to set air quality standards. Cities with seemingly intractable problems, such as Louisville, Kentucky, and Houston, have begun to take advantage of new regulatory approaches, such as the emission offset banking program, in order to facilitate planning and provide more certainty for industries wanting to locate there or to expand existing facilities. (U.S. National Commission on Air Quality 1981).

The acid deposition issue, usually associated with the northeastern states, is a growing problem in the South as well. Most of the Southeast and the coastal edge of the Southwest are sensitive to acid rain. Thus, cooperative interstate arrangements may be required to deal with this problem (U.S. General Accounting Office 1981; National Wildlife Federation 1982b).

STATE PROBLEM-SOLVING CAPACITY

States' capacity to deal with these and other environmental problems will depend on several factors, including:

* their awareness of the severity of problems and their capacity to anticipate emerging problems;
* the political will of states to manage problems, including the extent of public support for problem solving and the extent to which coalitions have formed in various problem areas;
* the financial capacity of states, including tax effort, tax burden, and percent of total revenue shared by state and local governments;
* the adequacy of institutional development, including legal, regulatory, and administrative structures; and
* the development of specific management tools which create incentives or sanctions for specific kinds of behavior.

Of these five factors, considerable attention has been given to financial capacity (*Business Week* 1981; Herbers 1981; Mosher 1982; Advisory Commission on Intergovernmental Relations 1982; Leathers 1982). Much less attention has been given to problem recognition, political will, and institutional capacity building. In many respects, these factors are prerequisites to developing specific management tools in substantive issue areas (Honadle 1981; Gargan 1981; Blumstein 1981). The remainder of this paper discusses indicators of Sunbelt growth management capacity in three areas: (1) social values and attitudes; (2) interest group activity; and (3) institutional arrangements for environmental protection.

Social Attitudes and Values

State responses to environmental problems occur within the broad context of social values and attitudes about the importance of environmental quality. Thus, public concerns about growth, economic trade-offs, and the conflicting pressures of energy needs directly affect how states choose to respond to these problems. At least three questions can be asked about public support: (1) is the public aware of environmental problems? (2) are they supportive of environmental goals? and (3) how do they view trade-offs between the environment and economic goals? Available data strongly suggest that broad public support for the environment does exist – goals generally are supported, problems are viewed as serious, and the costs of environmental protection are considered to be worthwhile (*Environment* 1982; Anthony 1982).

Residents of the South clearly expect environmental issues to be an ongoing problem. When asked to judge the "seriousness of different problems in the year 2000," most respondents in a national survey expected that air and water pollution and water shortages would be serious problems in the year 2000 (Roper Organization 1978). Over 70 percent thought air and water pollution would still be severe problems by the year 2000, and 56 percent thought that shortages of water supplies would be severe. Public opinion in the South about this question was similar to that found nationwide. Only the West viewed air and water pollution as more of a problem than did southerners.

Concerning potential changes in local air and water quality, clear regional differences emerged (Mitchell 1981a). Although respondents from the South Atlantic region (Florida, Georgia, South Carolina, North Carolina) rated local air and water quality as the lowest in the nation, they believed that significant improvements had been made since 1975 (see Figure 5-1).[2] In the East South Central states (Kentucky, Tennessee, Alabama, Mississippi), respondents

Figure 5-1: Rating Improvements in Local Air and Water Quality over the Past Five Years.

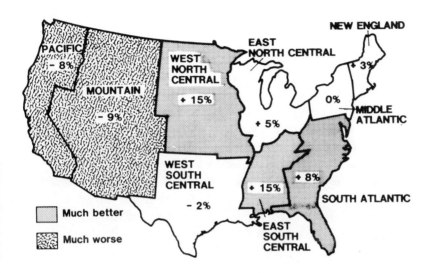

Balance of Those Who Believe Local Air Quality Has Improved Significantly In the Last Five Years Minus Those Who Believe It Has Significantly Worsened

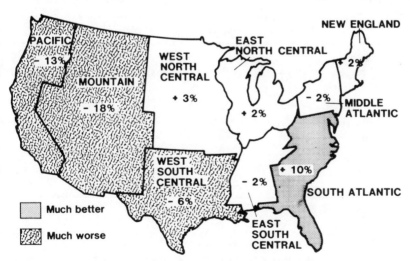

Balance of Those Who Believe Local Water Quality Has Improved Significantly In the Last Five Years Minues Those Who Believe It Has Significantly Worsened

Source: Mitchell 1981a, p. 12.

perceived considerable improvement in air quality (+15 percent), but deterioration in water quality (−2 percent). In the West South Central states (Arkansas, Louisiana, Texas, Oklahoma), residents expressed pessimism about water quality (−6 percent) and air quality (−2 percent).

In general, the public opinion data show that support for the environment comes from a broad base in society rather than from any special geographic or demographic subgroup: 60 percent of the respondents express sympathy for the environmental movement. Only three groups do not have a majority sympathetic to the movement − blacks, those without a high school education, and residents of the East South Central states of Kentucky, Tennessee, Alabama, and Mississippi (Resources for the Future 1980a, p. 42). These four states also had a relatively large number of respondents (39 percent) who replied "not at all" when asked if the term "environmentalist" applied to their interests (see Table 5-1) as did the West South Central states (30 percent).

TABLE 5-1
SELF-IDENTIFICATION AS AN "ENVIRONMENTALIST"[a]

Region[b]	Definitely	Somewhat	Not at all	Not Sure	(N)
South Atlantic	19%	51	25	5	(523)
East South Central	14%	44	39	4	(176)
West South Central	23%	46	30	2	(275)
Mountain, Pacific	16%	60	22	2	(519)
East and West North Central	16%	65	16	3	(784)
New England and Mid Atlantic	19%	50	29	2	(732)
Total U.S.	18%	55	24	3	(3,009)

N = sample size
[a]Question: "Now I am going to read you some phrases that describe different kinds of interests people have. As I read each one, would you please tell me whether it definitely applies to you, or only somewhat or not at all? . . . (b) an "environmentalist."
[b]U.S. Bureau of Census Regions.
SOURCE: Mitchell, 1981b; Resources for the Future, 1980a, p. 12.

As economic conditions have deteriorated, questions about trade-offs such as the cost of cleaning up the environment versus the acceptability of some environmental deterioration have become more important. Considerable attention is now focused on the trade-offs between specific environmental regulations and other public priorities such as economic growth, development of natural resources, and adequate supplies of energy. This is particularly true in the South, where there has been less development in the past in comparison with other regions (except for the Rocky Mountains) and a lagging income in comparison to the U.S. average.

One indicator of public reaction to environmental versus economic issues is whether pollution controls are perceived to be worth their costs. Between 1977 and 1980, the percentage of respondents who said that "protecting the environment is so important that requirements and standards cannot be too high, and continuing improvements must be made regardless of cost" declined from 55 to 42 percent (Resources for the Future 1980b). A recent poll (CBS/NY Times 1981) found that 40 percent of the respondents in the South supported this position compared to 48 percent in the East and West and 46 percent in the Midwest.[3]

However, those believing that pollution control "already costs more than it is worth" also declined 6 percent between 1977 (19 percent) and 1980 (13 percent). Thus, a middle position of "holding down costs rather than requiring stricter controls" gained support, from 20 percent in 1977 to 34 percent in 1980. As shown in Table 5-2, only in the East South Central region was more concern expressed for holding down costs (49 percent) than for continuing environmental improvements (34 percent) in 1980. Otherwise residents in the Sunbelt seem to have much the same priorities as the rest of the nation (Resources for the Future 1980a, 1980b; Mitchell, 1981b).

Interest Group Activity

In addition to general public support for environmental protection, the degree to which coalitions have formed to make demands on public sector agencies is an important stimulus to policy development (Latham 1965; Truman 1951). One indicator of the extent to which political coalitions have become active is interest group

TABLE 5-2
VIEWS OF SUNBELT RESIDENTS ABOUT POLLUTION CONTROL
IN 1980

Statement	South Atlantic[a]	East South Central[a]	West South Central[a]
Protecting the environment is so important that requirements cannot be too high, and continuing improvements must be made regardless of costs.	42%	34%	47%
We have made enough progress on cleaning up the environment that we should now concentrate on holding down costs rather than requiring stricter controls.	32%	49%	33%
Pollution control requirements and standards have gone too far; it already costs more than it is worth.	15%	10%	11%
Don't know, no answer, depends	12%	7%	9%

[a]U.S. Bureau of Census Regions.

SOURCE: Mitchell, 1981b; Resources for the Future 1980b, p. 13.

activity. In environmental policy, interest groups have played a critical role in getting problems on the public agenda, increasing information, and directly influencing the regulatory system through litigation (McFarland 1976).

Environmental interest groups are active in the Sunbelt, with every state having one or more local chapters of large national groups such as the Sierra Club or the National Audubon Society. However, environmental interest groups have been described as struggling to keep membership stable (Clark 1980). One recent assessment of the changing influence of interest groups at the state level describes environmental influence groups as "holding their own at best" (Peirce 1982, p. 377). Trends in membership levels for Sunbelt states in two of the most active national environmental groups lend some support to these views (see Table 5-3). The National Wildlife Federation, largest of the national environmental groups, has lost ground in the Sunbelt over the past six years, with membership totals down 32 percent. Losses in membership were greatest during the years of the Carter presidency (1976-80), lending

TABLE 5-3
CHANGE IN SUNBELT STATE MEMBERSHIP FOR THE
NATIONAL WILDLIFE FEDERATION, 1976-82

States	*1976*	*Percent Change*			
		76-78	*78-80*	*80-82*	*76-82*
Alabama	17,000	− 64	−14	− 14	− 94
Arkansas	4,500	0	−32	+ 6	− 28
Florida	12,500	+ 68	−67	+207[a]	+ 72
Georgia	6,697	− 9	−10	− 1	− 17
Kentucky	3,700	+676	− 8	− 43	+306
Louisiana	7,900	− 6	−25	+ 3	− 27
Mississippi	10,440	− 15	−41	+ 24	− 37
New Mexico	4,840	− 45	−31	− 44	− 79
North Carolina	30,680[a]	+ 4	−31	+ 36	− 2
Oklahoma	33,000[a]	− 5	−78	0	− 78
South Carolina	2,845	+129	− 5	+ 5	+126
Tennessee	12,000	0	+17	+ 14	+ 33
Texas	90,000	0	0	− 56	− 56
Sunbelt Total	236,102	+ 9	−23	− 19	− 32

[a]Yearly total not available, previous year substituted.

SOURCE: National Wildlife Federation 1978, 1982.

some support to the idea that environmental interest groups relaxed somewhat under an administration they viewed as supporting environmental goals (Clark 1980).

The changes in membership for individual states shown in Table 5-3 also suggest that from 1980 through 1982, many National Wildlife Federation chapters were successful in slowing the rate of membership losses and, in some cases, establishing gains in membership. For example, Arkansas, Florida, Louisiana, North Carolina, South Carolina, and Tennessee all showed increases in members for 1982 when compared to 1980. Of these, Florida, South Carolina, and Tennessee were able to establish overall gains in membership in 1982 compared to 1976. Alabama, New Mexico, Oklahoma, and Texas showed substantial losses in membership over the six years.

The membership picture for the Sierra Club in the Sunbelt is somewhat more positive. As Table 5-4 illustrates, after growth faltered during the 1976-80 period, membership increased in all

TABLE 5-4
CHANGE IN SUNBELT STATE MEMBERSHIP FOR
THE SIERRA CLUB, 1976-82

States	1976	Percent Change			
		76-78	78-80	80-82	76-82
Alabama/Georgia[a]	2,204	0	− 4	+100	+ 91
Arkansas/Missouri[a]	1,574	+50	− 1	+ 95	+187
Mississippi/Florida[b]	3,247	0	+18	+133	+175
Kentucky	1,076	0	− 1	+ 73	+ 72
Mississippi/Louisiana[b]	1,376	+20	+ 4	+ 70	+112
New Mexico	1,379	+34	− 9	+100	+145
North/South Carolinas	2,672	+28	−<1	+ 93	+148
Oklahoma	538	+36	− 1	+118	+193
Tennessee	886	+35	+ 6	+ 79	+156
Texas	3,892	+35	+ 9	+107	+206
Sunbelt Total	18,844	+22	+ 4	+101	+156
U.S. Total	156,397	+16	−<1	+ 87	+117

[a]Counted together until 1982.
[b]Counted together until 1980.

SOURCE: Compiled by authors from data supplied by The Sierra Club's
Member Services through correspondence and telephone communications,
December 1982.

states between 1980 and 1982. Membership doubled over the six
years, 1976-82, in every area except Kentucky, Alabama, and
Georgia. The Sunbelt's share of the Sierra Club's national membership increased from 12 percent to 14 percent.

Membership totals alone do not provide a complete picture of
active environmental support in the Sunbelt. Citizens who are
not members of an environmental organization may become involved
in local, regional, or state issues. Ad hoc coalitions have often formed
around specific issues. These environmental coalitions have been
active in some notable Sunbelt controversies, including the Cross
Florida Barge Canal and the Miami/Everglades jet port in Florida,
Oklahoma's Black Fox nuclear power plant, and the Tennessee-
Tombigbee Waterway.

As the Sunbelt experienced significant economic and population
growth, spurred in part by relocation of industry from the Frostbelt
(*Business Week* 1981), controversy over the costs and benefits of

such growth have increased. Controversy has included greater involvement of environmental groups in growth management questions from 1970 through 1978 (Gladwin 1980). In the Southeast states, local residents were involved in 24 percent of the conflicts, compared to 28 percent in the Southwest, 27 percent in the Midwest, 32 percent in the Far West, and 36 percent in the Northeast. Organized local or regional environmental groups were only involved in 15 percent of the conflicts in the Southeast, compared with 28 percent of those in the Southwest. National environmental groups were involved in 16 percent of the Southeast conflicts and 18 percent of the Southwest conflicts. This compares with 32 percent in the Far West where many such groups have national offices (Gladwin 1980).

Thus, evidence on environmental interest group activities in the Sunbelt presents some conflicting signals. Membership in the Sierra Club, typically associated with liberal easterners and westerners, has been making some substantial gains, particularly since the beginning of the Reagan administration in 1980. The National Wildlife Federation, the largest environmental interest group and one with a more moderate reputation lost some members in the Sunbelt during the Carter years but may be holding its own or improving its membership totals in some states. A study of controversy surrounding industrial facilities in the United States suggests that concerns over the potential environmental impacts of such facilities in the South have increased throughout the 1970s. However, local citizens and local or regional environmental interest groups were typically involved in a smaller proportion of these conflicts (in the Southeast) than were similar groups in either the Southwest or other parts of the country.

Institutional Development

Once problems have been recognized and political support has developed for their resolution, the development of appropriate institutional mechanisms is a key ingredient in states' capacity to manage growth (Advisory Commission on Intergovernmental Relations 1982; Mead 1979). In the past, the capacity of the states' legislatures to respond with innovative and appropriate actions was often questioned, based on such criticisms as their lack of representativeness, limited meeting periods, corruption, and lack of professional staff (Citizens Conference on State Legislatures 1971). However, a recent assessment of the state lawmakers concludes that patterns of reform over the 1970s have moved them toward "greater professionalism, increased openness, enhanced representativeness, and improved efficiency" (Advisory Committee on Intergovernmental Relations 1982). In a similar manner, the Office of Governor of the States has also undergone dramatic changes, leaving it stronger and more professional than in the past (Sabato 1978).

Executive branch reforms and reorganizations were also widely undertaken by states over the past several decades (Meier 1980; Advisory Committee on Intergovernmental Relations 1980). Particularly popular in these reorganizations was the functional, departmentalized approach emphasizing areas such as economic development and community affairs, energy, and environmental protection (Advisory Committee on Intergovernmental Relations 1982). Thus, one indicator of the development of institutional capacity is the extent to which environmental protection has received increased emphasis and improved management capacity through the existence of a state agency with primary responsibility for environmental protection.

In the Sunbelt, five states have developed centralized state regulatory agencies, while ten have more fragmented or unconsolidated institutions. As shown in Table 5-5, environmental agencies can be grouped into four models (Council of State Governments 1975; 1982). The Health Department model is found in states which have continued to use their health department to administer pollution control programs (Oklahoma, Alabama, Tennessee, South Carolina, and New Mexico). This reflects the historical relationship between environmental issues of air and water problems and the public's health. This model has three major advantages: (1) health departments are usually well-established politically; (2) they typically have effective relationships with local communities and regional groups; and (3) they are likely to have existing technical and laboratory support resources for coping with the increasing need to monitor chemicals and hazardous wastes. Disadvantages of this model are that environmental programs must compete with many other goals of health departments, and health departments are frequently not equipped to implement and enforce environmental regulations. A majority of public officials in states with the Health

TABLE 5-5
TYPE OF STATE ORGANIZATION FOR ADMINISTERING
ENVIRONMENTAL PROGRAMS

Health Department	Little EPA	Superagency	Partially or Unconsolidated Agency
Alabama	Arkansas	Georgia[a]	Louisiana
New Mexico		Mississippi	
Oklahoma	Florida	Kentucky[b]	Mississippi
South Carolina		North Carolina[c]	Texas
Tennessee		Louisiana	

[a]Includes conservation programs, coastal zone, and/or critical areas management.
[b]Includes conservation programs.
[c]Includes conservation, coastal zone management, industrial development, community assistance, law enforcement planning, and other programs.

SOURCE: Council of State Governments 1975, p. 20; 1982, pp. 603-4.

Department model reported dissatisfaction with the implementation of environmental programs in their states (Council of State Governments 1975).

The "Little EPA" model emerged in 12 states in the early 1970s in order to mirror program responsibilities of the federal EPA. In the Sunbelt, Arkansas and Florida have created this type of agency. New Mexico formerly had this type of agency but moved back to the Health Department model. The primary advantage of this model is that it creates an agency with a clearly defined mission, thus helping to legitimate that mission. It is also more likely to result in an agency which can effectively integrate its various tasks, including regulation, monitoring, and enforcement. The Little EPA model is more costly than integrating environmental protection into an existing agency, and it presumes that political support exists for establishing a centralized state regulatory agency.

The Environmental Superagency model, more comprehensive in scope than the Little EPA, is characterized by the consolidation of major pollution control, conservation, and natural resource management programs in one agency. In the Sunbelt, Georgia, Kentucky, North Carolina, Louisiana, and Mississippi use this approach. The major objections to this model focus on size and the negative impact of competition for agency resources. Supporters point to the political importance of the cabinet level status and the holistic perspective which such an organization fosters. Over 75 percent of the public officials questioned in states with superagencies expressed satisfaction with results in environmental program areas (Council of State Governments 1975).

A fourth model, the Unconsolidated Administration, describes the structure in states which have not attempted to reorganize. Texas is now the only state with an Unconsolidated Administration approach. Louisiana and Mississippi recently moved from this status to the superagency framework (Council of State Governments 1982). Some states with unconsolidated approaches have created coordinating groups such as interagency commissions or pollution boards in an attempt to better control environmental programs (Council of State Governments 1975).

A second indicator of institutional development is the extent to which states have responded to federal environmental programs. A recent survey dealing with the states' perspective toward federal programs (U.S. General Accounting Office 1980) shows that many states in the Sunbelt have placed more emphasis on environmental issues in the recent past (1974-78) than ever before (see Table 5-6). In fact, all but one (Tennessee) report that they have increased their emphasis on environmental issues over the past five years. The head of Georgia's lead environmental agency commented that the state "moved aggressively to keep state laws consistent with Federal." And according to Mississippi's administrator, the state "had been less environmentally aware than other states, but this started to change . . . as indicated by increasing State legislative support" (U.S. General Accounting Office 1980, p. 2.13). Officials in eight of twelve Sunbelt states have reported that their state's emphasis on environmental issues would be likely to increase during the next two years.

In addition to the development of regulatory agencies and the perceptions of state officials about increasing emphasis on environmental issues, an important indicator of state institutional development is the extent to which states have developed specific management tools in several problem areas. As discussed in the first section of this paper, the most significant problem areas in the Sunbelt are water resources, hazardous wastes, land use, and air quality. In many respects, states in the Sunbelt are just beginning to develop specific

TABLE 5-6

EMPHASIS ON ENVIRONMENTAL ISSUES, 1974-78 AND 1979-80

Question	Substantially Increased (Total N=13)	Somewhat Increased (Total N=20)	No Change (Total N=4)	Somewhat Decreased (Total N=8)	Decreased (Total N=0)
"In your opinion, during the past five years (1974-78) has your state's emphasis on environmental issues . . . ?"[a]	Georgia Mississippi South Carolina Arkansas Louisiana	Alabama Florida Kentucky North Carolina New Mexico Oklahoma		Tennessee	
"Overall, do you feel that during the next two years (1979-80) the emphasis your state places on environmental issues will . . . ?"[b]		Alabama Florida Kentucky South Carolina Arkansas Louisiana New Mexico Oklahoma	Georgia Mississippi North Carolina Tennessee		

[a]Respondents were the administrators for the states' lead environmental agencies; (N=45).

[b]Respondents were the administrators for the states' lead environmental agencies; Texas was the only state in regions 4 and 6 that did not respond; (N=45).

SOURCE: U.S. General Accounting Office 1980, pp. 2.13-2.18.

management strategies to deal with these problems. For example:

- while all eight states in the Southeast have regulated a few of the specific sources of ground water contamination, only two (North Carolina and Florida) have developed comprehensive management approaches which include water quality standards and a classification system (Science and Public Policy Program 1983);
- although most Sunbelt states are experiencing increased demands on water resources and many states have had shortages, water management systems generally have not been developed and virtually no intergovernmental mechanisms exist for addressing interstate problems;
- all seven states in the Sunbelt with coastal areas have developed their own legislation to control the use of their coastal areas (Science and Public Policy Program 1982). However, only Florida has developed a comprehensive management approach integrating protection of coastal zones with other valued lands and natural resources; and
- management of hazardous wastes will be an increasingly important problem for nearly all Sunbelt states. While most Sunbelt states have developed mechanisms to deal with solid wastes, these mechanisms do not deal specifically with hazardous wastes (U.S. Environmental Protection Agency 1980). A particularly important need is for states to develop siting procedures which facilitate the safe disposal of hazardous materials (Science and Public Policy Program 1982).

SUMMARY AND CONCLUSIONS

While growth in the Sunbelt will create many benefits, it also will generate many concerns about the availability and quality of natural resources. Among the most critical issues facing Sunbelt states will be water resources management, including ground water depletion, increased demands for surface water, and increased threats to water quality from industrial, municipal, and agricultural sources. The Sunbelt produces over 40 percent of the nation's hazardous wastes, and states will continue to have large responsibilities for managing the transportation and disposal of these wastes. The

Sunbelt states, so rich in coastal zone resources and wetlands which are increasingly under stress from economic and population growth, will be the primary decisionmakers in choosing among competing land uses. Air quality concerns are an emerging issue in many areas of the Sunbelt, including the increasing recognition of acid rain problems in the southeastern states.

State capacity to manage environmental growth issues is not simply a matter of the extent to which financial resources are available. This paper identifies several other indicators of management capacity which emphasize problem awareness, political will, institutional development, and availability of specific management tools. These indicators are:

- public recognition of problems;
- public support for environmental goals;
- growth of environmental interest groups;
- existence of state agencies with primary responsibility for environmental protection;
- the extent to which states have responded to federal environmental programs; and
- the development of specific management tools.

The picture that emerges from examining these indicators is generally positive. Available data strongly suggest that environmental problems are recognized and that strong public support exists for meeting environmental goals. In fact, residents of the Sunbelt generally reject the idea that meeting environmental goals will be too economically costly; and coalitions supporting environmental protection have been increasingly active across the Sunbelt. At least five Sunbelt states have developed centralized state regulatory agencies for environmental protection and the state legal framework for protecting natural resources is either in place or being developed. This institutional development corresponds with perceptions of state officials across the Sunbelt that emphasis on environmental issues has been increasing.

While these indicators suggest that states appear to have commitments to balance environmental and economic goals and a general framework for considering environmental policy issues, it is also clear that environmental management is a relatively recent phenomenon across the Sunbelt. Because of the relative newness of environmental concerns, and because many of these environmental problems have been subject to federal regulatory initiatives, Sunbelt states generally have not yet developed the specific management tools required to balance competing demands for their water, air, and land resources on a day-to-day basis.

NOTES

1. "Sunbelt" and "southern states" as used in this chapter refer to the 13 states in Federal Regions 4 and 6 (Alabama, Florida, Georgia, Kentucky, Mississippi, North and South Carolina, Tennessee; and Arkansas, Louisiana, New Mexico, Oklahoma, and Texas). These two regions are very close to the most frequently used classification of the Sunbelt (see Browning and Gesler 1979). Other states often mentioned as part of the Sunbelt are Arizona and California, while Kentucky is often excluded.

2. To calculate the percent change regarding air and water quality, the percentage of those rating present air or water quality at two or more steps lower (on a self-anchoring ladder) than five years ago was subtracted from the percentage of respondents rating present air or water quality as two or more steps higher than five years ago. Those who showed no change or less than two steps either direction were considered "no change".

3. The CBS/New York Times Poll defines "South" as Alabama, Arkansas, Florida, Georgia, Kentucky, Louisiana, Mississippi, North Carolina, Oklahoma, South Carolina, Tennessee, Texas, and Virginia.

REFERENCES

Advisory Commission on Intergovernmental Relations (ACIR). 1980. *State Administrators' Opinions on Administrative Change, Federal Relationships.* Washington, D.C.: Government Printing Office, December.

_____. 1981. *The Federal Role in the Federal System: The Dynamics of Growth; Protecting the Environment: Politics, Pollution, and Federal Policy.* Washington, D.C.: Government Printing Office, March.

_____. 1982. *State and Local Roles in the Federal System.* Washington, D.C.: Government Printing Office, April.

Anthony, Richard. 1982. "Trends in Public Opinion on the Environment." *Environment* 24(May): 14-20, 33-34.

Bean, Covery. 1981. "Nigh Urges Water Cooperation." *The Daily Oklahoman,* December 2, p. 21.

Blumstein, James F. 1981. "The Resurgence of Institutionalism." *Journal of Policy Analysis and Management* 1(Fall): 129-32.

Browning, Clyde, and Wil Gesler. 1979. "The Sunbelt – Snowbelt: A Case of Sloppy Regionalizing." *Professional Geographer* 31(1): 66-74.

Business Week. 1981. "Special Report: State and Local Government in Trouble." October 26.

"CBS News/New York Times Poll, September 22-27, 1981." News Special Projects. New York: New York Times, mimeographed.

Citizens Conference on State Legislatures (CCSL). 1971. *State Legislatures: An Evaluation of Their Effectiveness.* New York: Praeger.

Clarke, Susan E., and Mary L. Dodson. 1979. "Growth Management Innovation: Regional Distinctions." *The Environmental Professional* 1(2): 101-9.

Clark, Timothy B. 1980. "After a Decade of Doing Battle, Public Interest Groups Show Their Age." *National Journal,* July 12, pp. 1136-41.

Council of State Governments (CSG). 1975. *Integration and Coordination of State Environmental Programs.* Lexington, Kentucky: The Council.

_____. 1980. *Book of the States, 1980-81.* Lexington, Kentucky: The Council.

_____. 1982. *Book of the States, 1982-83.* Lexington, Kentucky: The Council.

Environment. 1982. "Spectrum: Poll Shows Support." 24 (December): 21.

EPA Journal. 1981. "Who's Who on the List." 7 (November/December): 16-17.

Florestano, Patricia S., and Vincent L. Marando. 1981. *The States and the Metropolis.* New York: Marcel Dekker.

Gargan, John J. 1981. "Consideration of Local Government Capacity." *Public Administration Review* 41(November/December): 649-58.

Gladwin, Thomas N. 1980. "Patterns of Environmental Conflict Over Industrial Facilities in the United States, 1970-78." *Natural Resources Journal* 20 (April): 243-74.

Hall, Timothy A., Irvin L. White, and Steven C. Ballard. 1978. "Western States and National Energy Policy." *American Behavioral Scientist* 22 (November/ December): 191-212.

Hebert, F. Ted, and Deil S. Wright. 1982. "State Administrators: How Representative? How Professional?" *State Government* 55(1): 22-28.

Herbers, John. 1981. "Shift to Block Grants Raising Issue of States' Competence." *New York Times,* September 27, pp. 1, 20.

Honadle, Beth Walter. 1981. "A Capacity-Building Framework: A Search for Concept and Purpose." *Public Administration Review* 41: 575-80.

Howells, David H. 1978. *A Summary Report: Southeast Conference on Legal and Administrative Systems for Water Allocation and Management, April 19-20.* Raleigh: North Carolina State University, Water Resources Research Institute of the University of North Carolina.

Jacobs, Jacqueline. 1982. "Report from the Executive Director." *South Carolina Out-of-Doors,* no. 9, p. 4.

Jones, Charles O. 1974. "Federal-State-Local Sharing in Air Pollution Control." *Publius* 4(Winter): 70-73.

Kyl, Jon. 1982. "The 1980 Arizona Ground Water Management Act: From Conception to Current Constitutional Challenge." *University of Colorado Law Review* 53(3): 471-505.

Latham, Earl. 1965. *The Group Basis of Politics.* New York: Octagon Books.

Leathers, Charles G. 1982. "The New Federalism and State Tax Efforts." *Texas Business Review* 6(September/October): 215-19.

Lieber, H. 1975. *Federalism and Clean Waters.* Lexington, Massachusetts: D. C. Heath.

Maugh, Thomas H., II. 1979. "Toxic Waste Disposal a Growing Problem." *Science* 204(May 25): 819-23.

McFarland, Andrew S. 1976. *Public Interest Lobbies: Decision-making on Energy.* Washington, D.C.: American Enterprise Institute.

Mead, Lawrence M. 1979. "Institutional Analysis for State and Local Government." *Public Administration Review* 39: 26-30.

Meier, Kenneth J. 1980. "Executive Reorganization of Government: Impact on Employment and Expenditures." *American Journal of Political Science* 24(August): 396-411.

Menzel, Donald C. 1981. "Implementation of the Federal Surface Mining Control and Reclamation Act of 1977." *Public Administrative Review* 41: 212-20.

Mitchell, Robert Cameron. 1981a. "Perceptions of Environmental Quality." *Resources,* Spring, pp. 11-12.

——. 1981b. Senior Fellow, Resources for the Future. Personal communication to author with unpublished data from the National Environmental Survey for the President's Council on Environmental Quality, the U.S. Department of Agriculture, the U.S. Department of Energy, and the Environmental Protection Agency. September 29.

Mosher, Lawrence. 1982. "Reagan's Environmental Federalism — Are the States Up to the Challenge?" *National Journal,* January 30, pp. 184-88.

National Wildlife Federation. 1978. "Affiliate and Associate Organization Fact Sheet Summary." Memorandum from the Secretary to NWF Affiliate Presidents, Secretaries, and Representatives, February 16.

——. 1982a. "Affiliate and Associate Organization Fact Sheet Summary." Memorandum from the Secretary to NWF Affiliate Presidents, Secretaries, and Representatives, April 2.

——. 1982b. "The Environmental Quality Index, 1982." Unpaged reprint from *National Wildlife* (January/February).

Nigh, George. 1982. Speech to the Annual Governor's Water Conference, December 7, Hilton Inn West-Airport, Oklahoma City, Oklahoma.

O'Hare, Michael. 1977. " 'Not on *My* Block You Don't': Facility Siting and the Strategic Importance of Compensation." *Public Policy* 25(Fall): 407-58.

Peirce, Neal R. 1982. "Is There the Will?" *National Journal,* February 27, pp. 374-78.

Resources for the Future. 1980a. "Final Results of the Resources for the Future National Environmental Survey for the President's Council on Environmental Quality." Unpublished questionnaire with preliminary summary data. August.

——. 1980b. *Public Opinion on Environmental Issues: Results of a National Public Opinion Survey.* Prepared for the Council on Environmental Quality, the U.S. Department of Agriculture, the U.S. Department of Energy, and the Environmental Protection Agency. Washington, D.C.: Government Printing Office.

Roper Organization. 1978. *Roper Report 79-1: Survey, December 2-9.* As cited in "Environmental Protection: An Idea That Has Come and Stayed." *Public Opinion* 2(August/September 1979): 21.

Sabato, Larry. 1978. *Goodbye to Goodtime Charlie: The American Governor Transformed, 1950-1975.* Lexington, Massachusetts: Lexington Books.

Science and Public Policy Program (S&PP). 1982. *Southern Regional Environmental Assessment: Environmental Status Report.* 3 vols. Norman: University of Oklahoma, Science and Public Policy Program.

_____. 1983. *Ground Water Report* (draft). Norman: University of Oklahoma, Science and Public Policy Program. Forthcoming.

Policy Program.

Sherwani, Jabbar K. 1980. *Public Policy for the Management of Ground Water in the Coastal Plain of North Carolina.* Raleigh: North Carolina State University, Water Resources Research Institute of the University of North Carolina.

Sierra Club. 1982. Data supplied by Member Services to authors in correspondence and telephone communications, December.

Truman, David. 1951. *The Governmental Process.* New York: Knopf.

U.S. Council on Environmental Quality, (CEQ) et al. 1980. *Public Opinion on Environmental Issues.* Washington, D.C.: Government Printing Office.

U.S. Environmental Protection Agency (EPA). Office of Solid Wastes. 1980. *Final Environmental Impact Statement Part I for Subtitle C, Resource Conservation and Recovery Act of 1976.* Washington, D.C.: Environmental Protection Agency.

U.S. General Accounting Office (GAO). 1980. *Federal-State Environmental Programs — The State Perspective; Supplement to a Report to the Congress.* Washington, D.C.: Government Printing Office.

_____. 1981. *Hazardous Waste Sites Pose Investigation, Evaluation, Scientific, and Legal Problems.* Washington, D.C.: Government Printing Office.

U.S. National Commission on Air Quality (NCAQ). 1981. *To Breathe Clean Air* (final report). Washington, D.C.: Government Printing Office.

Walker, Jack. 1969. "The Diffusion of Innovations Among the American States." *American Political Science Review* 3(September): 880-899.

6 Managing Urban Growth: Citizen Perceptions and Preferences

Susan A. MacManus

The problems and issues in growth management confronting Sunbelt cities are typified by those experienced by Houston, Texas, in the 1970s and 1980s. Houston is often described as "Boomtown, USA" and the "Golden Buckle of the Sunbelt." The city's population more than doubled between 1950 and 1970 when it passed 1.2 million. It increased another 29 percent between 1970 and 1980. Predictions are it will continue to be the nation's fastest growing city in the 1980s. In fact, one New York bank predicts that by 1985, Houston will lead the nation in three growth areas – employment, personal income, and department store sales (Donovan 1981).

Optimistic appraisals of Houston's continued prosperity and the assumed benefits of more growth are somewhat offset by escalating crime rates, snarled traffic, and increased social tensions that have resulted from mass migration to this "jobs mecca." In the 1970s, while Houston's population grew at a rapid pace, the number of murders rose by 127 percent, rapes and attempted rapes by 260 percent, burglaries by 79 percent, and robberies by 45 percent (Hammond 1981a, p. 18). Traffic jams have become a common phenomenon. The number of registered vehicles in Harris County is approaching two million and according to one report, there are an additional 377 cars on the road "every single morning when you back out your driveway" (Ashby 1982). The sizable influx of poor, unskilled workers who cannot find jobs in a city where a large proportion of the growth industries are technologically advanced has put pressure on the area's social service providers. For example, between

4,000 and 5,000 people are on waiting lists for public housing assistance (Hammond 1981a, p. 32). Those who see this less than rosy picture refer to Houston not as the city of the future, but as the "Baghdad on the Bayou" (Tempest 1982).

The challenge confronting public policymakers in Houston and other Sunbelt cities experiencing similar growth patterns is to develop growth management strategies that promote positive attitudes toward continued growth among their constituents, develop mechanisms to redress serious problems, and project an image of continued prosperity, rather than decline.

THE NEED TO EXAMINE CITIZEN PERCEPTIONS AND PREFERENCES

In order to succeed, growth management strategies typically must incorporate citizen attitudes toward growth, perceptions of growth-related problems, and relative preferences for various solutions, such as annexation, tighter land use restrictions, tax increases, service reduction, formation of area-wide governments, involvement of higher levels of government, and public/private sector partnerships (Brudney and England 1982). The purposes of this chapter are to: (1) identify such attitudes, perceptions, and preferences among Houston area residents; and (2) describe the impact such information has had on the development of growth management strategies and mechanisms in Houston, the Sunbelt's big boomtown.

The chapter is based on a number of public opinion polls taken by Houston researchers between 1975 and 1982.[1] Where possible, changes in public perceptions are highlighted.[2] These changes generally parallel changes in the immigration patterns between 1979 and 1982. In the late 1970s, newcomers were predominantly educated, white collar, and *skilled* blue collar workers. Not so by 1982. As the nation's economy worsened, especially in the Northeast and Midwest, the type of newcomer changed. The newer arrivals were often laid-off, semiskilled factory workers or unskilled workers who found it difficult to get a job in Houston once they arrived. Likewise, when the economy of Mexico worsened, there was a heavy influx of immigrants. These new illegal aliens differed from those of the 1970s in that most (60 percent) brought their spouses, intending to stay permanently instead of temporarily (*Houston Chronicle* 1982).

This chapter also compares the growth-related attitudes, perceptions, and preferences of several groups of citizens. Citizens are classified on the basis of *place of residence* and *length of residence*. Specifically, comparisons are made among inner city residents, residents of suburban municipalities, and residents of unincorporated areas of Harris County. One would expect citizen attitudes to vary according to place of residence since the initial decision about where to locate is an indication of certain policy preferences (tax-service packages) (Tiebout 1956). Comparisons on the basis of place of residence are especially important because many solutions to growth-related problems are dependent upon cooperative agreements between different units of local government. Consequently, determining whether there are marked differences among inner city, suburban, and rural residents is an important first step in sorting out and targeting policy alternatives.

Contrasts are also made of the attitudes of newcomers (who have lived in Houston less than five years) and oldtimers (residents for over 30 years). One common theory is that newcomers are often agents of change. They are thought to be less committed to the status quo than oldtimers and tend to bring with them new perspectives with regard to problems and solutions. The value of comparing these two groups is in identifying areas where public relations campaigns are necessary to lessen resistance of oldtimers and/or educate newcomers as to the legal constraints limiting adoption of certain policy options (e.g. state prohibitions against personal income taxes). Such analyses, and the strategies emanating from them, are very important and should be employed by policymakers in other growth-impacted Sunbelt cities.

GENERAL ATTITUDES TOWARD GROWTH

A June 1979 survey of 647 voters registered in Harris County asked if they, in general, thought growth was good, bad, or mixed (Thomas and Murray 1979). A majority of the respondents (59 percent) saw growth as having mixed results but the sample generally tended to be more positive than negative toward growth: 26 percent felt growth was a good thing and only 12 percent thought it was bad. Likewise, 43 percent believed growth had benefited them personally, whereas only 31 percent believed it had harmed them. The remainder said they were either unaffected by or unsure of the personal consequences of growth.

By October 1981 Houstonians had become less positive in their general attitudes toward growth (Center for Public Policy 1981). A similar survey of 637 voters showed that 62 percent viewed growth as having mixed results. It also showed a drop in the percentage of those who felt growth was good (19 percent) and an increase in the percentage of those who saw growth as bad (18 percent). This growing negativism toward growth paralleled increases in inflation, traffic, crime rates, and changes in the type of new immigrants. But in spite of the growing negativism toward growth in general, more people continued to view growth as personally beneficial (40 percent) than harmful (25 percent). No doubt many individuals weighed the social costs of rapid growth with individual economic benefits (employment) and concluded that growth was beneficial. As noted by one urban consultant, "You can't tell a guy who's come here looking for a job who's now working and is making money: 'Hey, bub, traffic's pretty bad, huh?' His answer will be short and sweet: 'Yeah, but I'm working'" (Hammond 1981b, p. 17).

Predictably, newcomers were more inclined to see growth as good (25 percent) and personally beneficial (54 percent) than old-timers (18 percent and 30 percent). Place of residence also had some effect on attitudes toward growth. Inner city residents and residents of unincorporated areas were more likely to view growth as good (22 percent and 18 percent, respectively) than suburbanites (10 percent). This negativism on the part of suburbanites is mostly due to a fear that immigrants will "invade" their homogeneous neighborhoods and change their character. This is confirmed by data presented below which shows that suburbanites have the greatest concern for neighborhood deterioration.

PERCEPTIONS OF MAJOR PROBLEMS FACING HOUSTON

The increasing negativism of Houstonians toward growth in general is reflected in the results of surveys asking them to identify the major problems facing the area. Most significantly, five times as many citizens (15 percent) ranked growth and overcrowding as a major problem in 1981 than in 1975 or 1979 (3 percent, see Table 6-1). In terms of more specific problems, a comparison of surveys

TABLE 6-1
CITIZEN RANKINGS OF MAJOR PROBLEMS
FACING THE HOUSTON AREA[a]

Ranking	Problem	% Citizens Ranking Problem First or Second[b]
	1975	
	(n = 1,000)	
1	Flood, drainage, sewers, subsidence	22
2	Mass transit	17
2	Pollution, decay	17
3	Crime	16
4	Maintenance of streets and roads	14
4	Traffic, congestion	14
5	Cost of utilities	9
5	Inflation, cost of living	9
6	Education	8
7	Inadequate social services	7
8	Drugs, alcohol	4
8	Law enforcement	4
9	Growth, overcrowding	3
9	Housing	3
9	Lack of recreational facilities	3
10	Lack of jobs	2
10	Local tax structure	2
11	Equal opportunity for minorities	1
11	Lack of planning and zoning	1
	1979	
	(n = 647)	
1	Inflation, cost of living	35
2	Mass transit	26
3	Maintenance of streets and roads	19
4	Traffic, congestion	13
5	Flood, drainage, sewers, subsidence	12
6	Crime	10
6	Pollution, decay	10
7	General energy shortage	5
8	Law enforcement	4
9	Education	3
9	Growth, overcrowding	3
9	Utilities costs	3
10	Drugs, alcohol	2
10	Local tax structure	2

Table 6-1, continued

Ranking	Problem	% Citizens Ranking Problem First or Second[b]
10	Too much government, red tape	2
11	Equal opportunity for minorities	1
11	Housing	1
11	Immigration, illegal aliens	1
11	Lack of recreational facilities	1
11	Lack of responsiveness of local officials	1
	1981	
	(n - 637)	
1	Traffic, congestion, mass transit	61
2	Crime	29
3	Neighborhood deterioration, decay	17
4	Growth, overcrowding	15
5	Maintenance of streets and roads	5
6	Flood, drainage	4
7	Immigration, illegal aliens, racial tensions	3
7	Inadequacy of city services	3
7	Cost of living	3
7	Provincialism, style of living, people	3
8	Lack of responsiveness of local officials	2
9	Education	1
9	Inadequacy of artistic, cultural activities	1

[a]Respondents were asked: "In your opinion, what are the one or two most important problems facing our community today?" (1975 and 1979 surveys). In the 1981 survey, respondents were asked: "What [2 or 3] things do you find least attractive about living in Houston?" Responses to the 1979 and 1981 surveys were classified in accordance with categories used in the 1975 survey.

[b]Figures do not add to 100 percent because of respondents' multiple answers.

SOURCES: Calculated from survey data reported in the following studies: (1) Alumni Educational Foundation, College of Business Administration, *Houston Community Study* (1976 data); (2) Robert D. Thomas and Richard W. Murray, *Survey of Harris County Residents* (1979 data); and (3) Center for Public Policy, University of Houston, *Policy Center Mayoral Election Poll* (1981). See Appendix for a detailed description of each survey.

taken at three different points in time shows a high level of consistency in the problems identified, but some shifts in the intensity of concern for them.

Consistencies in Identifying Problems

Over time, Houstonians have continued to rank traffic and congestion, crime, flooding and drainage, maintenance of streets and roads, and deterioration of neighborhoods as the area's most serious problems. With the exception of crime, these problems are largely capital-intensive. They reflect the inadequacy of local government physical structures and facilities to handle increased service demands caused by rapid growth. This represents the uniqueness of Sunbelt cities — the cross-pressure to expand facilities to keep up with new growth far away from the inner city while at the same time preventing further deterioration of the inner city's infrastructure.

Shifts in Intensity of Rankings

There have been some significant shifts in the intensity of public concern for certain problem areas, even though the rankings have remained fairly stable. For example, between 1975 and 1981, the percentage of citizens ranking traffic congestion and mass transit as a major problem almost doubled (31 percent to 61 percent).[3] Likewise, the percentage of individuals listing crime as a major problem nearly doubled (16 percent to 29 percent). (See Table 6-1). These results reflect the growth in traffic and crime statistics cited earlier.

Similarly, citizens increasingly identified social·tensions between newcomers and oldtimers and among racial groups as a major problem. The percentage ranking immigration, illegal aliens and racial tensions as a major problem, although small, tripled between 1979 and 1981 (from 1 to 3 percent). And the problem of dealing with different types of people (provincialism, style of living, people) first appeared in the 1981 survey (3 percent).

Immigrants have brought with them habits, cultures, and languages that are quite different from those of native Texans. Many native Texans have had difficulty adjusting to these new styles of living and the faster pace brought about by population diversification. Many oldtimers blame the newcomers for "causing the traffic jams, the increased crime, the loss of a once comfortable style of life in an overgrown Southern town that formerly called itself the Magnolia City, with more than a hint of Dixie in the background" (Boles 1982). On the other hand, non-Texans have had equal difficulty adjusting to the Texas style of living, characterized as being the epitome of "rugged individualism" and "frontierism." Said one newcomer from Milwaukee:

> I've been called snowbird and stupid Yankee. There's a deep down feeling of animosity that I don't understand. When I first came down here, I was very intimidated. I felt out of place and developed a severe depression and inferiority complex.

Said another:

> People here really like their town, and they're protective about it. They love their state and care about it. You almost feel that this is a country within a country (Hammond 1981b, pp. 17-18).

Tensions have also emerged among the new immigrants themselves, especially between low-skilled blue collar workers from other regions of the United States and illegal alien blue collar workers from Mexico. These groups must often compete for the same jobs (of which there are fewer and fewer), housing sites, etc. Further, many newcomers from the Northeast and Midwest have come from union backgrounds and resent the right-to-work laws which they say encourage employers to hire illegal aliens at lower wages.

Contrast of Perceptions by Place of Residence

There are some important distinctions in the intensity of citizen concern about certain problems, depending upon place of residence (Table 6-2), even though traffic, crime, and congestion are consistently ranked as most serious. Greater percentages of inner city residents than residents of suburban municipalities or unincorporated areas are concerned about maintenance of streets and roads, the overall quality of city service delivery, law enforcement, and

TABLE 6-2

CITIZEN RANKINGS BY PLACE OF RESIDENCE OF MAJOR
PROBLEMS FACING THE HOUSTON AREA, 1981[a]

Ranking	Problem	% Citizens Ranking Problem First or Second[c]
	INNER CITY RESIDENTS[b] (n = 421)	
1	Traffic, congestion	62
2	Crime	30
3	Deteriorating neighborhoods	16
4	Growth, overcrowding	14
5	Maintenance of streets and roads	7
6	Provincialism/style of living	5
7	Quality of city services	4
8	Flood control, drainage	3
8	Law enforcement	3
8	Immigration, illegal aliens, racial tensions	3
9	Cost of living	2
9	Quality of local government officials	2
10	Quality of art and culture	1
10	Education	1
10	Lack of social services	1
	RESIDENTS OF SUBURBAN MUNICIPALITIES[d] (n = 134)	
1	Traffic, congestion	51
2	Crime	31
3	Deteriorating neighborhoods	25
4	Growth, overcrowding	15
5	Flood control, drainage	8
6	Cost of living	5
7	Maintenance of streets and roads	4
8	Immigration, illegal aliens, racial tensions	1
8	Quality of city services	1
8	Law enforcement	1
8	Quality of local government officials	1
8	Provincialism/style of living	1
	RESIDENTS OF UNINCORPORATED AREAS[e] (n = 82)	
1	Traffic, congestion	73
2	Crime	22
3	Growth, overcrowding	20

140

Table 6-2, continued

Ranking	Problem	% Citizens Ranking Problem First or Second[c]
4	Deteriorating neighborhoods	8
5	Education	5
6	Flood control, drainage	4
6	Cost of living	4
7	Law Enforcement	2
7	Quality of local government officials	2
8	Immigration, illegal aliens, racial tensions	1
8	Quality of city services	1
8	Maintenance of streets and roads	1
8	Provincialism/style of living	1

[a]Respondents were asked: "What [2 or 3] things do you find least attractive about living in Houston?"

[b]Residents of the City of Houston.

[c]Figures do not add to 100 percent because of respondents' multiple answers.

[d]Residents of incorporated municipalities located within Harris County excluding residents of the City of Houston.

[e]Residents of unincorporated areas of Harris County.

SOURCE: Calculated from survey data reported in the Center for Public Policy, University of Houston, 1981, *Policy Center Mayoral Election Poll.* See Appendix for a detailed description of the survey.

social tensions between groups caused by immigration (Center for Public Policy 1981). This is indicative of the City of Houston's inability to sufficiently maintain and upgrade the infrastructure of the inner city because of the pressure to expand services and facilities to outlying, high-growth areas of the city. These perceptions also reflect immigration patterns. Most illegal aliens locate in inner city minority neighborhoods which are gradually expanding, causing a great deal of tension among the races as neighborhoods undergo transition.

Residents of suburban municipalities are more concerned about crime, deteriorating neighborhoods, and flood control and drainage than inner city or rural residents. Greater concern among suburbanites for crime and deteriorating neighborhoods is perhaps a consequence of the relative "newness" of these problems to suburbia. In the case of flood control and drainage, the primary reasons for greater concern are that these areas are more susceptible to flooding than the inner city and considerably more suburbanites have lived through a major flood, the last of which was in 1980. Only 5 percent of suburbanites have lived here less than five years.

Greater percentages of the residents of unincorporated areas are worried about traffic problems and the quality of education, although the differences are slight. These residents face much longer commutes to work each day on increasingly congested freeways. Their concern for education probably stems from the tendency of newcomers to regard southern schools as inferior and from the oldtimers' fear of school integration as a result of the influx of illegal aliens.

Contrast of Perceptions by Length of Residence

Length of residence appears to be much more important in explaining variations in citizen perceptions of growth-related problems than place of residence. Newcomers are somewhat more likely than oldtimers to criticize the quality of city services, law enforcement, and the general style of living (Table 6-3). This rating is predictable in light of Houston's reputation as being a low tax, low service city. On nearly every national comparison of municipal taxing and spending levels, Houston ranks among the lowest of the large cities (Hammond 1981a). For example, Houston ranks last among the nation's six largest cities in money per resident spent on police protection. It also falls well below the national average for the number of police officers per capita.[4]

In contrast, oldtimers are much more likely than newcomers to identify crime and deteriorating neighborhoods as major problems (Table 6-3). These problems have worsened noticeably over the past ten to twenty years, evoking much stronger reactions from long-time residents.

In summary, the perceived severity of specific problems confronting Houston varies somewhat depending upon where one lives in the metropolitan area and how long one has been a Houston resident. Not surprisingly, these differences extend to citizens' preferred solutions to the problems.

TABLE 6-3

CITIZEN RANKINGS OF MAJOR PROBLEMS FACING THE HOUSTON AREA: A COMPARISON OF NEWCOMERS AND OLDTIMERS, 1981[a]

Ranking	Problem	% Citizens Ranking Problem First or Second[c]
	NEWCOMERS[b] (n = 49)	
1	Traffic, congestion	57
2	Crime	20
3	Growth, overcrowding	14
4	Quality of city services	8
4	Provincialism/style of living	8
5	Deteriorating neighborhoods	6
6	Law enforcement	4
7	Maintenance of streets and roads	2
7	Cost of living	2
	OLDTIMERS[d] (n = 265)	
1	Traffic, congestion	52
2	Crime	36
3	Deteriorating neighborhoods	18
4	Growth, overcrowding	14
5	Maintenance of streets and roads	8
6	Flood control, drainage	5
7	Immigration, illegal aliens, racial tension	4
8	Cost of living	3
8	Quality of city services	3
8	Quality of local government officials	3
8	Provincialism/style of living	3
9	Education	2

[a]Respondents were asked: "What [2 or 3] things do you find least attractive about living in Houston?"
[b]Newcomers are those who have lived in Houston less than 5 years.
[c]Figures do not add to 100 percent because of respondents' multiple answers.
[d]Oldtimers are those who have lived in Houston over 30 years.

SOURCE: Calculated from survey data reported in the Center for Public Policy, University of Houston, 1981, *Policy Center Mayoral Election Poll.* See Appendix for a detailed description of the survey.

144 / THE FUTURE OF THE SUNBELT

ATTITUDES TOWARD SOLUTIONS TO
GROWTH-RELATED PROBLEMS

Among the most commonly cited solutions to growth-related problems are annexation, tougher land use restrictions, tax increases or service reductions, regionalization (shifting of a local function to a regional or metropolitan-wide government), and the direct imposition of solutions by state and federal government. In a sense, these solutions can be visualized as falling along a continuum, with annexation representing a purely local solution and federal intervention representing the highest form of an externally-imposed solution. In general, Houstonians' preferences have traditionally been for locally-initiated solutions.

Annexation

Houston's liberal annexation authority has been cited as one way to manage the growth of the area by preventing the formation of an overly-fragmented maze of local governments competing for revenue.[5] Annexation also is seen as a way to prevent the decline of the inner city by eliminating any tax advantages one might gain from moving to suburbia. Historically, Houston's development process has been geared toward future annexation of developed areas as the city deems appropriate. Between 1970 and 1980, Houston annexed more than 100 square miles (Rice Center 1981, p. 1).

In spite of this traditional method of "managing" growth and the benefits stemming from its use, surveys show that most Houston residents are either unaware or unconvinced of its utility. By 1981, only about one-fourth of the population (26 percent) believed the power of annexation was a good thing; almost half (45 percent) believed it was not a good thing. Another 29 percent had no opinion or were not sure (Center for Public Policy 1981).

Not surprisingly, negativism toward annexation was much stronger among residents of unincorporated areas on the fringe of Harris County and suburban municipalities than among inner city residents: 61 percent of the ruralites, 54 percent of the suburbanites, but only 40 percent of the inner city residents regarded annexation as not good. Inner city residents generally are more supportive of annexation because they tend to resent suburbanites who do not pay Houston property taxes yet work inside the city and use city services frequently. In contrast, suburbanites tend to oppose the general principle of annexation and defend the right of neighborhood residents to form units of local government. Ruralites oppose annexation for two other reasons. First, they fear it will increase their taxes. Second, they fear they will not get city services within a reasonable amount of time after being annexed even though the state mandates that the city must provide newly-annexed areas with a level of public services equal to comparable areas within the city within three years after annexation (Rice Center 1981, p. 1).

The city's inability to provide services to one newly-annexed area, Clear Lake City, a community of some 23,000 located around NASA headquarters, brought about a number of lawsuits petitioning for disannexation. Much of the negativism toward annexation in general may have been created by exposure to a high level of anti-annexation publicity following the 1978 annexation of this area. (The 1981 Center for Public Policy survey showed that 68 percent of the respondents did not think the City of Houston should have annexed Clear Lake City.)

Negativism toward annexation also is stronger among newcomers than oldtimers. Newcomers tend to locate in the areas outside the city limits where housing is more available and affordable. (This does not hold true for immigrants from Mexico.) Also, many newcomers are from states where annexation procedures are much different than in Texas.[6]

These survey results show that strategies to promote the continued use of annexation as a growth-management tool must further convince inner city residents of the equity of annexing the fringe areas. In turn, those living in unincorporated areas must be sold on the idea that taxes will remain stable, or even go down,[7] and services will increase following annexation.

Tighter Land Use Restrictions

Houston is a city without zoning. Proponents of zoning attribute many of the city's problems, especially traffic congestion, neighborhood deterioration, pollution, and flooding and drainage problems, to the city's lack of traditional zoning ordinances and its market-oriented approach to urban development. In contrast, opponents of zoning, namely Houston's builders and developers, argue that the absence of zoning ordinances has aided growth and economic prosperity and helped keep the price of new homes below the national average (Simmon 1981; *Houston Chronicle* 1981). They also argue that the city's system of building code requirements and deed restrictions is as effective as zoning in ensuring the quality of development. Other opponents of zoning maintain that the ability to use land for diverse·purposes within the same neighborhood (e.g. small shops, restaurants, homes, offices, art galleries), precisely because of the lack of zoning restrictions, has been the main force behind rapid revitalization of two deteriorating inner city neighborhoods – the Heights and Montrose areas.

As with annexation, Houstonians have some rather strong ideas about use of zoning to manage growth. In surveying City of Houston residents, it was found that 62 percent favored adoption of a zoning ordinance (Center for Public Policy 1981). Support for zoning is much stronger among newcomers than oldtimers, since most of them have come from areas where zoning is a fact of life. Over 70 percent of the city's newcomers favor adoption of a zoning ordinance while 55 percent of the oldtimers regard it as a good strategy for managing growth.

Based on these results, it appears that strategies to enact tougher land use restrictions must be aimed at convincing policymakers, many of whom initially were elected to office with the support of the city's developers, that public support is broad enough and strong enough to mandate such restrictions. In turn, developers would have to be sold on the idea that growth will not be negatively impacted and, instead, will be further promoted as a result of tighter land use restrictions.

Tax Increases, Service Reductions

To meet the increased need and demands for services and facilities resulting from rapid growth, local governments typically are limited to two choices: raise taxes or reduce or eliminate services. There has been a tendency on the part of many Sunbelt local government officials to assume that the first option is not politically viable (MacManus 1981). However, the results of citizen surveys in Houston do not show this always to be the case (Thomas and Murray 1979;

Center for Public Policy 1981). Much depends upon the local govern-ment's ability to convince citizens that without a tax increase, important basic services will have to be cut.

Almost two-thirds of the Houstonians polled responded nega-tively to the statement: "Local taxes should be cut, even if this means some services will have to be eliminated" (Thomas and Murray 1979). As with the other growth-management polls, there were some variations in citizen responses based upon length of residence. Old-timers were somewhat more likely to agree with the statement than newcomers (11 percent and 2 percent, respectively). The explanation for this difference lies in the fact that newcomers are more likely to recognize Houston's relatively low tax rate *and* its low service levels. For example, 39 percent of the newcomers strongly agreed with the statement: "Compared to other parts of the country, local taxes in Houston are not high." Only 30 percent of the oldtimers shared this belief.

Residents of incorporated areas (inner city; suburban munici-palities) were less supportive of service cuts for the sake of tax stability or reduction than rural residents. The reason for this differ-ence is the variation in who delivers basic services: government or private entities. Residents of incorporated areas receive many more basic services (e.g. police protection, garbage pickup, water) from government whereas those living in unincorporated areas rely more on the private sector for these services. Obviously, those relying upon government for delivery are much less likely to support reductions in services just to get a tax cut, especially when taxes are already low.

Based on these results, it appears that strategies to raise taxes to cover the growth-related costs of expansion can be successful if: (1) Houston's residents are convinced that taxes are relatively low; and (2) tax increases are linked to increases in specific basic services.

Regional or Metropolitan Government

The formation of a regional or metropolitan government often is mentioned as a solution to problems involving many local govern-ments. Houstonians are favorably disposed to such a solution — much more than they are toward annexation or tax increases. Of those surveyed, 23 percent strongly agreed and 36 percent somewhat agreed that such a governmental entity should be established, whereas only 11 percent somewhat disagreed and 20 percent strongly disagreed (Thomas and Murray 1979). (The remainder did not have any opinion or were not sure.) This same survey found non-inner city residents to be more opposed to a regional or metropolitan government than residents of the City of Houston (39 percent and 27 percent, respectively). Much of the fear of the residents of outlying areas is that in a metropolitan or regional-type government, the decision-making structures would be dominated by inner city residents.

Where regional or metropolitan governments have been formed, great efforts have been taken to ensure that all areas are formally represented in legislative bodies. Another successful approach has been to give individual local governments the option of joining. Finally, in cases where a general purpose regional government is not politically viable, a successful approach has been to create area-wide special purpose governments (special districts) to handle specific problems viewed as metropolitan-wide in nature. Such strategies are still wise ones, especially in a highly-fragmented, decentralized local government arena like Houston.

Intervention of Higher Levels of Government

Citizens of this Sunbelt city clearly prefer state intervention to federal intervention, with 60 percent strongly or somewhat agreeing that state government should be involved in local problem solving (Thomas and Murray 1979). In contrast, only 42 percent strongly or somewhat agree that the federal government has to be involved if local problems are to be solved.

Opposition to federal intervention is strongest among the residents of suburban municipalities and unincorporated areas. Resistance to federal intervention is less characteristic of inner city residents, in large part because minorities make up a significantly greater proportion of the inner city population. Many minorities either have participated in federally-funded programs, such as CETA, or have friends or relatives who have. And the city gets far more federal funds than either suburban municipalities or counties (which provide services to residents of unincorporated areas).

Strategies that have successfully sold Houstonians on the idea that some federal intervention is good have usually done so by:

(1) popularizing the notion that Houston should get back its fair share in federal taxes paid by Houstonians; (2) arguing that the federal government *should* help underwrite the costs of Houston's expansion (and that of other Sunbelt cities as well) because it is offering employment opportunities to many Americans migrating from other regions of the country who previously had no jobs; and (3) focusing on the use of federal aid for capital improvements, rather than for social services and employment programs (highly unpopular federal programs in this city).

Opinions on the need for state intervention do not vary as much by place of residence, although the patterns are the same as for opinions on federal intervention. In the past, successful strategies for involving state government in the solving of Houston area problems have played up several themes. One theme is that the primary interests of the State and Houston, namely continued growth and prosperity, are identical and, in fact, inseparable. Another theme is that state intervention is preferable to federal intervention because of a difference in the nature of the intervention. State intervention generally is perceived as being in response to requests *initiated locally*. Federal intervention, on the other hand, is viewed as being Washington-initiated and often not in the best interest of local governments in Houston, Texas.

INCORPORATING CITIZEN PREFERENCES INTO GROWTH MANAGEMENT STRATEGIES

There is a great deal of evidence to suggest that citizen preferences for dealing with growth-related problems have been carefully analyzed by policymakers in the Houston area and incorporated into strategies used to "sell" certain growth-management tools. The approach has been to package all these tools and market them according to consumer preferences. When there is a difference in consumer preferences, the tendency is to sell compromise and, thus, incremental solutions.

Annexation

In response to high levels of negativism toward annexation, the city halted all annexation activities between 1978 and 1982.[8] But in July 1982, city council gave its approval to go ahead with the annexation of almost 13 square miles of land, containing some 23,000 people. The strategies adopted by the city to sell this idea were aimed at diffusing the antagonism of suburban and rural residents, while at the same time strengthening the support of inner city residents for annexation of outlying areas.

In publicity surrounding the announcement of the proposed annexations, great care was taken to establish the legitimacy of the action. The stated purpose was

> to increase the city's revenue base and to even out some rough city boundaries [which] have led to confusion among residents as well as the city over where the city should provide police and fire protection along with street repairs and drainage improvements (Kennedy 1982a).

Guarantees also were made that services would be extended to the newly-annexed areas immediately. To diffuse concerns about the dilution of minority voting strength, statistics showing the negligible population make-up changes that would occur were widely disseminated. Finally, to ease residential tax-related opposition, it was stressed that a large part of the area being annexed was commercial property, not residential property.

At the same time she was expressing support for these annexations, the mayor publicly stated she supported the *idea* of a plan for disannexing Clear Lake City. However, she made it equally clear that nothing would be done with regard to Clear Lake City "that would set a precedent that would hamper future annexation programs . . . essential to the long-term financial strength of the city of Houston" (Snyder 1982).

The cumulative effect of these strategies, based on citizen preferences identified earlier, was that the city's first successful annexation in over three-and-a-half years was accomplished with a minimum of public opposition.

Tighter Land Use Restrictions

In response to strong public support for tighter land use restrictions (reflected by public support for a zoning ordinance), the Houston City Council passed a Development Ordinance on June 22,

1982. The "tough" sell in passing this ordinance came not in convincing the public at large, but rather the city's developers who had to be assured that the ordinance was not a first step toward zoning. The councilwoman who sponsored the ordinance repeatedly stressed that "it is not a zoning ordinance and that its primary aim is to give the Houston City Planning Commission more authority over the layout of thoroughfares and other streets" (Carreau 1982b). The ordinance created minimum requirements for setbacks — 10 feet for all developments, with 25-foot setbacks for all developments on major thoroughfares, excluding the downtown business district. It established minimum block lengths and gives the city the authority to require the extension of existing streets through new developments. It also mandates annual reviews and city council approval of a major thoroughfare plan drawn up by the City Planning Department.

Supporters of the ordinance, which passed unanimously, view it as a first step in the direction of systematic comprehensive planning. It also is the first step toward tighter land use restrictions, even though it is not zoning. For the first time, the city has an ordinance "controlling subdivision development as well as planning for large commercial projects where land is not broken into smaller parcels" (Carreau 1982b).

A Tax Increase Linked to a Basic Service

In 1982, Houston City Council approved a one cent property tax rate increase. The city's new mayor, Kathryn J. Whitmire, was able to sell this tax increase in spite of a series of events which would normally lead one to predict taxpayer revolt at the mere thought of such an announcement.

The tax increase took place in spite of an active Tax Protest Group which had come close to convincing voters to approve a very restrictive tax limitation measure in November of 1981 (defeated 52 percent to 48 percent) and in spite of a citywide revaluation of property which resulted in average valuation increases of 200 to 300 percent. The tax increase was approved in spite of another tax-related episode — a highly publicized lawsuit filed in 1981 against the City (*Ginther* v. *City of Houston*). Plaintiff charged that certain personal property had been omitted from the city's tax rolls in return for political favors — and the courts agreed.

The successful strategy employed to sell the tax increase was to link it to police protection — a high-priority basic service that was regarded as insufficient to meet the area's needs. In justifying the increase, the mayor said:

> I think in this particular case the need for this increased police protec-
> tion is critical enough to set a tax rate of 44 cents instead of 43. The
> one-cent difference is really very small in relation to the increased
> police protection we will be able to provide (Kennedy 1982b).

She stressed that the tax rate increase appeared to be the only way to pay for police overtime and the hiring of more civilians to relieve officers of administrative work. In recent years, Houstonians have been subject to considerable publicity about the relatively low number of police officers patrolling the city's streets. Since crime rates are perceived by nearly all Houstonians as a major problem, this strategy of linking tax increases to police service expansion was very effective.

Regionalization: The Formation of Special Purpose Area-wide Governments

Houstonians' willingness to support the *concept* of regionalization while at the same time exhibiting reluctance to dissolve existing general purpose governments has resulted in the formation of a number of special districts to handle metropolitan-wide problems: Harris County Flood Control District, Harris-Galveston Coastal Subsidence District, Gulf Coast Waste Disposal Authority, Metropolitan Transit Authority, and the Harris County Tax Appraisal District. While authorization for the formation of such districts comes from the state legislature, the initial requests generally come from the local area involved, as does the final approval.

Again, the importance of linking new governments (and new taxes) with services deemed critically important, and lacking, is apparent. For example, Houstonians voted to create the Metropolitan Transit Authority (MTA) and pay an additional one cent sales tax at the height of the Proposition 13 taxpayer revolt, simply because the sponsors of the MTA proposal presented it as the "only" alternative to the mass transit problem that was ranked as so important by large numbers of Houstonians in 1975 and 1979. This proposal also was sold by allowing suburban municipalities the option of joining the MTA and by guaranteeing representation of suburban areas on the MTA Board of Directors.

External Intervention: Preference for Public/Private Partnerships

Rare is the solution at the local level that does not require state authorization and/or approval. In the case of Texas, it has often approved locally-initiated efforts to solve growth-related problems. Much of this state assistance is due to the political clout of Houstonians in the legislature, the presence of a number of Houstonians on important state boards and commissions, and the fact that Houston's growth has become a symbol of Texas' growth. In a survey of local government officials' attitudes toward state block grants created as a result of federal legislation, an overwhelming number preferred dealing with the State of Texas than with the federal government (MacManus and Stein 1982).

Houstonians always have been skeptical of the federal government's ability to solve local problems, as cited earlier. Consequently, when the Reagan administration pushed reductions in the federal budget through Congress, there was little public outcry. A survey conducted in October, 1981, showed that only 19 percent thought the budget had been cut too much. In fact, 37 percent felt further cuts were needed; 35 percent thought the budget had been cut by about the right amount (Center for Public Policy 1981). The irony of this is that in recent years, federal aid for capital projects (sewer plants, airports, highways, fire and police stations, parks, water mains, etc.) has stimulated the growth and development of Sunbelt cities, such as Houston. However, most people do not regard this type of money as "federal aid," but rather, only money for social services.

In recognition of the preference of many Houstonians for locally-initiated solutions, their support for the principles of Reagan's new federalism, and their preference for dealing with the State of Texas, a number of growth-management solutions have been adopted. Most of these, including public/private partnerships, reiterate the historical preference of Texans for "solving local problems locally" using free-market oriented approaches. Reagan's new federalism is viewed as merely a restatement of Texas' old "rugged individualism."

There has always been a great deal of cooperation between the public and private sectors. In fact, the growth of the Houston area can be viewed in the following way:

> The product of a number of private and public actions and decisions. . . . The timing and placement of urban development in Houston is largely determined by the response of private developers to the market [but] a number of local, state, and federal agencies also participate in the process (Rice Center 1981, p. 1).

While public/private cooperation is important as a stimulant to growth, it also is crucial in devising solutions to problems generated by that growth. There are a number of recent examples of how public and private resources (financial, institutional) have been merged toward this end. Several stand out: the development of a regional mobility plan aimed at providing solutions to traffic congestion, the formation of a reinvestment zone (a tax increment finance district), and the creation of an industrial revenue bond program to help revitalize deteriorating neighborhoods in the inner city.

In February 1982, the transportation committee of the Houston Chamber of Commerce proposed a $16.2 billion regional mobility plan "designed to offset the stiffling traffic congestion that threatens to put brakes on Houston's growth" (Stancill 1982). The 15-year plan took two years to develop and was drafted by transportation planners from the Chamber, city, county, Texas Department of Highways and Public Transportation, Metropolitan Transit Authority, and Texas Turnpike Authority. The plan was presented for adoption to each of the governments involved. Adoption of the plan was fairly easy. The difficult part lies in funding the proposal. Only $6.9 billion of the total is expected to be supplied by existing funding sources. The remainder will have to come from increased federal and state funding, tolls, increased fares for bus service, revenue bonds, special assessment districts, and public and private joint development efforts (tax increment financing, or TIF).

In December 1981, the city council created Reinvestment Zone Number One, a TIF district, for the purpose of beautifying and improving the Buffalo Bayou area (adjacent to downtown). The TIF mechanism was made possible as a result of a constitutional amendment approved by Texas voters on November 3, 1981. As a result of its creation, all increased revenue in city, Houston Independent School District, and Harris County real property taxes levied in the designated area will be used to finance bonds for street, bridge, sewer, flood control, and park improvements. Planning for the Buffalo Bayou improvements is being conducted by the non-profit Buffalo Bayou Transformation Corporation.

Another example of a creative financial mechanism being used to revitalize the inner city is Houston's industrial revenue bond program. This program was authorized in February 1982, by city council for the purpose of creating jobs and bolstering the property tax base in the city's blighted area. It was approved by the Texas Industrial Commission, the state agency that regulates industrial bond sales. The bonds are issued by the nonprofit Houston Industrial Development Corporation. The first neighborhood targeted for improvement is Houston's far East End (the Harrisburg/Wayside area). This area has a population of over 36,000, 90 percent of which is Hispanic, including many undocumented aliens. A coalition composed of the Houston Council of Human Relations, the East End Progress Association, the City of Houston, and the Houston Chamber of Commerce has been formed to develop the plan for the revitalization of this area. Members of the coalition see this project as a model for other neighborhoods and as a primary example of the strategy of leveraging public and private sector resources. Says the chairman of the coalition:

> You have to see that there is a time for redevelopment and a time for revitalization of used land just as there is a time for development of raw land. When the conditions are right for development, the private sector will step in, invest and make money. It is just like owning a piece of land that is too far out of town. Until the town gets there, the conditions aren't right for development. I think the conditions are changing, and they are going to be ripe for inner-city revitalization (Janowski 1982, p. 40).

In summary, public/private partnerships, while given a boost by the Reagan administration's heavy emphasis on private sector initiatives, are right in line with the laissez-faire psychology which has always characterized Houston.

The Success of Growth Management Strategies

The long-term nature of many of the more complex growth-management strategies that have been adopted (e.g. the regional mobility plan, the reinvestment zone, industrial revenue bond program) makes it difficult to make a definitive statement about the relative success or failure of the growth management package. In terms of citizen outlook, it appears that Houstonians have a slightly more optimistic than pessimistic attitude toward the future (Tarrance and Associates 1982). More see the quality of life five years from now as being good (45 percent) than as bad (32 percent). The remainder see the future in somewhat neutral terms (neither good nor bad).

Most optimistic about the future of Houston are the newcomers (see Table 6-4). Naturally, they are less inclined to criticize the future of a place to which they have just migrated in hope that their fortunes will improve. As one observer has noted: "Houston still presents a high level of opportunity for vertical mobility, even for those way down. It gives them a sense of the 'possible'" (Hammond 1981a, p. 32).

CONCLUSION

Growing pains are characteristic of all Sunbelt cities. The ability to alleviate those pains, at least to the point of tolerance, will determine the degree to which the "boom" will continue. This examination of the experiences of Houston, Texas, has shown that at the very least, growth management strategies must take into account the attitudes, perceptions, and policy preferences of citizens impacted by the growth.

This review of various public opinion polls conducted since 1975 has shown that among Houstonians there is generally:

- a positive attitude toward growth from a personal perspective but an increasingly negative attitude toward growth in general;
- a high level of consensus among various subgroups of the population as to what are the most serious problems facing Houston; these problems are traffic and congestion, crime, neighborhood

TABLE 6-4
CITIZEN RATINGS BY PLACE/LENGTH OF RESIDENCE OF QUALITY
OF LIFE IN HOUSTON

	Percentage Rating Good/Very Good[a]		
Place/Length of Residence	*1978*	*1982*	*1987*
Inner City (n=133)	78	62	37
Suburban/Rural Area[b] (n=267)	76	81	48
Newcomers[c] (n=124)	56	75	52
Oldtimers (n=84)	89	65	33
All (n=400)	77	73	45

[a]Citizens were asked to respond to three questions: (1) "Thinking back to five years ago [1978], how would you rate the quality of life then? Would you say it was very good, good, neither good nor bad, bad, or very bad?" (2) "How would you rate the quality of life in Houston today [January, 1982]?" (same choices); (3) "Concerning the future, what do you think the quality of life will be like five years from now?" (same choices).

[b]Not possible to distinguish responses of residents of unincorporated areas from those of residents of suburban municipalities.

[c]Newcomers are defined as those living in Houston since 1975. Oldtimers are native Houstonians.

SOURCE: Calculated from survey data reported in Tarrance and Associates 1982, *Houston Report*. See Appendix for a detailed description of the survey.

deterioration, flooding and drainage, and maintenance of streets and roads;

- a growing concern for the social tensions associated with immigration of individuals with markedly different cultures, languages, and life-styles;
- some variation in the relative concern for problems depending upon place of residence within the metropolitan area and length of residence in Houston; inner city residents are more concerned about maintenance of streets and roads, the overall quality of city service delivery, law enforcement, and social tensions between groups caused by immigration; residents of suburban municipalities are more concerned about deteriorating neighborhoods,

flood control and drainage; ruralites are worried more about traffic problems and the quality of education. Newcomers are more concerned about the quality of city services, law enforcement and the general style of living than oldtimers who are more worried about crime and deteriorating neighborhoods;

- greater support for locally-initiated solutions to growth-related problems, even though newcomers tend to be less committed to such solutions; newcomers are agents of change and
- a feeling that in spite of all the growth-related problems, living in Houston is still preferable to living in declining, economically-depressed regions of the United States.

The attitude of most Houstonians is summed up by the following statement: "Houston's problems are those associated with growth. They are indeed better than the problems associated with decline, depression and despair" (Cox 1981). When asked whether Houston is still a good place to live, one oldtimer replied: "It's not as good as it used to be, but what is?" (Hammond 1981b, p. 17). And in spite of the intensifying problems confronting the city, "There's still life to the city and a sense of optimism. This is one of the last frontiers; it's an urban frontier" (Hammond 1981a, p. 16). The fact that there's still optimism probably is the first tangible evidence that the city's growth management strategies adopted in the early 1980s may be successful in meeting the challenge of promoting positive attitudes toward growth, and preventing the economic decline of this Sunbelt boomtown.

NOTES

1. With the exception of the 1982 poll by V. Lance Tarrance & Associates, these were publicly disseminated polls. They were not polls conducted for political candidates or sold on a subscription basis to private customers.

2. Certain questions were asked only once (e.g. attitudes toward federal and state involvement, formation of a regional government, zoning laws) prohibiting any analysis of change. In addition, certain classifications (e.g. place/ length of residence) varied somewhat across the polls.

3. In the 1981 survey (Center for Public Policy), mass transit was included in the "traffic, congestion" problem area.

4. Houston spent $58.13 per capita for police protection in 1979. The other five cities averaged $98.68. Dallas, the seventh largest city, spent $71.09.

Likewise, FBI figures show that U.S. cities of over 250,000 population average 3.4 officers per 1,000 residents. Houston, with its 3,100 officers for almost 1.6 million residents, has 1.9 officers per 1,000 population (Hammond 1981a, p. 18).

5. Texas law reserves to its urban municipalities the right to "veto" the incorporation of an unincorporated area within their extraterritorial jurisdiction (ETJ). Houston's ETJ extends five miles. Thus, any area wishing to incorporate must first gain the city's approval — which is rarely given. Conversely, a city has the right to *unilaterally* annex any unincorporated territory within its ETJ.

6. Unlike Texas (see note 5), in many states annexation can occur only after a majority of the voters in both the area to be annexed and the city doing the annexing grant their approval.

7. There is some evidence that residents of certain unincorporated areas pay higher taxes than inner city residents. Specifically, the taxes assessed by municipal utility districts (covering unincorporated areas) often exceed the property taxes which would be levied by a municipality following annexation.

8. Another factor which has reduced the city's rate of annexation is the preclearance requirement of the Voting Rights Act of 1975, which requires the U.S. Justice Department to okay any boundary changes to prohibit dilution of the minority vote.

REFERENCES

Alumni Educational Foundation, College of Business Administration. 1976. *Houston Community Study* (Survey of 1,000 Harris County residents). Houston, Texas: University of Houston, August.

Ashby, Lynn. 1982. "'Houston Facts' Tell Us We're Still Getting Bigger." *Houston Post*, July 25.

Boles, John B. 1982. "Houston Has Always Been A City of Newcomers." *Houston Chronicle*, August 20.

Brewton, Pete. 1982a. "Council Gives Go-Ahead for Annexation Planning." *Houston Chronicle*, July 29.

———. 1982b. "City Council OKs Restrictions on Commercial Development." *Houston Chronicle*, May 7.

Brudney, Jeffrey L. and Robert E. England. 1982. "Urban Policy Making and Subjective Service Evaluations: Are They Compatible?" *Public Administration Review* 42 (March/April): 127-134.

Carreau, Mark. 1982a. "FM 1960 Annexation Linked to Services." *Houston Post*, July 13.

———. 1982b. "Proposed Ordinance Would Help Control Development in the City." *Houston Post*, May 7.

Center for Public Policy. 1981. *Policy Center Mayoral Election Poll, 1981.* Houston, Texas: University of Houston, October.

Cox, Clayton. 1981. "Bad Publicity for City Undeserved, Orton Says." *Houston Post*, May 13.

Donovan, Sharon. 1981. "Houston's Lead in Growth Areas Predicted." *Houston Chronicle*, December 3.

Hammond, Ken. 1981a. "Growth and Our Threatened Quality of Life." Part I. *Texas: Houston Chronicle Magazine, December 6.*

_____. 1981b. "Growth and Our Threatened Quality of Life." Part II. *Texas: Houston Chronicle Magazine*, December 6.

Houston Chronicle. 1981. "Builders Here Praise Lack of Zoning." *Houston Chronicle*, December 15.

_____. 1982. "Study Finds Most Illegal Aliens Prefer Houston; Dallas; Want to Be Citizens." *Houston Chronicle, April 7.*

Janowski, Patrick. 1982. "Can the Private Sector Turn the East End Around?" *Houston*, May, pp. 36-40.

Kennedy, Tom. 1982a. "City Studies Annexations." *Houston Post*, July 21.

_____. 1982b. "Whitmire Will Ask for Boost in Taxes: One-Cent Rate Increase Would Pay for Putting More Police on Streets, Mayor Says." *Houston Post*, June 23.

King, Fred. 1982. "Aliens Taking Away Jobs, Economist Says." *Houston Post*, January 23.

MacManus, Susan A. 1981. "Special District Governments: A Note on Their Use As Property Tax Relief Mechanisms in the 1970s." *Journal of Politics* 43 (November): 1207-1214.

MacManus, Susan A. and Robert M. Stein. 1982. "The Effect of Federal Budget Cuts on Houston." *Texas Business Review* 56 (November/December): 281-284.

Rice Center. 1981. *Houston Initiatives Phase One Report.* Houston, Texas: Rice Center, June.

Simmon, Jim. 1981. "Lack of Zoning in Houston Cited as Lead to Follow." *Houston Post*, December 16.

Snyder, Mike. 1982. "Whitmire May Face Uphill Fight Under Disannexation Plan." *Houston Chronicle*, September 18.

Stancill, Nancy. 1982. "$16.2 Billion Traffic Plan is Proposed for City." *Houston Chronicle*, February 22.

Tarrance, V. Lance and Associates. 1982. *Houston Report.* Houston, Texas: January. Tables II-1, II-2, II-3.

Tempest, Rone. 1982. Cited in "Magazine Warns Michiganders of Perils of Fleeing to Houston." *Houston Chronicle*, May 8.

Thomas, Robert D. and Richard W. Murray. 1979. *Survey of 647 Harris County Residents.* Houston, Texas: University of Houston, Department of Political Science.

Tiebout, Charles. 1956. "A Pure Theory of Local Expenditure." *Journal of Political Economy* 64 (October): 416-424.

United Press International. 1981. "Houston Will Be Fastest Growing City of '80s, Chase Study Says." *Houston Chronicle*, October 26.

_____. 1982. "British Paper Calls Texas A Rugged Land of Capitalism." *Houston Chronicle*, September 21.

APPENDIX

Bases of Studies

1. Alumni Education Foundation. College of Business Administration, *Houston Community Study* (Houston: University of Houston, August 1976). The study was based on a telephone survey of 1,000 randomly selected male and female heads of household residing in Harris County, stratified by race, gender, and place of residence. The survey was conducted in the summer of 1975.
2. Thomas, Robert D., and Richard W. Murray, *Survey of Harris County Residents* (Houston: University of Houston, Public Affairs Research Center 1979). The study was based on a telephone survey of 647 randomly selected Harris County registered voters, stratified by race and place of residence. The survey was conducted in June 1979.
3. Center for Public Policy, University of Houston. *Policy Center Mayoral Election Poll* 1981 (Houston: University of Houston, Center for Public Policy 1981). The study was based on a telephone survey of 637 randomly selected registered voters in Harris County, stratified by race, socioeconomic status, and place of residence. The survey was conducted October 20-25, 1981.
4. Tarrance, V. Lance, and Associates. *Houston Report: January 1982.* (Houston, Texas: V. Lance Tarrance & Associates 1982). The study was based on a telephone survey of 400 randomly selected Harris County residents over 18 years of age. The survey was conducted in January 1982.

7 Intergovernmental Issues in Managing Sunbelt Growth
James L. Regens and
Robert W. Rycroft

For the Sunbelt,[1] growth in both population and industrial base has not been accomplished without adverse consequences, and future development poses a host of potential impacts. An array of issues, including air and water quality degradation, inadequate waste disposal, loss of prime agricultural lands, traffic congestion, urban sprawl, and overburdened social service delivery systems reflect not only the results of growth but also its inherent trade-offs. Each of these issues is to some degree scientific and technological in nature.[2] Environmental protection, public health and safety, and other concerns associated with growth are driven in part by the introduction of sophisticated energy and nonfuel mineral technologies, to name only a couple of the most obvious examples (see Price 1982).

The management and control of these issues largely is a function of the development and use of complex, new technology by federal, state, and local governments as well as the generation of scientific and technical analytical and evaluative capabilities at each level of the federal system. Unfortunately, the intergovernmental aspects of growth and its management have been assigned a relatively low priority in domestic policy. This has contributed to fragmented,

A previous version of this chapter was prepared for presentation at the 1982 Annual Meeting of the Southwestern Social Science Association, San Antonio, Texas, March 17-20. The opinions, findings, and conclusions expressed are those of the authors and do not necessarily reflect the views or policies of the United States Government or the Environmental Protection Agency.

uncoordinated, and often unresponsive reactions to pressures generated by growth. Equally troublesome is the inadequate attention devoted to the potential role of intergovernmental science and technology (S&T) in resolving these problems. While this situation always has been part of the reality of the federal system (see Sapolsky 1971; Roessner 1979), it appears especially dysfunctional in light of the Reagan administration's proposed "new federalism" which promises to restructure federal/state/local relations. This is because the Reagan initiative does not include a role for the S&T enterprise in managing growth. Instead, it systematically undercuts the foundation upon which an intergovernmental S&T partnership might evolve. This chapter examines the major implications of the Reagan administration's failure to link S&T policy to the growth management needs of the U.S. Sunbelt.

GROWTH MANAGEMENT, SCIENCE, AND TECHNOLOGY

Growth confronts state and local policymakers with a range of problems, but two sets of issues appear to be central: inadequate financing to meet the demands of increased population and development, and a lack of planning expertise and information to respond effectively to these problems (Science and Public Policy 1980, p. 231). Most policies for growth management, therefore, involve efforts to modify federal, state, and local tax structures, efforts to increase impact assistance and to target it to affected parties, and the development and dissemination of techniques and programs to improve the problem-solving and anticipatory capabilities of various communities, state, regional, and national organizations.

Science and technology traditionally has been a politically attractive resource in each of these sets of activities. Whether manifested in broad support for funding of research and development (R&D) or faith in the effectiveness of the quick "technological fix," the use of S&T to help resolve issues such as those presented by rapid growth has a long track record. But the scientific and technological enterprise largely has been guided by the priorities and goals of the federal government. Justifications for the domination of the federal perspective range from the public good character of scientific knowledge to the capital-intensive nature of many complex technological endeavors.

In the face of mounting pressure, however, the first outlines of a partnership among the various levels of government began to emerge in the late 1960s. Over the next decade, the areas of S&T which were of common interest and concern to federal, state, and local officials were clarified and some policy mechanisms were created. Shapley et al. (1980) identified four components of inter-governmental S&T policy as we entered the decade of the 1980s:

- direct federal funding of R&D projects in state and local governments;
- technology transfer and utilization assistance programs from federally sponsored R&D;
- capacity-building, or improving the state and local governments' capabilities to use S&T; and
- intergovernmental agenda setting and implementation, in order to increase the involvement of state and local governments in federal policy.

Each of these components is relevant for growth management.

Given limited state and local resources, it is no surprise that one of the key intergovernmental S&T responses has been direct federal support for R&D projects at the state and local levels. Most federal funding (about $182 million in 1977) has had a very applied orientation. There has been a heavy emphasis on growth-related programs, such as education, social services, and crime prevention. Although state and locally funded efforts (together amounting to some $440 million in 1977) have had a similar focus, they have tended to support health, energy, or environmental problem solving (National Science Foundation 1980).

Technology transfer from federally sponsored R&D to state and local users has followed a similar pattern. Important roles in the transfer process have been played by a number of federal agencies whose missions clearly have direct growth-related impacts, such as the Department of Transportation or the Environmental Protection Agency (EPA), as well as by agencies whose growth management importance is a function of indirect spin-offs or spillovers, such as the Department of Defense or the National Aeronautics and Space Administration.

Capacity-building generally has the objective of aggregating the S&T resources of various communities, states, or regions. The National Science Foundation (NSF) has played a pivotal role in this process through its support of regional innovation groups, state legislatures and governors' offices, and various urban and community networks and consortia.

Intergovernmental agenda setting and implementation initiatives were the responsibility of the Intergovernmental Science, Engineering, and Technology Advisory Panel (ISETAP), located in the White House's Office of Science and Technology Policy (OSTP). Following its creation in 1976, ISETAP provided a forum (its membership has included governors, state legislators, county and regional representatives, mayors, and city managers) in which major state and local problems amenable to S&T solutions could be delineated.

By the end of the Carter administration, this basic framework had been in place for several years and analysts could argue with validity that "despite small budgets, much progress and many contributions had been made by intergovernmental science and technology" (Wells and Morrison 1981, p. 4). Evaluations of intergovernmental S&T projects revealed significant payoffs in terms of reduced costs and improved services at state and local levels (see Killian and Becker 1980; CONSAD Research Corporation 1980; Conway and Simay 1977). However, based on a review of 140 case studies of technological innovations in state and local services, Robert Yin and his associates (1976) maintained that even when successful, those activities were not necessarily attributable to federal policies. Moreover, a recent survey of 341 state legislators in eight states (two of them in the Sunbelt) demonstrated that "many legislators were profoundly ambivalent about the contribution that S&T information might make" (Feller et al. 1979, pp. 433-34).

Such caveats suggest basic incompatibilities may exist between the way in which the federal government historically has been organized to provide S&T assistance and those elements which influence the effective utilization of that assistance by state and local governments (Feller 1980). Thus, the entire intergovernmental S&T enterprise appears to be extremely vulnerable to modifications in the federal system as well as having the liability of not necessarily being central to any of the major national, regional, state, or local actors.

INTERGOVERNMENTAL RELATIONS
AND THE NEW FEDERALISM

The Reagan administration has found decentralization reforms politically attractive because they promise to reduce costs, improve services, more effectively utilize resources, and democratize organizations. The first phase of this latest version of new federalism has emphasized reductions in the size and scope of federal programs, especially those that previously had been the sole domain of the states and localities and those which originated in the "new social regulation" climate of the late 1960s and early 1970s. In addition to these budget cuts, the administration has consolidated some 57 federal aid programs into nine new block grants that account for about $7.5 billion (Stanfield 1981; Walker, Richter, and Colella 1982).[3]

The second phase has been more controversial. In his 1982 State of the Union address, President Reagan proposed a major reshaping of the domestic policy responsibilities and fiscal relationships underlying U.S. federalism. As originally outlined, this proposal involved an approximately $48 billion transfer of national programs to the states. The transfer would occur over the balance of the decade, commencing in fiscal year (FY) 1984. The rationale for such an approach is that it would foster a balance of responsibilities within the federal system while lessening presumed decision, management, and fiscal overload on the federal government. Central to such an approach is the premise that, unlike a generation ago, a variety of structural changes, such as governmental reform, reapportionment, and reduced regional economic disparities, have strengthened state and local government capacity to perform as full partners in the intergovernmental system (Advisory Commission on Intergovernmental Relations 1981).

Naturally enough, most of the early debate over the Reagan initiative focused on fiscal implications for the states. The administration maintained that its suggested functional realignment would produce no significant net financial gain or loss for any individual state if one considered a "swap" assignment of state responsibilities for food stamps and Aid to Families with Dependent Children (AFDC) and a "turnback" component (transfer of categorical and block grant programs to the states) not to be separable. Medicaid savings were projected to increase from $19.1 billion in FY 1984 to $25 billion in FY 1987, exceeding the costs to the states of assuming sole responsibility for both food stamps and AFDC. The differential presumably would be available to release an increasing proportion of the state's own tax base (Executive Office of the President 1982a).

The transfer of other federal programs would be financed by means of a proposed $28 billion annual trust fund (Executive Office of the President 1982b). Originally, revenues were to be obtained from existing major federal excise taxes and a portion of the windfall profits tax on oil.[4] During the turnback component's first phase (FY 1984 to FY 1987), state allocations from the trust fund would be based on their historic FY 1979 to FY 1991 share of those federal grants scheduled for revision to the states. An adjustment for any gains/losses attributable to the Medicaid-welfare exchange would be provided. States would have the option throughout the initial transition period (the first four years) to use trust fund revenues to either continue receiving federal grants designated for turnback,[5] or, to the extent they opted to forego those programs, receive them directly as a "no strings" super revenue sharing allotment.[6] Grant programs included in the turnback component would be terminated at the federal level starting in FY 1988 (as the second phase, FY 1988 to FY 1991). Trust fund payments and the corresponding federal excise taxes to support the fund also would be reduced 25 percent ($7 billion) per year with the trust fund scheduled to expire after FY 1991.

IMPLICATIONS FOR THE SUNBELT

The proposal outlined above encountered significant disagreement and mounting opposition in the months after its promulgation. Although they were dissatisfied with existing intergovernmental arrangements, Sunbelt officials generally were equally skeptical about the Reagan initiative. Growth management issues were at or near the top of the hierarchy of problems fueling this skepticism.

Reservations about the administration's initial effort to transfer functions to the states and localities did not stem primarily from the plan's conceptual underpinnings, although some critics have objected on the basis of philosophical considerations. Instead, debate typically has focused on uncertainties about both its ultimate content and the stability of revenue sources to meet programmatic needs, especially after FY 1991 when federal financial supports would cease (Stanfield 1982a).

The precise nature of the concerns being expressed varied somewhat depending on the level of government. At the state level, because of the cuts in domestic social welfare programs which started in the FY 1982 budget and continued in FY 1983, the states clearly face a policy dilemma. State officials can either opt to implement scaled-down programs or to increase state funding to maintain current social service levels. Neither is a particularly attractive option politically. The decision is further complicated by uncertainty over whether sufficient capability exists to finance even reduced programs with those revenue-generating mechanisms earmarked for the states under the turnback component. For example, Governor George Nigh (D-Oklahoma) noted: "The state simply cannot afford to replace, dollar for dollar or program for program, the loss of Federal funds and programs" (Pear 1982). This is an assessment from the governor of one of the few states anticipating major budget surpluses at the end of this fiscal year.

According to a survey conducted by the National Conference of State Legislatures, or NCSL (1982, p. 3), seven of the 13 Sunbelt states expect to conclude their current fiscal year "in the red" or with a balance below one percent. These problems fueled concern among local officials as well as program beneficiaries that the net effect of the Reagan proposal would be a reduction in services (Stanfield 1982b; Peirce 1982; Pilcher 1982). Responding to this concern, President Reagan, in a February 9, 1982, speech to the Indiana legislature, said: "I will give you a flat and binding pledge: there will be no net winners or losers. This will not be a roll of the dice" (Stanfield 1982a).

Yet, the conventional explanation for the rise of the Sunbelt rests, in part, on a presumption of winners and losers. The assumption that "a region is stimulated to grow when all federal expenditures received by the area exceed all federal tax receipts coming from the area" commonly is a key element in discussions of subnational development (Pack 1982, p. 177). According to that viewpoint, regional economic growth primarily is a function of differential impacts of federal activity, especially the flow of federal funds, rather than responses to the market. However, Janet Pack (1982,

p. 187) concludes that "most of the overall differences in federal expenditure-revenue ratios are accounted for by taxes, not expenditure disparities" for the period from 1952 to 1976. Such a finding raises the question of whether state governments generally and those in the Sunbelt in particular, possess adequate capacity to generate revenues through excise tax or oil windfall profits tax allocations sufficient to sustain program needs.

About 60 percent of the trust fund, as originally proposed, would have come from revenues generated by the windfall profits tax on petroleum production. While the vast majority of oil production activities are located in the Sunbelt, only three or four states would capture significant taxes on oil production. Of course, the other states could simply increase their excise taxes on oil products — by substituting a tax on gasoline, for example. Although such a substitution makes sense in theory, those states without major petroleum production sectors within their boundaries may find such a strategy very difficult to implement. Some analyses have suggested that taxes as high as 14 cents per gallon of gasoline might have to be added by a state to replace the federal windfall profits revenues (Stanfield 1982b).

Excise taxes in general have the critical flaws of being small, stable, and regressive. For the purposes of the Reagan plan, these weaknesses may prove to be fatal. In the existing system, federal aid programs are funded by the larger, more productive, and progressive federal income tax. By substituting excise taxes on alcohol, tobacco, gasoline, and telephones for current revenues, the administration risks presenting the states with insufficient and inflexible sources of funds and of extracting these monies at the expense of the lowest economic classes. Moreover, the states do not have equal capabilities in raising money through the excise tax mechanism. An analysis of the relative ability of the states to use the federal cigarette and gasoline taxes to pay for a portion of the turnback effort found wide variations in excise tax capacity. Sunbelt states generally exhibited greater overall fund-raising potential through the use of these taxes than would be necessary to provide program support. But these generalizations mask some crucial differences within the Sunbelt. For example, Texas has more than twice the excise tax capacity of South Carolina (Stanfield 1982b).

The other principal uncertainty has to do with the planning dimension of the proposal. Here the concern is with the extent to which reductions in resources available for federal departments and agencies will constrain the ability of state or local governments to assume increased programmatic responsibility. Lawrence Mosher (1982) alludes to the importance of the federal government's traditional role in providing technical support services, particularly in those areas where most other levels of government lack expertise. For example, when state program specialists encounter new or unusual problems, they most often turn to their counterparts in federal agencies or to their national associations for expert assistance. Thus far, cuts in federal programs have not been assessed in terms of their potential damage to state capabilities, but there is concern at the state level that further budget reductions could force cancellation of technologically complex and costly administrative functions. On the other hand, it must be noted that the states already play key roles in a variety of very sophisticated programs linked to growth management. These include state oversight of handling drinking water, sewage construction and discharge permitting, and air pollution control.

Responding to these concerns, the administration has modified its federalism initiative. In a speech to the National Association of Counties, on July 13, 1982, the president outlined a new reform package (Executive Office of the President 1982c). The most important changes in the proposal were as follows:

- the proposed separation of domestic social welfare functions was changed by dropping the food stamp program from the swap;
- general revenue funds were proposed as a substitute for oil windfall profits tax revenues as a source of money for the trust fund; and
- the turnback component was reduced from some 40 programs to about 30, with the most important deletions taking place in the area of transportation. Similarly, the scope of the transfer was reduced from the $48 billion suggested in the initial proposal to about $39 billion in this latest version.

These compromises, however, left most of the basic financing and planning questions unanswered. And, as Governor Richard Snelling (R-Vermont), Chairman of the National Governors' Association (NGA), has observed, these issues "go to the very heart of the fairness of the federal initiative" (Omang 1982). Frustration with the Reagan approach has also become apparent in the Congress, where even republican leaders have questioned the plan's structure and its host of equity problems (*Washington Post* 1982).

A FUTURE ROLE FOR INTERGOVERNMENTAL S&T IN THE SUNBELT

Faced with financial and planning uncertainties, S&T policy has taken on greater potential importance for Sunbelt states seeking to manage the impacts of growth. The challenges facing the Sunbelt are substantial and have been complicated by recent modifications in the federal system. Proposals to implement an even more far-reaching initiative pose a range of opportunities and risks for state and local governments in the South and Southwest. The resolution of many of the toughest growth-related issues, such as environmental management, might well hinge on the continued development and imaginative use of intergovernmental S&T mechanisms.

It does not seem to be an exaggeration to suggest that never before has the opportunity been greater to support state and local growth management activities through the use of such mechanisms as direct federal R&D, the transfer and utilization of technology, capacity-building, and cooperative federal/state/local agenda setting and policy implementation efforts. The Reagan administration, however, has ignored the potential advantages of linking S&T policy to its bureaucratic reform plan. Instead, at the very time state and local governments are being asked to assume more complex functions, each of the major intergovernmental S&T components has been damaged by the administration's philosophy regarding the use of the public sector's resources in areas such as growth management, the altered policy priorities assigned to S&T, and the changed assumptions about the costs and benefits of intergovernmental relations. Taken together, these policy shifts have been translated into drastically lower funding for the intergovernmental S&T enterprise.[7]

Direct federal funding for R&D projects by state and local governments and technology transfer and utilization assistance programs from federally sponsored R&D have been reduced because of the separation, for policy purposes, of research from development (with the latter viewed as tasks better suited for the private sector), a lower priority attached to R&D in the social and behavioral sciences, and a higher priority for defense programs. Reflected in the 1983 budget, this new R&D orientation makes it very difficult for the federal government to play as active a role in growth management policy.

Even more damage has been inflicted upon capacity-building and agenda setting programs. The NSF intergovernmental program was eliminated at first and then restored to a minimal level by the budgetary process. This outcome left a host of NSF-sponsored networks, consortia, and other capacity-building programs highly vulnerable. Included in this category are such highly regarded services as those provided by the NGA and the NCSL.[8] In fact, without more funding, it is very likely that a good portion of the capacity-building apparatus simply will disappear. Such an outcome would leave the states and localities in very different circumstances with regard to their indigenous S&T capabilities.

The fate of intergovernmental S&T agenda setting and implementation already may have been sealed. As of February 1982, the OSTP's only intergovernmental component, ISETAP, no longer exists. Thus, in an era when many technological activities may be turned back to the states and localities, there is no formal structure to assure intergovernmental S&T policy coordination at the highest level of the federal government. Ironically, the decision to terminate ISETAP came at a time when some experts were calling for its expansion into a more comprehensive body, perhaps encompassing a larger number of private as well as public sector S&T representatives (National Governors' Association 1982).

When viewed as a whole, these factors have heightened uncertainty about the future of intergovernmental S&T and of its potential role in resolving complex issues such as growth management in the Sunbelt. The ongoing controversy surrounding attempts by the Reagan administration to shift primary responsibility for environmental protection to the states provides a stark illustration of the underlying implications of the demise of intergovernmental S&T mechanisms when coupled with the latest new federalism reforms. As Mosher (1982, p. 184) has observed:

> Proponents of these changes promise that they will lead to a more efficient system of environmental protection at much less cost. But critics warn that the Reaganites are ruthlessly destroying the federal

environmental machinery with no guarantees that the states can or will pick up the pieces.

Regardless of who are right, it's now clear that by this summer, the Administration's new environmental policy direction will become almost impossible to reverse, at least through most of this decade. In that respect, President Reagan's New Federalism doctrine could be described as the great environmental gamble of the 1980s.

A recent study by the Science and Public Policy Program of the University of Oklahoma (1982) underscores the significance of growth-induced environmental problems facing the states of the Sunbelt. Expanding industrial and population needs clearly will place great pressures on the Sunbelt region's water availability, air and water quality, hazardous waste management, and land use and coastal zone control. As an indication of the range and magnitude of these threats, consider the following:

- mobile source (vehicle) emissions continue to be a major source of air pollution in the larger cities of the Sunbelt, especially Houston, Dallas, the Piedmont area of North Carolina and South Carolina near Charlotte and the Miami-Ft. Lauderdale and Tampa-St. Petersburg area in Florida;
- marine fisheries are affected by the quality of the coastal environment and the intensity of human utilization. The Gulf Coast white shrimp fishery, for example, has been depleted by coastal pollution, salt water intrusion, and by reduction in nursery grounds by dredging and landfills. Despite increased fishing effort, the harvest of the resource has declined;
- ground water depletion is an immediate problem for the Sunbelt which will worsen over the next decade. It is most serious in the southern High Plains (Ogallala Aquifer), along the Texas Gulf Coast and South Atlantic Gulf (Biscayne Aquifer in Florida and the coastal areas of Georgia and South Carolina);
- point source (those facilities that discharge pollutants from a pipe or other conduit) pollution of water currently is a widespread problem in the Sunbelt. Municipal point sources seriously affect 91 and 100 percent of the basins in the Southeast and South Central regions respectively. Industrial point sources seriously affect 74 and 70 percent of these basins; and

- managing hazardous wastes will be a problem throughout the next several decades because of the growth of key driving forces (chemicals and allied products, stone, clay, and glass production, fabricated metals, petroleum and coal products, textile mills, and primary metal industries) and the number of unknown disposal sites.

Meeting the challenges posed by these changes will test severely the resources and capacities of the Sunbelt states. And while the states of the South and Southwest have come a long way in the development of indigenous problem-solving capabilities, including S&T resources and skills, there still is wide variation in their ability to deal with those issues. Moreover, many of the most serious ecological threats posed by growth simply are beyond the abatement capacity of any single state. Intergovernmental cooperation appears to be a requisite in such a situation. As we have seen, however, the future of intergovernmental partnerships in S&T is highly uncertain. This is especially the case in the environmental protection area, where the EPA has reduced substantially its assistance to the states.

The major mechanism through which the EPA provides support for the states is the use of direct grants-in-aid, although there are other technical, financial and information assistance programs. For grants-in-aid, the pattern that emerges is one of a steady reduction in both absolute and current dollar terms from FY 1981 to FY 1983. Total grants-in-aid have been reduced almost 18 percent for the various media programs (i.e., air, water, waste management, pesticides, toxic substances, and radiation). And these budget cuts were substantially smaller than those originally proposed by the administration. For example, had the administration's proposed FY 1983 EPA budget been accepted by the Congress, air pollution control activities would have been reduced almost 22 percent, drinking water programs would have been cut 25 percent, and water quality grants would have had a reduction of about 22 percent (Congressional Research Service 1982). But even though Congress refused to make these more substantial reductions in the EPA's level of support, the outlook for future intergovernmental assistance cannot be described as promising. The EPA Administrator, Anne Gorsuch, has indicated that the agency "intends over the long term to phase out state grants entirely" (*Inside E.P.A.* 1982, p. 3). Both the NGA (1982, p. 11) and the NCSL (1982, pp. 92-94) maintain that major reductions in, let alone termination of, grants will preclude state capabilities to deal effectively with environmental issues. The NGA has gone so far as to label environmental management one of the six "emerging deficiencies" in the scientific and technological structure of this country.

Although the longer-term impacts of these shifts in federal policy are highly uncertain and are likely to have mixed effects on the various regions (see Muller 1982), it is clear that efforts such as the latest new federalism proposal have at least three negative near-term consequences for the states of the Sunbelt. First, such reforms heighten uncertainty about the intergovernmental rules of the game and make the development of anticipatory strategies much harder to implement. Planning for growth management, a difficult task in the best of circumstances, is presented with almost insurmountable obstacles when sources of funding, expertise, and information are destabilized. Second, there are some indications that the administration's policies are contributing to the postponement of crucial infrastructure investments in the Sunbelt, in order to respond to budgetary exigencies (see Nathan et al. 1982). In the area of environmental protection, for example, the instability generated by the administration's reforms may be forcing postponement of capital improvements in water and sewage treatment facilities in rapidly growing Sunbelt cities. Finally, decentralization and budget reductions may exacerbate disparities among states both within and outside the Sunbelt region. Many states in the South already are among the poorest in the nation, and the Reagan administration initiatives appear likely to increase rather than reduce the fiscal gap between these and other, more prosperous, areas. In such a situation, there may be a tendency toward the weakening of environmental standards, in order to attract and maintain industrial activities.

Faced with such serious implications, efforts to reform intergovernmental affairs appear to be stalemated. At a December 1982 meeting of the NCSL, Senator David Pryor (D-Arkansas) argued that the Reagan plan is "dead in the water" as far as the Congress is concerned, because "We have too many fires to put out to be thinking about New Federalism" (Kurtz and Williams 1982). Science and technology can help put out many of these "fires," but until S&T resources are linked to intergovernmental relations in a more comprehensive manner, the short-term pressures toward conflict and competition are likely to dominate the federal system.

NOTES

1. For the purposes of this study, the definition of the Sunbelt is limited to Federal Regions 4 and 6, including the following states: Florida, Georgia, South Carolina, North Carolina, Kentucky, Tennessee, Alabama, Mississippi, Arkansas, Louisiana, Oklahoma, Texas, and New Mexico. See Science and Public Policy Program (1982, p. 1).

2. "Science and technology" is used throughout this chapter to refer to the research and development programs administered by federal mission agencies as well as the National Science Foundation.

3. Included in this consolidation are preventive health, maternal and child health services, alcohol, drug abuse, and mental health, primary care, social services, community services, low-income energy assistance, community development, and education programs.

4. In the original proposal, for the period from FY 1984 through FY 1987 inclusive, the following dedicated receipts would be allocated to the maintenance of the trust fund at its proposed $28 billion annual level: oil windfall profits tax ($16.7 billion per year); tobacco excise tax ($2.7 billion per year); two cents per gallon gasoline tax ($2.2 billion per year); and telephone excise tax ($0.3 billion per year). In theory, upon completion of the turnback component, the federal excise taxes would be eliminated and available in addition to sales and property taxes as optional sources for state and local revenues.

5. States would be permitted to continue participating in all or some of the federal programs identified under the original turnback proposal. In that case, a state's trust fund share would be used to reimburse those federal agencies from whom the state received grants with the state being required to abide by all federal conditions and rules for those grants.

6. States could elect to withdraw from some or all of the affected federal grant programs prior to FY 1988 by giving one-year notice of voluntary withdrawal to the federal government. Such action would have to be approved by the state legislature and governor following consultation with affected interests. Subsequent to voluntary withdrawal, certain mandatory pass-through of the super revenue sharing allotment would be required. The three pass-through conditions included in the proposal to ensure participation and equitable treatment of local governments during the transition included: (1) 100 percent pass-through to local governments if states opt out of direct federal-local grant programs (i.e., urban development action grants, mass transit, etc.); (2) 15 percent pass-through to local units of government based on general revenue sharing formula if states opt out of other federal programs; and (3) no pass-through of education funds because those programs generally are not within the jurisdiction of general units of local government.

7. Ironically, these cutbacks came at the very time many experts in the field were calling for expanded intergovernmental S&T activities. For instance, Congressman George Brown (D-California) has proposed the creation of a National Technology Foundation to consolidate most federal technology-related functions and to give deliberate direction to nondefense S&T applications. See National Governors' Association (1982).

8. It should be noted that not all intergovernmental capacity-building efforts have been well received at the state and local levels. Many of the federally-sponsored programs have been criticized on the basis of a low level of perceived need for the particular capabilities, and because of low acceptance of federal technical aid and advice. See Jones and Doss (1978).

REFERENCES

Advisory Commission on Intergovernmental Relations. 1981. *State and Local Roles in the Federal System.* Washington, D.C.: Advisory Commission on Intergovernmental Relations.

Congressional Research Service. 1982. *The Environmental Protection Agency's Support of State and Local Programs, FY81-FY83.* Washington, D.C.: Library of Congress.

CONSAD Research Corporation. 1980. *Evaluation of the Experimental Phase of the Urban Technology System.* Washington, D.C.: CONSAD Research Corporation.

Conway, Nicholas T., and Gregory L. Simay. 1977. "The Energy Research and Development: A Partnership Between Federal and Local Government." *Public Administration Review* 37 (November/December): 711-13.

Executive Office of the President. 1982a. "The President's Federalism Initiative: Basic Framework." Washington, D.C.: White House Office of the Press Secretary, January 26.

———. 1982b. "Text of an Address by the President on the State of the Union before a Joint Session of Congress." Washington, D.C.: White House Office of the Press Secretary, January 26.

———. 1982c. "Text of Remarks by the President to the National Association of Counties Convention, Baltimore Convention Center, Baltimore, Maryland." Washington, D.C.: White House Office of the Press Secretary, July 13.

Feller, Irwin. 1980. "Science and Technology in State and Local Governments: Problems and Opportunities." In *The Five-Year Outlook*, vol. 2, edited by National Science Foundation, pp. 639-47. Washington, D.C.: Government Printing Office.

Feller, Irwin, Michael R. King, Donald C. Menzel, Robert E. O'Connor, Peter A. Wissel, and Thomas Ingersoll. 1979. "Scientific and Technological Information in State Legislatures." *American Behavioral Scientist* 22 (January/February): 417-36.

Inside E.P.A. 1982. "Gorsuch Tells States EPA Has Long-Term Goal of Ending All State Grants." September: p. 3.

Jones, Jr., William A. and C. Bradley Doss, Jr. 1978. "Local Officials' Reaction to Federal 'Capacity-Building.'" *Public Administration Review* 38 (January/February): 64-69.

Killian, Vicki M., and Ann L. Becker. 1980. "Public Works and Public Utilities Case Study: Implications for Federal R&D Decision-Making." Prepared for the American Association for the Advancement of Science under contract with the National Science Foundation. June.

Kurtz, Howard, and Juan Williams. 1982. "Reagan May Meld 30 Domestic Programs into Several Block Grants, Adviser Says." *Washington Post*, December 10, p. A19.

Mosher, Lawrence. 1982. "Reagan's Environmental Federalism – Are the States Up to the Challenge?" *National Journal* 14 (January 30): 184-88.

Muller, Thomas L. 1982. "Regional Impacts." In *The Reagan Experiment*, edited by John L. Palmer and Isabel V. Sawhill, pp. 441-57. Washington, D.C.: Urban Institute Press.

Nathan, Richard P., Philip M. Dearborn, Clifford A. Goldman, and Associates. 1982. "Initial Effects of the Fiscal Year 1982 Reductions in Federal Domestic Spending." In *Reductions in U.S. Domestic Spending*, edited by John W. Elwood, pp. 315-49. New Brunswick, New Jersey: Transaction Books.

National Conference of State Legislatures. 1982. *Fifty State Survey: The State of the State Budgets*. Washington, D.C.: National Conference of State Legislatures, February 11.

National Governors' Association. 1982. "Utilizing America's Technological Resources: New Challenges to the States." A background paper prepared for the Winter Meeting of the National Governors' Association Task Force on Technological Innovation, Washington, D.C., February 21.

National Governors' Association and National Conference of State Legislatures. 1982. *The Proposed FY 1983 Federal Budget: Impact on the States*. Washington, D.C.: National Governors' Association and National Conference of State Legislatures.

National Science Foundation. 1980. *Research and Development in State and Local Governments: Fiscal Year 1977*. Washington, D.C.: National Science Foundation.

Omang, Joanne. 1982. "Governors' Chairman Lists New Federalism's Flaws." *Washington Post*, July 15, p. A2.

Pack, Janet R. 1982. "The States Scramble for Federal Funds: Who Wins, Who Loses?" *Journal of Policy Analysis and Management* 1 (Winter): 175-95.

Pear, Robert. 1982. "Few States Seek to Ease Effects of Costs for Poor." *New York Times*, January 12, pp. A1, A12.

Peirce, Neal R. 1982. "The States Can Do it, But Is There the Will?" *National Journal* 14 (February 27): 374-78.

Pilcher, Dan. 1982. "Sorting Out the Federal System: The Prospects." *State Legislatures* 8 (February): 7-12.

Price, Kent A. ed. 1982. *Regional Conflict and National Policy*. Baltimore, Maryland: Johns Hopkins University Press.

Roessner, J. David. 1979. "Federal Technology Policy: Innovation and Problem Solving in State and Local Governments." *Policy Analysis* 5 (Spring): 181-200.

Sapolsky, Harvey M. 1971. "Science Policy in American State Government." *Minerva* 9 (July): 322-48.

Science and Public Policy Program. 1980. *Energy from the West: A Technology Assessment of Western Energy Resource Development*. Norman: University of Oklahoma Press.

Science and Public Policy. 1982. *Southern Regional Environmental Assessment: Environmental Status of the Sunbelt.* Volume III. Norman: University of Oklahoma, Science and Public Policy Program.

Shapley, Willis H., Albert H. Teich, Gail J. Breslow, and Charles V. Kidd. 1980. *Research & Development AAAS Report V.* Washington, D.C.: American Association for the Advancement of Science.

Stanfield, Rochelle L. 1981. "For the States, It's Time to Put Up or Shut Up on Federal Block Grants." *National Journal* 13 (October 10): 1800-05.

———. 1982a. "A Neatly Wrapped Package With Explosives Inside." *National Journal* 14 (February 27): 356-62.

———. 1982b. "'Turning Back' 61 Programs: A Radical Shift of Power." *National Journal* 14 (February 27): 369-74 .

Walker, David B., Albert J. Richter, and Cynthia C. Colella. 1982. "The First Ten Months: Grant-in-Aid, Regulatory, and Other Changes." *Intergovernmental Perspective* 8 (Winter): 5-22.

Washington Post. 1982. "Reagan Remarks on 'New Federalism' Called 'Baloney' by Senate Panel Chief." July 13, p. A9.

Wells, William G., and Mary E. Morrison. 1981. *Partnerships for the 1980s: An Overview of Intergovernmental Science and Technology.* Washington, D.C.: American Association for the Advancement of Science.

Yin, Robert K., Karen A. Heald, Mary E. Vogel, Patricia D. Fleischauer, and Bruce C. Vladeck. 1976. *A Review of Case Studies of Technological Innovations in State and Local Services.* Santa Monica, California: Rand Corporation.

8 Energy Management and Economic Development in Mississippi

Timothy A. Hall

The 1980 census indicates that Mississippi has the lowest per capita income of all 50 states – a ranking the state has held for several decades (*National Journal* 1981; McCarthy and Biggs 1981). During 1981, the Mississippi Research and Development Center and the Mississippi Department of Energy and Transportation began investigating possibilities of developing Mississippi's extensive lignite resources in a manner that would foster industrial development and benefit the state's economy. Radian Corporation, an engineering/ environmental services firm active in the development of Gulf Coast lignite, was asked to evaluate the extent to which Mississippi lignite might satisfy future energy demand, the nature and size of the resource, its technological applications, regulatory constraints and incentives for lignite development, and measures the state can implement to expedite lignite development in a socially and environmentally-acceptable fashion.

The author wishes to acknowledge the considerable contributions of his colleagues at Radian Corporation to the research reported in this chapter. Primary among these colleagues have been R. Leon Leonard, Robert J. Davis, and David M. White. In addition, I wish to acknowledge the funding provided by the Mississippi Research and Development Center and the Mississippi Department of Energy and Transportation to support the background research upon which this chapter is based. The author is solely responsible for the views and conclusions expressed in the chapter.

This chapter draws heavily from the Radian work (Radian Corporation 1981; 1982) and, in part, from the results of other efforts by the Mississippi Research and Development Center and Mississippi Department of Energy and Transportation. It overviews the role energy development plays in Mississippi's economic future and discusses actions the state can undertake to reduce the barriers to coal and lignite utilization. The concluding section summarizes findings from the study and offers several observations about the management of Mississippi energy development and research needs to further this development.

ENERGY DEVELOPMENT: KEY TO MISSISSIPPI'S ECONOMIC GROWTH

Industrial development offers an attractive means of improving Mississippi's economy and the welfare of its citizens. Industrial development creates jobs from both direct employment and indirectly in the form of personal and support services. Increasingly, however, the availability and cost of energy is becoming a major factor when industrial firms consider locations for new plants. This is especially the case for "heavy industries," such as chemical and fertilizer production, which involve energy-intensive manufacturing processes.

With respect to industrial electric utility rates, Mississippi is already at a competitive disadvantage with surrounding states. As of early 1980, electric rates for industrial users in Louisiana and Arkansas were 25 percent lower than in Mississippi; rates in Tennessee and Alabama were 16 and 8 percent lower, respectively (Leonard 1982; U.S. Department of Energy 1980). Given its current reliance on out-of-state energy in general[1] and high-priced oil and gas, in particular, it is crucial that Mississippi develop a source of low-cost energy to fuel industrial expansion. Such resource development is required if the state is going to compete effectively for future economic growth with neighboring Sunbelt states.

Coal and Lignite Alternatives

Forecasts of future industrial fuel costs for the state demonstrate the economic advantages of using coal or lignite over competing fuels such as oil and natural gas. According to one forecast, coal (or lignite) prices will range from one-fourth to one-fifth that of oil and gas by 1990 (Tenneco 1980, Book 2, Appendix B, Table 37). These forecasts are driven largely by a pessimistic domestic gas supply scenario and assumptions that world oil prices will increase by 10 percent in real dollars (i.e., adjusted for inflation) accompanied by a 10 percent overall inflation rate, thus creating a 21 percent annual increase in oil prices. Although the figures differ, most other national forecasts of comparative fuel prices indicate similar results — a substantially lower price per Btu for coal compared to competing industrial and utility fuels.

Even if economics did not favor coal and lignite, its future use is virtually mandatory; electric utilities and industry are prohibited by federal law[2] from building new oil and gas boilers. Although nuclear remains an option for electric generation, cost overruns, delays in construction, and problems of waste disposal have reduced its attractiveness. No new nuclear units have been ordered by electric utilities since the accident at Three Mile Island on March 28, 1979 (*Nucleonics Week* 1981). Thus, it seems certain that barring dramatic changes in energy pricing, such as changes in the current requirements to deregulate natural gas prices in 1985 or a sudden large price reduction by foreign oil producers, the fuel choice for new energy-intensive industries and electric generating facilities will be coal or lignite.

Currently, less than 10 percent of Mississippi's energy demand is met by coal. Almost all of the 3.6 million tons of coal used in the state is consumed by electric utilities as boiler fuel, and all of it is imported from other states — Colorado, Utah, Kentucky, Illinois, and Alabama (U.S. Department of Energy 1981a). In addition, the price of coal delivered to Mississippi utilities is the highest in the nation (U.S. Department of Energy 1981b). The primary contributor to this high cost is transportation, accounting for over one-half of the total cost of western coal and one-third the cost of Illinois Basin coal delivered to Mississippi utilities. Imported coal prices remain the subject of much controversy and are subject to potentially large increases in the future (Gross 1982). Indeed, during the past decade transportation costs for hauling coal have risen dramatically (especially rail transportation), and several coal producing states have increased the severance tax rate on coal.

Faced with the prospects of ever-increasing costs of imported coal, several utilities in Texas, Louisiana, and Arkansas which had originally built units to burn western coal are developing new capacity by building lignite units located at the mine site (minemouth plants). The economic advantages of these minemouth plants are significant. For example, the fuel costs of minemouth plants in Texas and North Dakota are less than half the delivered price of imported coal to Mississippi and from five to seven times less expensive than the equivalent energy from oil delivered from use in U.S. power plants (Radian Corporation 1982, pp. 6-7; U.S. Department of Energy 1981b).

However, because coal and lignite facilities require larger boilers and expensive pollution control equipment, their capital costs are much higher than similar costs of oil and gas units. Therefore, an important comparison among competing fuels — gas, oil, coal, and lignite — is the busbar cost of producing electricity. This accounts for fuel, capital, and operating costs. For a typical power plant built in the late 1970s burning gas at $2.50 per million Btu (average cost of gas purchased by Mississippi power plants), the cost of electricity at the busbar is roughly 3.5 to 4.0 cents per kilowatt-hour. By comparison, lignite power plants built in the 1970s burning Texas lignite produced power at 2.0 to 2.5 cents per kilowatt-hour (Mississippi Power Company et al. 1981).

Unless one assumes that Mississippi lignite utilization will incur markedly higher costs than elsewhere in the Sunbelt, it appears that minemouth lignite plants offer the best opportunities for providing competitive electric power and raw energy to attract new industry, and for holding down future electric rates for Mississippi electricity consumers.

Import Economics

Currently, Mississippi is a net importer of energy. As of 1979, the equivalent of approximately half of the energy consumed was produced in the state. Approximately 25 percent of the electricity consumed was generated in other states (Mississippi Department of Energy and Transportation n.d., p. 6). Regardless of the form this energy takes, the importation results in transfer of income from

Mississippi consumers to energy producers, royalty owners, energy processors, and governments in other states. Also, to the extent that Mississippi resources could have provided this energy, it represents lost economic opportunities.

More specifically, it is estimated that for coal imports in 1980 alone, Mississippi "lost" $285 million in personal income in transfers to other states and an additional $80.2 million in personal income gain which would have been generated from the use of Mississippi lignite as a substitute for imported coal. Based on these figures, Mississippi state government revenues in 1980 would have been $30.4 million higher had Mississippi lignite been used instead of imported coal (Opitz 1981).[3]

Up to this point the discussion of economic growth based on lignite development has focused on the attractiveness to industry of low cost power. However, with careful planning and management coupled with an effective public-private sector dialogue, lignite could provide a series of "value-added" industries — each taking lignite derived products and, through further processing, adding value to that product. By encouraging the processing to occur in Mississippi, job opportunities and other economic benefits would accrue to the state. For instance, if lignite were mined in Mississippi and transported out of state, the benefits in terms of jobs, tax base, and economic stimulus would be minimal. However, if the lignite were burned in a minemouth power plant as discussed above, additional benefits would be recognized. Moreover, if the lignite were used as a raw material for synthetic fuels and chemical feedstocks which, in turn, were further processed in-state into a variety of chemical products and refined fuels, the economic stimulus would be even greater. Lignite is especially attractive for this kind of use. Because of its physical and chemical properties, the resource is unlikely to be shipped out of the area in which it is produced, and it appears well suited for utilization as a synthetic fuels feedstock (Lee 1982; White, Kaiser, and Groat 1981).

CURRENT LIGNITE OWNERSHIP AND USE

Of the states in the Gulf Coast lignite province, Mississippi ranks second only to Texas in total tonnage of near-surface lignite resources with an estimated five billion tons[4] (Table 8-1). If fully

TABLE 8-1
GULF COAST LIGNITE RESOURCES BY STATE

State	Resources [a] *(billion tons)*
Texas	23.4
Mississippi	5.0
Arkansas	2.5
Louisiana	1.7
Alabama	1.4
Tennessee	1.0

[a]Estimated in-place tonnage; seams ⩾3 feet thick and to a depth of 200 feet.
SOURCE: White, Kaiser, and Groat 1981, p. 4.

recoverable, Mississippi lignite (based on this estimate) would be comparable in energy content to 60 years of the state's current level of total energy use or 240 years of the current energy use by the state's electric utilities (Radian Corporation 1981, p. 4-1). A more recent resource estimate based on knowledge of the current status of exploration and development activities suggests that the state may contain up to 10 billion tons of lignite at surface mineable depths plus substantial additional tonnages at greater depths (Minshew 1981). In combination with the above economic observations, these estimates indicate that the state's lignite offers good prospects of providing a much needed low cost energy source.

Major Activities

Although a number of private companies and individuals have been involved in the exploration for Mississippi lignite over the past decade (Williamson 1976, pp. 12-13; Minshew 1981), lignite properties of potential significance appear to be held by just three companies — Phillips Coal Company, Tenneco Coal Company (as a major partner in a joint venture with Entex Coal Company and Falcon Coal Company), and Consolidated Coal Company. Of the total estimated lease acreage in Mississippi of 450,000 acres, these three companies are estimated to control approximately 90 percent of the productive acreage (Beckett 1981).

Of these lease holders, Phillips is the largest with an estimated three billion tons in resource under lease (Van Reenen 1981). The most actively discussed prospect has been the Delta Star Project located in the state's northwest corner (northeastern Quitman County, just west of the towns of Crenshaw and Sledge). As proposed, the Delta Star Mine would supply nine million tons of lignite annually for two 750-megawatt minemouth electric generating units.

Tenneco's estimated holdings of 815 million tons of lignite resource are in three separate holdings in Winston, Neshoba, and Kemper Counties (Almon 1981). Tenneco proposed the construction of a large scale synfuels plant which would have converted 16.5 million tons of lignite mined yearly into 125 million cubic feet per day pipeline quality synthetic natural gas and 23,000 barrels of high-octane gasoline per day (Tenneco Coal Conversion Company 1980, pp. 1-1). Tenneco's request to the U.S. Department of Energy for feasibility study funding for the proposed project was not approved, and the project is currently inactive.

Consolidated Coal's lease holdings are located in Kemper and Lauderdale Counties and are estimated at approximately 400 million tons (Atwater 1981). No announcements have been made regarding plans for development of Consolidated's reserves.

Lignite Utilization

The utilization of lignite can be accomplished by three basic routes: direct combustion, gasification, and liquefaction. The direct combustion of coal and lignite accounts for almost all of the coal used in the United States and will continue to be a major use of coal in the foreseeable future for steam generation. Gasification represents a route to supplement natural gas supplies and to displace a portion of the domestic and foreign oil consumed in Mississippi. Liquefaction technology (converting coal or lignite to liquid fuel products) is receiving less attention primarily because coal liquefaction products cannot compete with the current price of crude oil. Each of these three routes can play some role in the state's future energy plans as discussed in the following paragraphs.

A recent energy demand analysis for the state of Mississippi (Radian Corporation 1981) indicates that approximately 1850 megawatts of electric utility load growth in Mississippi between

1980 and 2000 could be constructed to use Mississippi lignite. All but 250 megawatts of this total would occur in the 1990s. To supply this demand would require an annual production of at least 10 million tons by the year 2000. If half of the energy demand to meet new direct industrial energy requirements for the year 2000 were to be met by lignite, another 4 million tons per year of lignite production would be required.[5]

Based on this projection, the total of utility and industrial lignite requirements to meet in-state demands for the year 2000 is estimated at 14 million tons or about four times the volume of coal currently imported into Mississippi from other states. The estimated five billion tons of near-surface lignite resource could support an annual production figure of 50 million tons for 100 years. Thus, the development of Mississippi lignite appears to be demand-limited rather than supply-limited. The 14 million tons projection could be increased significantly by any one or combination of the following developments:

- cancellation of some or all of the planned nuclear power plants serving Mississippi consumers anticipated to come on line between 1980 and 2000;
- use of Mississippi lignite as a fuel for power generation facilities for electricity demand in adjacent states; or
- construction of one or more large synthetic fuels facilities. The proposed Tenneco synfuels plant would require some 16.5 million tons of lignite per year to produce synthetic gas and gasoline, products which would ultimately be consumed mostly in other states.

As shown in Figure 8-1, in combination these events could easily require the annual production of 50 million tons or more per year by 2000. This compares with approximately 30 million tons of lignite mined in Texas, the nation's largest lignite producer in 1980 (George and Harner 1980).

RESEARCH NEEDS FOR ENERGY DEVELOPMENT

Although forecasts for Mississippi lignite use appear promising, utility and industrial decisionmakers need additional information on

Figure 8-1: Year 2000 Demand for Mississippi Lignite (Millions of tons per year)

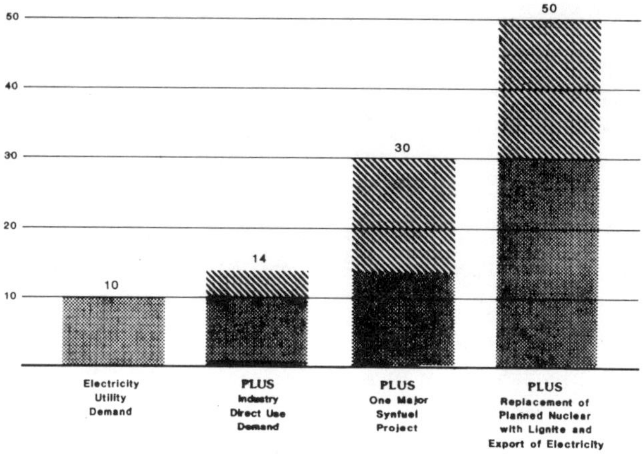

Source: Compiled from Radian 1981, pp. 3-9 to 3-12.

the state's resource endowment, cost of mining, technological feasibility of use, and environmental/socioeconomic impacts of lignite mining and utilization. While lignite must be developed primarily by the private sector, there are several actions the state can undertake to reduce the technical and institutional barriers to lignite development. Like any investment, these actions will require upfront expenditures in the form of state appropriations. However, the long term return on these investments could be immense in the form of increased tax bases, personal incomes, and overall economic activity. The alternative of no action and the risk of prolonged loss of economic opportunities must be weighed against the risks posed by impacts associated with development activities.

Within this context, five possible areas of state action and their objectives are outlined below. It should be noted that although these activities relate specifically to Mississippi's attempts to plan for and manage its lignite development, the actions generally are transferable to other states investigating the potential for developing indigenous resources. In addition, meeting the objectives of any one of these projects will require careful coordination between state agencies responsible for monitoring state resources, lease holders, and other parties at interest.

Conduct an Integrated Technology Assessment of Mississippi Lignite

Technology assessments examine a broad range of impacts associated with the development of a technology. Technology assessments are used as a way of anticipating impacts which may occur and proposing policy alternatives which might be considered to eliminate, reduce, or mitigate those impacts (White, Ballard, and Hall 1978). As such, technology assessment can be an effective tool for structuring a research agenda for the development of a technology.

The objectives of this study would be to evaluate and compare technological options for Mississippi lignite use; to examine the social and environmental consequences of various levels of lignite development; to identify and evaluate policies to stimulate development and mitigate adverse impacts; to suggest lignite-related research needs; and to coordinate statewide lignite research.[6] It would address such areas as the adequacy of current state and local environmental regulations to accommodate lignite development, marketability of Mississippi lignite, and strategies to maximize the value-added concept of lignite development.

The timing for carrying out such a study is critical. It should be done when the technology is well enough developed so that a reasonable forecast of impacts can be made. However, the assessment should be done early enough to precede major development so that anticipated impacts will still be amenable to effective mitigation.

Conduct a Regional Analysis of the Mississippi Lignite Resource

Current estimates of the lignite resource in the state are, as discussed above, about five billion tons within 200 feet of the surface. Although the extent of this resource is large, it also is important to know the location of the resource and whether mineable tracts might be available. The purpose of a regional analysis would be to assess the extent of the lignite resource; that is, to determine more accurately and completely the quantity, quality, ownership, and cost of extraction. In other states, efforts to determine more accurately the quantity of coal or lignite resources usually have resulted in increases in the estimate of the extent of resource, with associated increases in opportunities for development. Because most of the resource is held under lease by private corporations, the cooperation of major lignite holders is vital to the success of this type of analysis.

Conduct a Test Burn and Sample Reclamation Project

Much uncertainty surrounds the development of Mississippi's lignite in terms of combustion characteristics of the resource and potential environmental effects. This activity would reduce the uncertainty in the use of the state's lignite by demonstrating mining, reclamation, and combustion characteristics at a specified pilot site (or sites). Specifically, an estimated 4,000 to 5,000 tons of Mississippi lignite would be mined from a test pit and analyzed for various combustion features. The tests would demonstrate the feasibility of using lignite as a boiler fuel and suggest the type and level of emission control requirements.

Once the lignite is mined and the pit filled, alternative methods of reclamation could be evaluated. Because test burns usually are conducted as part of marketing analyses, the private lease holders would play a lead role in this work. The state should participate in the project primarily in the reclamation research and investigation of environmental impacts.

Conduct a Feasibility Study of the Gasification Potential of Mississippi Lignite

The decision to use Mississippi lignite as a feedstock or fuel has been limited by the lack of past experience. The absence of commercial experience makes cost estimates for the state's lignite utilization more uncertain than estimates that can be made of other lignites or coals already in use. There appears to be acceptance of the potential of Mississippi lignites as a power source for electricity generation (White 1982). But of equal interest, especially for its value-added industry potential, is the use of lignite as a feedstock for synthetic fuel (Lee 1982). This feasibility analysis would seek to reduce some of the uncertainties associated with the gasification of Mississippi lignite. Bench-scale tests developed by various gasification technology vendors (e.g., Lurgi, Westinghouse, Texaco) could be used to determine reaction characteristics of lignite samples.

With its access to major interstate gas pipelines, the Mississippi lignite belt is well located as a future source area for synthetic gas. As noted above, development of one or more synfuels projects is essential if efforts to use lignite as a stimulus for economic growth are pursued and if the demand for Mississippi lignite is to exceed the relatively modest in-state needs forecast through the year 2000.

Conduct Other Research and Development Activities

Of lesser priority than the first four activities are several other studies which could reduce financial and regulatory barriers to lignite development. In particular, a study evaluating various financing strategies for lignite-fired power plants (including, for example, tax-free bonds for a publicly-owned entity) could be conducted. To expedite the permitting of large new lignite facilities, the legislature could provide additional funding to support development of a program for coordinating and expediting review and permitting processes for major industrial facilities. A Business Permitting Advisory Council has been established to help in this regard. The Council includes representatives of state agencies, business and commerce, labor and environment, and federal agencies.

Other states have established coordinating councils, "one-stop" permitting structures, and other methods to facilitate the permitting of new industrial facilities or energy facilities. Notable are the programs in the State of Kentucky, which has a one-stop permitting system, and the State of Colorado, which has a joint review process for major energy and mineral resource development projects. At the present time, 13 states have joint review or consolidated review processes which might serve as models for a Mississippi program (see, for example, Camp, Dresser, and McKee, Inc. 1981).

Finally, to facilitate siting and environmental impact assessments, the state needs to consider the establishment of a single multiagency natural resources data service. This would allow environmental and socioeconomic data currently collected and stored in several state agencies to be centralized, thereby providing an institutional base for coordinating data acquisition and compilation.

SUMMARY AND OBSERVATIONS

As discussed in this chapter, Mississippi has clear incentives for encouraging the development of its in-state lignite resources. Such development is closely tied to the interests and strategic plans of the owners of the resources, and relationships between the public and private sectors are only now being forged with regard to development of these resources. One certainty, however, is the impact of energy on the regional economy, generally, and its measurable effect on personal income growth, specifically. When the economic costs of imported energy are added to the traditional cost elements of energy production, a more meaningful total cost of energy emerges. The users of this energy must pay the total cost, both directly and indirectly, through higher prices, slower income growth, higher taxes and, ultimately, declining services and standard of living.

Mississippi has set an objective of lowering the total cost of energy as a key component of its development strategy. Compared to neighboring states, Mississippi is a "late comer" in the development of coal/lignite resources. Although this probably has resulted in lost opportunities, it also may prove fortuitous in that it provides an opportunity for utility, industry, state, and local leaders to consider lignite development which incorporates the best features of the value-added concept and joint public-private sector planning.

An example of such development would be an energy industrial park located close to several lignite mines. The nucleus of the park could be a synfuel plant which provides raw materials for colocated chemical and refining plants and pipeline-quality synthetic gas for export. The carefully planned location of the industries permits dramatically improved energy use efficiencies through a process known as cogeneration. In cogeneration the otherwise wasted heat energy produced in electric power generation is used by adjacent industries with a need for low-grade steam.[7] Mississippi may be particularly well-suited for the energy industrial power park concept for two additional reasons: (1) the lignite resource is controlled by a small number of large energy companies, thus avoiding some of the institutional and planning barriers to an energy-industrial park posed by an ownership pattern characterized by many smaller interests; and (2) many of the Mississippi lignite-bearing areas are located in and adjacent to deposits of bauxite and iron ore, suggesting the possibility of coordinated extraction and processing of these resources in an energy-industrial park.

As a result of previous energy policy decisions and because of the long lead times necessary to develop new energy resources and concepts like industrial parks, the state's energy future is relatively determined for the next 30 years. However, as suggested here, the state does have a proper role in initiating and coordinating research to encourage other types of developments utilizing lignite. It can play a major role in removing the barriers and uncertainties surrounding lignite development, thus expediting the evolution of a policy agenda to capitalize on the benefits which accrue from the use of Mississippi's own energy resources.

NOTES

1. As of 1979 Mississippi produced an equivalent of approximately half the energy consumed in the state (Mississippi State Oil and Gas Board 1981; U.S. Department of Energy 1979).

2. The Powerplant and Industrial Fuel Use Act of 1978 basically prohibits new steam electric and industrial boilers above 100 million Btu per hour from using oil or gas unless an exemption is obtained. Title III of the Act, which required that existing gas-fired powerplants cease using natural gas by 1990, was repealed in 1981.

3. This estimate excludes any revenues which might have been levied in the form of a lignite severance tax.

4. "Near-surface lignite resources," as commonly defined in the Gulf Coast region, refers to the tonnage of lignite occurring in the ground in seams equal to or greater than three feet thick and at depths less than 200 feet. "Reserves" are a measure of the quantity of "resource" that actually can be recovered given current mining technology and economics. Due to uncertainty with regard to mining characteristics of Mississippi lignite, no estimate has been made of what percentage of the "resource" will yield "reserves." All numbers contained in this chapter are based on estimated "resources." The data source for the five billion ton lignite resource figure is Luppens (1978).

5. The energy forecast for Mississippi in the year 2000 is based on a regional (Mississippi, Alabama, Georgia, Florida, South Carolina, North Carolina, Tennessee, and Kentucky) forecast developed by the U.S. Department of Energy (1980). It was assumed that Mississippi's share of regional energy use in the year 2000 would be proportional to its current share of the region's population. This demand forecast was compared to Mississippi electric utility projections and industrial boiler modeling studies to estimate demand for Mississippi lignite. For elaboration see Radian Corporation 1981, pp. 2-1 to 2-13.

6. Past technology assessments of this type have included a technology assessment of Texas lignite development (Radian Corporation 1979), the Ohio River Basin Energy Study (ORBES 1981), and an integrated technology assessment of western energy resource development (Science and Public Policy 1981).

7. The economic attractiveness of lignite-fired cogeneration is substantial. A calculation of product costs (in dollars per million Btu's of product) for a planned site in neighboring Arkansas shows the fuel costs of a Wyoming coal-fired power plant to be $8.44, a lignite-fired power plant at $4.15, and a lignite-fired cogeneration arrangement between a utility and two industries to be $1.75 (Opitz 1981).

REFERENCES

Almon, B. 1981. Manager of Coal Marketing, Tenneco Coal Company, Houston, Texas. Telephone communication with D. M. White, Radian Corporation, July.

Atwater, R. 1981. Vice president for Eastern U.S. Sales, Consolidated Coal Company, Pittsburgh, Pennsylvania. Telephone communication with J. R. Haarstad, Radian Corporation, July.

Beckett, F. 1981. Bruce, Mississippi. Telephone communication with D. M. White, Radian Corporation, July.

Camp, Dresser, and McKee, Inc. 1981. *Permit Requirements for Development of Energy and Other Selected Natural Resources for the State of Colorado.* Prepared for Four Corner Regional Commission and United States Geological Survey. Wheat Ridge, Colorado. August.

George, F. M., and D. D. Harner. 1980. "Supply and Demand Considerations for Future Industrial Use of Gulf Coast Lignite." In *Coal Technology '80,* Vols. 1 and 2, pp. 133-45. Proceedings from the Third International Coal Utilization Exhibition and Conference, November 18-20, Houston, Texas.

Gross, Lisa. 1982. "Mining Its Own Business." *Forbes,* December 6, p. 106.

Lee, C. 1982. "Use of Mississippi Lignites as a Feedstock for Synthetic Fuel." Presented at Seminar on Mississippi Lignite and Petroleum Resources, May 18-19. Jackson, Mississippi. Mimeographed.

Leonard, R. Leon. 1982. "Forecasts of Industrial Electric Rates." Memorandum submitted to Mississippi Research and Development Center, January 4. Austin, Texas: Radian Corporation. Mimeographed.

Luppens, J. A. 1978. "Exploration for Gulf Coast U.S. Lignite Deposits: Their Distribution, Quality and Reserve." In *Coal Exploration,* Vol. 2. Second International Coal Exploration Symposium, October, Denver, Colorado.

McCarthy, M., and H. Biggs. 1981. *The Recession and the Mississippi Economy.* Jackson: Mississippi Research and Development Center. Mimeographed.

Minshew, V. 1981. Director, Mississippi Mineral Resources Institute, University of Mississippi. Personal communication with D. M. White, Radian Corporation, July.

Mississippi Department of Energy and Transportation. n.d. *Mississippi Lignite Development.* Jackson, Mississippi.

Mississippi Power Company, Southern Mississippi Electric Power Association, and Greenwood Utilities. 1981. Personal communications from respective spokesmen with R. J. Davis, Radian Corporation, December.

Mississippi State Oil and Gas Board. 1981. *Mississippi Oil and Gas Production, 1980 Annual Report*. Jackson, Mississippi.

National Journal. 1981. "The Rich Stay Rich, The Poor Stay Poor, but the Gap Narrows." August 29, p. 1557.

Nucleonics Week. 1981. "Presidential Study Group Concludes Nuclear Has Reached Deadend." October 15, p. 1.

Opitz, J. H. 1981. "A Development Aspect of the Total Cost of Energy." Jackson, Mississippi: Mississippi Research and Development Center and Mississippi Department of Energy and Transportation, November 27. Mimeographed.

ORBES Core Team. 1981. *Ohio River Basin Energy Study (ORBES): Main Report*. Washington, D.C.: Environmental Protection Agency, Office of Research and Development, Office of Environmental Engineering and Technology.

Radian Corporation. 1979. *Integrated Assessment of Texas Lignite Development*. Prepared for the Texas Energy Advisory Council. Washington, D.C.: Environmental Protection Agency.

____. 1981. *Mississippi Lignite Development: Final Report*. Austin, Texas: Radian Corporation.

____. 1982. "Mississippi Lignite Development: An Overview of Opportunities and Recommended State Actions; Report to the Mississippi State Legislature." Austin, Texas: Radian Corporation.

Science and Public Policy Program. 1981. *Energy from the West: A Technology Assessment of Western Energy Resource Development*. Norman: University of Oklahoma Press.

Tenneco Coal Conversion Company. 1980. *Mississippi Coal Conversion Project: Application for Feasibility Grant Under DOE Solicitation No. DE-PS01-80RA-50412*. Books 1 and 2, Vol. 1. Houston, Texas, September 30.

U.S. Department of Energy. 1979. *State Energy Data Report*. DOE/EIA-0214(79). Washington, D.C.: Government Printing Office.

____. 1980. *Typical Electric Bills — January 1, 1980*. DOE/EIA-0040(80). Washington, D.C.: Government Printing Office.

____. 1981a. *Coal Distribution, January-December, 1980*. Washington, D.C.: Government Printing Office, April 30.

____. 1981b. *Cost and Quality of Fuels for Electric Utility Plants, 1980 Annual Report*. DOE/EIA-0191(80). Washington, D.C.: Government Printing Office, June.

Van Reenen, J. E. 1981. Vice President for Marketing, Phillips Coal Company, Richardson, Texas. Letter to D. M. White, Radian Corporation, July 31.

White, D. M. 1982. "Overview of Mississippi Lignites as a Power Source for Electricity Generation." Presented at Seminar on Mississippi Lignite and Petroleum Resources, May 18-19, Jackson, Mississippi. Mimeographed.

White, D. M., W. R. Kaiser, and C. G. Groat. 1981. "Status of Gulf Coast Lignite Activity." Presented at Eleventh Biennial Lignite Symposium, June 15-17,

San Antonio, Texas. Mimeographed.

White, I. L., S. C. Ballard, and T. A. Hall. 1978. "Technology Assessment as an Energy Policy Tool." *Policy Studies Journal* 7 (Autumn): 76-83.

Williamson, D. R. 1976. *Investigations of Tertiary Lignites of Mississippi.* Jackson, Mississippi: Mississippi Geological Survey.

9 Long Range Planning for Managing Growth and Change
Victor L. Arnold

INTRODUCTION

The future of Texas will be influenced greatly by the rich legacy of the past, by changing conditions of the present, and by national and international factors — many of which are beyond the control of the state and its people. Rather than yield the future to a course of events imposed from outside, Texans choose to rely on a great, long-standing asset: the determination to shape their own destinies. Consequently, Texas must manage its growth. The work of the Texas 2000 Project and the Texas 2000 Commission has been dedicated to understanding how Texas state government, in carrying forward its basic functions, can contribute to this management process. The commission was also dedicated to serving as a catalyst to galvanize the energies of the Texas community as a whole. Texas, clear about its goals and acting to achieve them, can shape its own destiny and play a significant role in setting constructive national policies.

The first sections of this chapter briefly describe the purposes and operation of the Texas 2000 Project and the Texas 2000 Commission as they help develop the basis for managing growth and

The author shares credit for this chapter with the other members of the Texas 2000 Commission drafting committee: Bo Byers, T. R. Fehrenbach, Leslie Geballe, Guy Marcus, Harvey McMains, Walt Rostow, Freeman Smith, Robert Weatherford, and Meg Wilson.

change in Texas. This is followed by a discussion of the problems and issues associated with some of the areas of particular concern for the State of Texas and recommendations of the commission for dealing with these concerns. The final two sections present some general findings and conclusions about growth issues facing Texas in the future and the role of efforts like the Texas 2000 Commission in helping to plan for and manage growth and development.

THE TEXAS 2000 PROJECT

Purpose and Operation

The Texas 2000 Project was created by Executive Order in April 1980, by Governor William P. Clements, Jr. (The State of Texas 1980). At the signing ceremony, Governor Clements said:

> In these times of momentous change, it is imperative that Texas State government look to the future and map a wise course for the years ahead. The dramatic population and economic growth experienced in Texas during the 1980s is expected to continue throughout the rest of the century. We will be increasingly challenged to use our natural resources productively and carefully, provide government services that are essential and economical, and maintain and improve our quality of life.

The Texas 2000 Project staff, working under the guidance of a bipartisan steering committee composed of the governor, lieutenant governor, and Speaker of the House, developed a long-range planning information base and coordinated the preparation of briefs on issues critical to the future of Texas. The planning information base developed with cooperation of Texas state agencies and the private sector was published in 1980 as *Texas Trends*. Trend data on Texas' population, finance, economy, human services, education, natural resources, transportation, and communication were available for the first time in one document. The volume was used immediately by members of the Texas Legislature, state agencies, and the private sector. Additionally, thousands of copies were printed and distributed free of charge to educators for classroom use as well as to any citizen who wished to have a copy. *Texas Trends* now enjoys the status of a primary source book on Texas.

The issue briefs, prepared by recognized experts in the respective areas of concern, were published by the Texas 2000 Project in 1981 as *Texas Past and Future: A Survey*. This document provided projections and insights on issues that would become the Texas 2000 Commission's agenda. While providing a foundation for the commission's work, the document also forms a permanent addition to the knowledge of the state and its concerns. It is used as a textbook in one of the state's universities. In addition, over 15,000 copies have been ordered by members of the public interested in the future of Texas.

As the Texas 2000 Project gained credibility and visibility as source of objective information on Texas issues, the Texas Legislature reinforced the importance of the effort by appropriating $250,000 per year for fiscal year 1982 and 1983. This financial support made possible a statewide long-range planning effort based on information and analysis.

Growth and Development Trends

The reports of the Texas 2000 Project indicated that the extraordinary momentum in recent years is the product of special circumstances, among them the rapid rise in energy prices, the state's generally warm climate, extensive job opportunities, and a favorable environment for private enterprise. In determining the setting for the 1980s and 1990s it was learned that Texas had experienced unprecedented economic and population growth.

- as of 1980 personal income per capita in Texas was $9,513, which was 100.5 percent of the national average of $9,458. In 1960 Texas' income per capita was only 87 percent of the national average;
- over the period of 1959-1978 Texas' rate of growth in real Gross State Product was 4.8 percent compared with the nation's growth rate in real Gross National Product of 3.6 percent. Mainly the surge in Texas' growth rate after 1974 accounts for this difference. Between 1974 and 1979 real Gross State Product increased in Texas to an average annual rate of 6.1 percent, compared with the national rate of 3.6 percent.

- population in Texas increased at an annual rate of 2.7 percent between 1970 and 1980, compared with the national rate of 1.0 percent; and
- unemployment in Texas has been below the national average. For example, over the period of 1974-1980 it averaged 5 percent, compared with the national average of 6.8 percent.

It is also learned that despite the historical records, Texas cannot count on automatic persistence of the high economic growth rates. The Texas 2000 Project estimated that the population of Texas by the year 2000 will be approximately 22 million, a 50 percent increase over 1980. The projected age structure of this population is such that 170,000 new jobs must be created each year to keep the growing work force employed. This is a formidable challenge.

TEXAS 2000 COMMISSION

Purpose and Operation

In April 1981, Governor Clements created the Texas 2000 Commission with Executive Order WPC-22 (The State of Texas 1981). The commission, appointed by the governor and composed of citizens from all regions of the state, was charged with continuing and expanding the work begun by the Texas 2000 Project and the steering committee. Its 30 members, who were organized into functional committees, contributed a broad cross-section of knowledge and experience relevant to its work. Its first task was to work closely with the Texas 2000 Project staff and study the issues critical to the continued health and vitality of the Texas economy and quality of life. Then, it focused on determining recommendations for action that are consistent with the appropriate roles of Texas state government. These recommendations were published in 1982 as part of the *Texas 2000 Commission Report and Recommendations*.

The commission benefited from volunteer assistance from business, education, and state and local government. With staff support from the Texas 2000 Project, the commission as a whole met one day every five weeks and each committee met at least once a month. The basic research and data gathering had been completed before the creation of the commission so the commission members focused their attention on long-term strategies and recommendations for Texas. It had many meetings with individuals and groups to discuss its efforts and to obtain insight and suggestions. It encouraged the creation of regional Texas 2000 projects to provide localized input and was gratified with the response. The East Texas and West Texas Chambers of Commerce created task forces which focused on the seven areas of concern as well as on population and the state's economy. These efforts provided significant regional perspectives and recommendations. All four regional Chambers of Commerce initiated Texas 2000 efforts within their organizations. Also, a number of communities have created projects focused on the year 2000. Among these are Amarillo, Austin, Fort Worth, Houston, Laredo, and San Antonio. Bryan-College Station presented its project report to the commission.

Agenda of Concerns

Population growth and changes in the Texas economy were accepted as driving forces that will, to a large degree, influence Texas' future; and in that context, issues related to water, energy, agriculture, transportation, research and development (R&D), state and local finance, and relations with Mexico were examined. These seven areas of concern constituted the first agenda of the commission. There are other issues important to the future; for example, education, health, housing, human services, and recreation. The state's capacity to deal with these human resource issues, however, will depend on its success in meeting the economic development challenges.

The seven topics that formed the commission's agenda are areas of concern that, if not well handled, are virtually certain to slow down the state's economic growth — making it difficult to provide the jobs required by an expanding work force and jeopardizing the public services demanded by the common desire for a high quality of life. The following is a brief description of the areas of concern:

Water. Present and foreseeable acute water shortages affecting urban life, agriculture, and industry are the concern of Texas. Water use in the year 2000 is projected to be 21.6 million acre-feet. This exceeds dependable supplies in that year by 2.5 million acre-feet —

202 / THE FUTURE OF THE SUNBELT

even with cutbacks in irrigation — and by 8.5 million acre-feet, if irrigation demand is to be met.

Energy. A declining trend in Texas' oil and gas production has significant implications for state revenues as well as for every sector of the Texas economy. Texas' energy production from present conventional sources is projected to decline at an annual rate of 1.4 percent, despite the projected substantial increase in lignite production.

Agriculture. A slowdown in the rate of increase of Texas' agricultural productivity and a lack of access to markets are a future concern. The rate of increase in agricultural productivity was halved between 1973 and 1978. If present trends are not reversed, agricultural production and productivity will decline in Texas as a result of the increasing cost of inputs.

Transportation. Inadequacies in transportation in both urban and rural areas are a real problem as we enter a period of rapidly increasing requirements. Vehicle traffic, for example, is expected to more than double in Texas between now and 2000. Highway, rail and waterway maintenance, and improvements are not keeping pace with increasing use and need.

Research and Development. A lack of understanding of the value of R&D and an inadequate level of investment in R&D focused on the key areas of concern of the state. U.S. expenditures for R&D (private and public) are $216 per capita, but Texas expenditures are only $126 per capita.

Government Finance. The uncertain outlook for state and local revenues will be determined largely by the degree of success in dealing with five preceding topics.

Relations with Mexico. These important relations depend greatly on national rather than state policy. However, Texas can both influence national policy and initiate certain actions on its own.

Guiding Principles

The pervasive, self-confident optimism and can-do attitude of Texans, the good fortune of a rich endowment of natural resources, and an expanding technological base provided by the universities and the private sector together create the ideal conditions for sustained progress in the state. Progress is the combined result of many individuals' efforts — of the private decisions made at home, in business, and in other organizations. The role of Texas state government in this process is to provide the basic services that support and permit progress. In reviewing the state role, the commission faced the challenge of protecting the freedom of the individual Texan while guarding the common interest of all Texans. In studying the seven areas of concern and developing recommendations, the commission adhered to three broad principles as a foundation for its work:

* to keep the role of government at a minimum. Our recommendations are focused primarily on improving the performance of state government as it is presently organized. Thus, any recommendation suggesting a new governmental entity was examined very critically;
* to assure that the favorable business climate, which has been a major factor in the growth of Texas' economy, is preserved and enhanced; and
* to preserve to the greatest extent possible the tradition of local autonomy and responsibility.

As examples of the type of information provided by the Texas 2000 Project and Commission, the following three sections briefly describe the problems, issues, and recommendations associated with water, energy, and research and development concerns.

WATER

PROBLEMS AND ISSUES

Ensuring an adequate supply of usable water in the next 20 years is one of the most important challenges facing Texas. The state's healthy economic condition and recent rapid growth have been possible because there usually has been enough water for all sectors. If immediate action is not taken, that will not be the case in the future. Forecasted increases in demand for water and lead times of 15 to 30 years to complete major water projects make immediate action necessary (Kramer 1981, p. 210).

Texas has a wide assortment of water and water-related problems; (1) frequent drought; (2) frequent flooding; (3) man-made pollution; (4) natural pollution and contamination from salt and mineral deposits; (5) excessive ground water use causing land subsistence, salt water encroachment, and aquifer depletion; (6) need for water purification, transportation, storage, and distribution; (7) potentially insufficient water supplies for our growing industrial economy; (8) inadequate management of freshwater inflows; and (9) potentially insufficient water supplies for food and fiber production, and for energy production.

Extensive use of ground water and increasing demand for surface water, along with the probabilities for major droughts and devastating floods, demonstrate that Texas must pay more attention to the development and protection of its water resource supplies as the state's population and economy grow. Over the next two decades Texas cities and water authorities will need to invest in a wide range of facilities to supplement existing water supplies and meet the growing water needs of cities, business, and industry. According to the Texas Department of Water Resources estimates, the sewage treatment, flood protection, and water supply projects will cost approximately $30.2 billion through the year 2000.

In addition, the future of Texas' important agricultural sector is dependent upon the availability of adequate water supplies for irrigation. Thus, water conservation, quality protection, and development financing activities need to be accelerated to avert a water crisis in Texas. An aggressive planning effort, backed by implementation authority, is a major first step.

RECOMMENDATIONS

1. A statewide water plan should be developed, adopted, and implemented as soon as possible. A plan should include a priority list of surface water development and transfer projects, with options for interjurisdictional (including interstate and international) transfers; water-sharing mechanisms within use categories for times of short- and long-term shortages; a mechanism for allocating water under the preference list in Section 11.024 of the Texas Water Code; conservation strategies; water quality protection strategies; and financing strategies for water development, conservation, treatment, and quality control.
2. The state should design and implement a financing strategy for the plan called for in the preceding recommendation.

3. Authority should be granted to the Texas Department of Water Resources to initiate, sponsor, or undertake water development projects that involve interbasin transfers of floodwater, floodwater in storage, water in conservation storage and joint use of conveyance facilities and reservoirs in accordance with a state water plan.
4. The Texas Department of Water Resources should be authorized to develop and implement a statewide system for ground water management. This should be done as part of the revised water plan in cooperation with the special districts in Texas that currently have management responsibility for underground water.
5. The state should increase financial support for research and assist in technology transfer in the areas of desalinization, water modification, aquifer geology and mechanics, water quality enhancement, conservation methods, water reuse and recycling, economies in agricultural water use, and water treatment process improvements.

ENERGY

PROBLEMS AND ISSUES

Historically, Texas' energy resources have played a major role in the state as well as in the nation. A full quarter of all the energy ever produced in the United States, including 40 percent of the nation's historic production of oil, gas, and gas liquids, has been produced in Texas. The state's current contribution to the nation's energy output has declined somewhat from historic levels, but still stands at an impressive 21 percent. Through 1980 some 542 quadrillion Btus of energy (equivalent to 97.6 billion barrels of oil) have been produced in Texas.

There are four key facts which summarize Texas' energy situation:

1. Conventional production of oil and gas is declining at a time when energy consumption in Texas continues to rise.
2. The important Texas refining and petrochemical industry has become dependent on imported oil.
3. Thus far, state finances and Gross State Product have been shielded from the decline in energy production by the rapid

rise of oil and gas prices since 1973. It is not known, however, what path oil and gas prices will follow over the next 20 years, and it would be unwise to count on continued price increases compensating fully and indefinitely for a continuing decline in Texas' energy production.

4. Texas' economic future will be dictated largely by how successful efforts are to stem the decline in conventional oil and gas production, to increase the production of surface lignite, uranium, and synthetics, and to develop the state's submarginal energy resources — such as deep lignite and oil and gas produced by nonconventional recovery techniques, e.g. infill drilling.

RECOMMENDATIONS

1. The state should pursue policies that promote exploration, development, and production of nonrenewable conventional energy sources — including lignite — and that encourage development of renewable energy sources.

2. The state should work with the federal government to develop measures which provide appropriate incentives to maximize efficient energy production and insure that the state has equal geographic and price access to natural gas.

3. Public and private energy R&D efforts should be concentrated on development of subeconomic, marginal resources, chiefly nonconventional oil and gas and deep basin lignite, and renewable resources such as biomass, solar, and wind energy.

4. The state, in concert with the federal government, should pursue both the continued use of nuclear technology and the technical resolution of waste disposal issues, while devoting the highest priority to protection of public health and safety.

5. The state should seek to ensure an adequate supply of trained personnel and teachers to meet the demands of local energy industries for skilled and professional employees.

6. The state, in collaboration with the private sector and universities, should develop and maintain a more accurate body of information and projections on energy production, consumption, and prices.

7. Educational, financial, and technical programs that augment energy conservation should be supported by the state.

RESEARCH AND DEVELOPMENT

PROBLEMS AND ISSUES

A congressional study points out that "industrial innovation is at the core of the economic well-being of the United States and is a major contributor to economic growth. Innovation helps combat inflation, stimulates productivity, employment and the ability of U.S. products to compete both in domestic and world markets" (U.S. Congress, Joint Economic Committee 1980, p. ii). This statement applies directly to Texas.

Increased commitment to research and development in Texas over the next generation is imperative for three basic reasons: 1) to improve the use of the current resource base; 2) to help provide Texas with a resilient, well-diversified industrial base to counter possible deceleration in basic resource-dependent sectors; and 3) to take advantage of the new round of emerging technologies on which Texas' industrial growth will be increasingly based.

These reasons are based on an underlying assessment: steady economic growth will be required to accommodate the projected increase in population and to sustain a high quality of life in Texas. Traditional growth sectors — agriculture, oil and gas, and petrochemicals — must be supplemented by an expanding, diversified industrial base to create needed jobs and economic activity. Technological advances will stimulate both expansion and diversification; research and development will thus be the key to economic strength and development.

Specific requirements for R&D have been identified. They include, but are not limited to, genetic engineering, especially as it applies to agriculture, animal husbandry, and forestry; techniques for improving recovery of conventional and nonconventional oil and gas reserves; energy alternatives such as nuclear fusion and *in situ* burning of lignite; biomass as an energy source and as an input to agricultural production; water conservation; additional advancements in aeronautics, communications, and microelectronics; and improvements in construction and maintenance methods such as those used for transportation systems.

In addition, the necessary expansion and diversification of industry will depend on an ample supply of highly qualified people. High technology industry is attracted to areas that have first-class technical competence and an adequate supply of educated, skilled people to take the jobs.

The majority of funds for R&D in Texas come from the federal government and go to industries and public universities. State government historically has played a minimal role in supporting R&D at its universities or through state agencies. Federal priorities, which may not adequately address Texas' needs, and uncertainty about future federal R&D funding required that the governor and legislature evaluate state research and development funding levels and programs. If Texas is to maintain a competitive position in the nation and sustain its own economy, it must expand R&D efforts and focus them on areas most important to the state. Development of strong R&D partnerships among Texas government, universities, foundations, and the private sector will foster this expansion and sharpening of focus.

RECOMMENDATIONS

1. The state, in cooperation with the private sector, should design and implement communications programs to create greater awareness among corporations, universities, foundations, and the Texas Legislature of the vital role of research and development.
2. The state should establish a Science, Technology, and Research and Development Advisory Council composed of representatives from the public and private sectors.
3. The state should ensure that universities have sufficient financial, physical, and human resources to conduct research and development in high priority areas beneficial to the public and private sectors.
4. The state should recognize that R&D is a legitimate and essential university responsibility and support these functions by adjusting current teaching load and compensation formulas.
5. The state should evaluate ways in which state agencies, universities, and the private sector can develop and exploit communication technologies to further education and R&D activities.
7. The state should work with the federal government to improve legal, regulatory, and financial incentives for private sector research and development.

GENERAL FINDINGS

There are four general findings which transcend the specific areas of concern examined by the commission. First, basic issues in each area are closely interwoven. For example, agricultural productivity in the future is heavily dependent on what Texans do about water and energy supplies and transportation facilities, as well as on the new technologies that agricultural R&D may yield. Achieving the diversified energy base that Texas needs will not only require R&D, but also solutions to water and transportation problems. Similar interdependencies exist in the other areas.

Second, the commission believes that an increased and strategically focused R&D effort is fundamental to Texas' future. This effort is needed for two rather different purposes: (1) to help solve water, energy, agriculture, and transportation problems; and (2) to assure that Texas becomes a leader in the new technology-based industries rapidly emerging throughout the world — industries which inevitably will constitute the new leading sectors in future economic growth. R&D is a complex process, stretching from fundamental scientific research through multiple phases of experiment, development, and application. A successful R&D program requires close cooperation among creative scientists, engineers, and private entrepreneurs, as well as management by people who understand the crucial role of R&D.

Third, federal resources available to help finance activities of state and local government are being cut severely. Looking ahead, the policies of future national administrations and Congress are expected to vary on this matter. The citizens of Texas would be wise to assume that states will have to rely increasingly on their own resources. For example, it is up to Texans to solve Texas' water, energy, agricultural, and transportation problems and to build the R&D capacity necessary to solve such problems. No one else is going to do these things for Texas.

Fourth, the commission's report should be regarded as the beginning of a sustained process. It is important that Texas commit itself to an active and permanent long-range planning process, with the resulting information made available to the public and private decision makers around the state.

CONCLUSION

During the 1960s and 1970s Texas experienced a period of economic growth that greatly expanded the range and capacity of its industries, dramatically increased its per capita personal income, and brought the state to a position of national economic prominence. Business, industrial, and agricultural sectors flourished, supported by a plentiful supply of water, energy, land, and technology relatively unrestricted by government regulation.

The very existence of a Texas 2000 Commission is evidence of a widespread consensus that a new phase of Texas economic history is beginning. For this new era to be as productive as the one just past, new resources and an adequate infrastructure will be required. Growth during the next two decades and beyond will be achieved through innovation, efficient use of resources, investment to maintain and improve permanent structures, and success in applying new technologies.

In examining sectors of the Texas economy, the commission observed an intricate relationship of mutual dependence coupled with intense competition for the same resources: land, water, energy, and government services. Competition necessitates that both public and private choices be made. The broad implication is that, to make informed choices, Texas must engage in planning. Planning is the process of defining goals and devising means to achieve them. The commission has begun this process, setting as a goal "the continued health and vitality of the Texas economy and the quality of life" (Texas 2000 Project 1982, p. 1). Specific recommendations have been directed toward achieving that end. What now must follow is the development of a number of individual plans, each related to the commission's recommendations. Any plan, of course, should include the means of measuring progress toward reaching its goals.

The process initiated by the Texas 2000 Project has not completed one full cycle. Therefore, it is difficult to ascertain how successful it has been in stimulating concerted and sustained public action for managing growth. The first cycle will be completed during the current biennial session of the Texas Legislature. The Texas 2000 recommendations have been subjected to extensive review and discussion by members of the legislature and interim committee. A growing awareness of the growth management issues is evident among elected officials.

To other states and regions contemplating a growth management planning process similar to Texas 2000 three cautions are in order. First, senior elected public officials must be committed to the process and willing to provide the public visibility necessary for success. Second, the planning process must be open to anyone who wishes to participate. In a republic no plan works unless those who carry it out participate in its creation. A plan which emerges by analysis, debate, and consensus should command the support of a substantial majority and it should be carried out not only through existing public institutions, but also by private institutions and through public-private cooperation. It should, above all, be a dynamic and flexible process, changing as we experiment and learn what works and does not work.

REFERENCES

Kramer, Maxine. 1981. "Water in Texas Part II: Water Availability and Use." In *Texas Past and Future: A Survey*, Texas 2000 Project, pp. 209-229. Austin: Office of the Governor.

The State of Texas, Executive Department, Office of the Governor. 1980. *Executive Order WPC-16 Establishing The Texas 2000 Project*, Austin, Texas.

———. 1981. *Executive Order WPC-22 Establishing The Texas 2000 Commission*, Austin, Texas.

Texas 2000 Project. 1980. *Texas Trends*. Austin: Office of the Governor.

———. 1981. *Texas Past and Future: A Survey*. Austin: Office of the Governor.

———. 1982. *Texas 2000 Commission Report and Recommendations*. Austin: Office of the Governor.

U.S. Congress, Joint Economic Committee. 1980. *Research and Innovation: Development in a Dynamic Economy*. Special Study on Economic Change. Washington, D.C.: Government Printing Office.

10 Policy and Research Needs
Dwight F. Davis

Contributors to this volume have chronicled growth in the Sunbelt and asked a variety of questions about how growth can be managed. Emphasis has been placed on four categories of management issues: intergovernmental relations, state capacity building, local problem-solving, and the role of long-range planning. The substantive issues addressed include energy development, environmental protection, and social service delivery. Among other contributions, this volume clearly indicates the complexity of growth in this region and the diversity of issues associated with this growth. Rather than review each of the individual chapters, this conclusion will review three general questions found in the previous nine chapters: (1) What is different about the Sunbelt? (2) What are the short-term growth management needs? and (3) What are the long-term research needs?

WHAT IS DIFFERENT ABOUT THE SUNBELT

Sunbelt growth is interesting because it is relatively new, it is occurring during a period of national economic stagnation, and it is contrary to trends in most other areas of the United States. But, it is also interesting because the Sunbelt has other characteristics that differentiate it from the rest of the country. A review of the previous chapters suggests that Sunbelt states are different with regard to at least the following characteristics:

- economically disadvantaged throughout most of modern U.S. history;
- historically dominated by three economic sectors — agriculture, tourism, and fossil fuel development;
- perceived to be a region of very attractive climate, recreational opportunities, smaller cities, and lower taxes;
- extremely rapid growth in population and rate of employment since 1970; and
- a region which is very likely to continue to experience substantial growth in the foreseeable future.

While some of these characteristics also exist in other regions, it is their combination or cumulative effects which differentiate the Sunbelt and its growth management concerns. For example, because of its history and relative economic deprivation, the states and people of the region have been actively encouraging growth. As long as the states in this region continue to lag behind other areas in benefits, such as per capita income, they are very likely to continue to pursue growth actively.

Yet several factors about growth in the Sunbelt increase management difficulties. First, the pace of growth is rapid; few states have the luxury of gradually accommodating economic and population change. Second, there is a lack of historical experience within the region in managing rapid growth. Third, there is a lack of parallel experience outside the Sunbelt which could provide useful lessons; for example, recent growth in the West is largely an energy boom and much less pervasive than Sunbelt growth. Fourth, a variety of values are evident in the South which suggest that growth will need to be tempered; for example, clear concerns exist for preservation of resources, providing adequate services, and integrating new populations.

IMMEDIATE GROWTH MANAGEMENT CONCERNS

One dilemma in managing Sunbelt growth is that growth is both a blessing and a curse. With growth comes lower unemployment, higher personal income and higher capital investment for the common good; but growth also brings a host of maladies as well, which the previous authors have summarized. Dealing with these negative consequences of growth, therefore, is ironic — handling the problems of growth may require more growth. Paying for the consequences of growth is expensive, and states would like to avoid losing the positive benefits of growth. Balancing positive and negative consequences of growth is one of the most difficult public policy problems.

If a balance is to be achieved, planning and coordination will be required to link growth to natural resource protection and provision of social services. However, effective planning which impacts policy choice is frequently a very difficult task. Plans may fail because they are inadequately informed, because they include logically contradictory or ambiguous elements, or because of the complexities of policy formation and implementation.

It is often suggested that with adequate financial support, scientific and technological studies will allow for improved growth management. However, planning is much more complex. For example, many efforts to plan for growth fail on informational grounds alone. Thus, efforts to integrate and evaluate existing information sources for their applicability to future management concern, such as those developed by the Texas 2000 Commission (Chapter 9), may be particularly significant innovations.

Planning also can be constrained by the complexities of the political process. Most critics of governmental planning have observed that planning requires consensus on key values. Political processes typically inhibit this consensus, especially within the context of a highly fragmented political system like that of the United States. Examples of this problem are legion in law, as nearly every evaluation researcher or auditor has discovered.

Even the best technical information can be misrepresented or defused in the policy process. Consequently, policy action may be guided by incongruous, ambiguous, or vague mandates. A classic illustration of this tendency is the legal requirement for diverse participation in governmental planning for social services, capital investment, and other policy areas. This practice not only relieves public officials from the responsibility for plans, it makes logically coherent planning close to impossible. Of course, such broad participation in planning may help to coopt competing interests and to enhance public support for policy decisions, but it is still problematic for planning.

Implementation also can be an important constraint on government programs. This has been a major theme in the scholarly evaluation research literature of the past decade. While there are many causes for this, perhaps the most general explanation is, again, governmental fragmentation. In brief, in a fragmented political system such as ours, substantial discretion exists at each level of decision making. Indeed, the traditions of federalism and localism in this country make fragmentation virtually inevitable. In addition, during the past 20 years or so support for fragmentation and local discretion in several policy matters has been supported by both the right and left wings of the political spectrum. It is frequently argued that current changes in U.S. federalism are being brought about partly in response to strong lobbying for greater policy discretion by states and communities. While this fragmentation has many advantages, it also makes implementation more difficult and, frequently, of greater consequence to the ultimate results of policy than the adoption and formulation of the policy itself.

LONG-TERM RESEARCH NEEDS

This volume primarily contributes to our understanding of the kinds of problems which Sunbelt states will continue to face. However, it also suggests the need to refine our understanding of Sunbelt growth, since formation of policies to deal with growth should be related to these causes. For example, if attempts by Sunbelt states to attract business investment by means of generous tax benefits have little affect on capital investment decisions, as Daniel McGovern suggests (Chapter 3), then Sunbelt policymakers need to reconsider their understanding of the causes of investment.

Similarly, if policymakers are going to deal effectively with the consequences of growth, they need to understand its causes. If they do not adequately understand the causes of growth, then the variety of policy needs suggested in this volume become much more risky. Most of the authors of this volume advocate more future-oriented approaches to policy making — better planning, research and development, and linking growth policy to natural resource policy. The effectiveness of these efforts will be reduced if they are not premised on a reasonable understanding of the factors which are creating growth and change.

The issues discussed in this volume suggest at least four areas for which further research is particularly needed: underlying causes of growth, interdependence among regions, international factors, and infrastructure and human capital factors. As Chapter 1 by Roberts and Butler suggests, precisely characterizing the causes of Sunbelt growth is extremely difficult. Describing growth in terms of absolute and relative population shifts, per capita income changes, and changing employment patterns, among other variables, is important knowledge for improving management capabilities, but a better understanding is needed for why these trends are occurring if long-term management is to be successful. This volume does suggest that the most important intermediate causes are a reversal of domestic migration patterns and a shift of capital from Frostbelt to Sunbelt states. However, further research in this area needs to address why these phenomena occurred, how they are related to each other, and how long they will last.

Conventional wisdom is that both people and capital are attracted to the Sunbelt by the attributes of these states. Collectively, these attributes contribute to what is called a "favorable business climate." Lower costs of living and lower business operating costs resulting from generally lower wage, lower taxes, less governmental regulation, and lower annual fuel costs contribute to this climate. However, the irony of Sunbelt growth is that it may well be causing a reversal in these traditional attractions — many of these factors are changing in the direction of the rest of the country. For example, rapid growth in the Sunbelt has been accompanied by rapidly rising inflation, higher costs for operating businesses, and increased governmental regulation at the state and local level. A better understanding of these trends and possible reversals is necessary if we are to accurately project future growth trends.

Several authors of this volume (Roberts and Butler, James, McGovern) suggest the significance of understanding the interdependence of Sunbelt states with the rest of the United States. Obviously, the most recent Sunbelt population growth is related to dramatic economic decline in some northern states. Also, Sunbelt growth is affected by the nature of contemporary federalism in the United States. Several authors emphasize how changes in U.S. federalism will affect the ability of Sunbelt states to cope with growth, but these changes may affect growth itself. For example, if the states receive increasing authority over social programs at the same time that they receive decreasing fiscal support for these programs from the national government, disparities among the state regarding these programs are likely to increase. If that happens, population migration patterns might be affected. Explanations of Sunbelt growth must include factors outside of the Sunbelt as well as within.

The interdependence of the Sunbelt with rest of the country also means that it is affected by international events. For example, illegal aliens fleeing war, oppression, or economic adversity have moved disproportionately to the U.S. Sunbelt states. Indeed, if it was possible to get accurate estimates of the number of illegal aliens in the Sunbelt states, estimates of absolute and relative rates of population growth would probably have to be adjusted upward. Capital investment in the Sunbelt is also influenced by international events. As production cost differences between northern and Sunbelt states are reduced, it is likely that capital flight from the Sunbelt to foreign countries in Asia and South America will increase. There are several foreign countries whose economic policies are geared specifically to attracting investment by U.S. entrepreneurs in manufacturing enterprises in those countries. Daniel McGovern (Chapter 3) implies just such a possibility in his analysis of capital flight from the Frostbelt. Policymakers in the Sunbelt should consider factors beyond the borders of the United States as they wrestle with the causes and consequences of Sunbelt growth.

There also are a variety of factors related to infrastructure and human capital that require further research. For example, McGovern mentions the effects of improvements in transportation in the Sunbelt, especially the interstate highway system. The development and expansions of major airports in Sunbelt cities such as Atlanta, Dallas/Fort Worth, and Tampa have probably affected Sunbelt growth. Additionally, business investment is affected not only by the ready availability of a relatively inexpensive labor force, but also by the technical competence of that labor force. Historically, Sunbelt states have not fared well in ratings of educational performance of the states. Teachers' salaries, educational expenditure per capita, pupil performance on standardized exams, etc., all tend to be lower in Sunbelt states compared to northern states. What effect, if any, have these tendencies had on Sunbelt growth? Are recent Sunbelt investors cognizant of changes regarding these matters that have not been well publicized? More investigation of the effects of technological factors on Sunbelt growth is needed.

CONCLUSION

It is safe to conclude that developing appropriate governmental responses to Sunbelt growth is likely to be difficult. When one considers that Sunbelt growth is fairly recent, this conclusion is not surprising. Additionally, several factors will make it difficult to benefit from the historical experiences of other regions of the country. First, until the previous two decades, economic growth was considered to be beneficial. Consequently, extensive analysis of the negative effects of growth is of recent origin. Second, the Sunbelt is different from other parts of the country in several respects. Third, Sunbelt growth is occurring during a time of substantial economic dislocation and interdependence among nations. Consequently, historical parallels are difficult to find. Fourth, we are much more sophisticated than we used to be about the frailties of planning. Plans are normally quite uncertain both in design and execution. Finally, a review of studies of economic growth in this country indicates that while our understanding of the causes of growth has increased markedly, there is still room for further investigation.

So much for limitation. Is there anything positive we can do? Certainly there is. First, Sunbelt states need to learn from each other, since historical comparisons with other parts of the country may not be completely parallel. Part of this sharing of information should involve analysis of the distinguishing features of Sunbelt states compared to the rest of the United States and to each other. We also need to disseminate this information about the attempts of Sunbelt states to manage growth. The mechanisms for this already exist in the Southern Governors' Conference, and the Conference of State Legislatures.

Second, there is need for more and better research on private sector decisions resulting in Sunbelt growth. Daniel McGovern's contribution to this volume is in the right direction. His research suggests that state policymakers need to understand the factors that cause the influx or flight of capital in the Sunbelt. Only with such understanding can Sunbelt policymakers formulate appropriate responses to growth in their region.

Third, the concept of state and local capacity for managing growth needs elaboration and refinement. The contributions by Steven Ballard, Elizabeth Gunn, and Susan MacManus touch on several of the major elements of this concept, but there is still much to learn. Analysts interested in this issue might benefit from consulting the most recent international development literature. Building problem-solving capacity has been a major concern of the U.S. Agency for International Development, the World Bank, and other organizations involved in international technical assistance for some time. Basically, what is needed with regard to the U.S. Sunbelt is specification of the necessary conditions for the management of growth and understanding of the constraints to establishing these conditions.

Additional Readings

The selections that follow address the general theme of growth and development in the Sunbelt. They are intended to supplement but not duplicate the material referenced at the end of each chapter. Only materials published since 1977 have been included. We have emphasized material that discusses issues which are regional in scope or which have implications for many areas throughout the Sunbelt.

JOURNALS AND PERIODICALS

Abbott, Carl. 1979. "The American Sunbelt: Idea and Region." *Journal of the West* 18(July): 5-18.

Adams, Jerry. 1977. "Organizing the South Isn't So Easy." *South Magazine*, November/December, pp. 16-18.

Allmon, Dale, and Don M. Bechter. 1981. "State and Local Governments: Their Stake in Federal Budget Reform." *Economic Review*, November, pp. 20-27.

Alonso, William. 1978. "Metropolis Without Growth." *The Public Interest* 53(Fall): 68-86.

Avery, David M., and Gene D. Sullivan. 1982. "Southeastern Oil Industry Booming Again." *Economic Review*, January, pp. 32-38.

Ayer, Harry W., and Paul G. Hoyt. 1977. "Industrial Growth in the U.S. Border Communities and Associated Water and Air Problems: An Economic Perspective." *Natural Resources Journal* 17(October): 585-614.

Barkley, David L. 1981. "Regional Manufacturing Employment Cycles Revisited." *Annals of Regional Science* 15(March): 66-83.

Bartlett, Robin L., William L. Henderson, Timothy I. Miller, and Charles Poultan-Callahan. 1982. "Migration and the Distribution of Earnings in the South." *Growth and Change* 13(April): 40-47.

Beyle, Thad, and Patricia Dusenbury. 1982. "Health and Human Services Block Grants: The State and Local Dimension." *State Government* 55(1): 2-14.

Breckenfield, Gurney. 1977. "Business Loves the Sunbelt (and Vice Versa)." *Fortune*, June, pp. 132-46.

Briggs, Vernon, M., Jr., and Brian Rungeling. 1980. "Economic Development: A Poverty Solution for the Rural South?" *Growth and Change* 11(October): 31-36.

Brown, Anthony. 1980. "Technical Assistance to Rural Communities: Stopgap or Capacity-Building?" *Public Administration Review* 40(January/February): 18-23.

Brown, David L. 1981. "Spatial Aspects of Post 1970 Work Force Migration in the United States." *Growth and Change* 12(January): 9-20.

Browne, Lynn. 1980. "Regional Investment Patterns." *New England Economic Review*, July/August, pp. 5-23.

———. 1980. "Narrowing Regional Income Differentials." *New England Economic Review*, September/October, pp. 35-56.

———. 1980. "Narrowing Regional Income Differentials: II." *New England Economic Review*, November/December, pp. 40-59.

———. 1982. "Two Years of Stagnation: A Regional Perspective." *New England Economic Review*, September/October, pp. 35-44.

Burns, Mark. 1982. "Domain Consensus in Alabama Health Systems Agencies." *Administration and Society* 14(November): 319-43.

Business Week. 1978. "A Push to Tie Federal Spending to Area Needs by Regions." January 30, pp. 66-68.

Carter, Charlie. 1981. "The Effects of Proposed Federal Spending Cuts on the Southeast." *Economic Review*, June, pp. 4-12.

Clarke, Susan E. 1979. "Determinants of State Growth Management Policies." *Policy Studies Journal* 7(Summer): 753-62.

Cobb, James C. 1977. "Urbanization and the Changing South: A Review of Literature." *South Atlantic Urban Studies* 1: 253-66.

Cohen, Richard E. 1981. "In The Conservative Politics of the 80s, The South Is Rising Once Again." *National Journal*, February 28, pp. 350-54.

Congressional Quarterly Weekly Report. 1977. "Regionalism in Congress: Formulas Debated." 35: 1747-52.

_____. 1982. "Growth, Diversity Reshape Sun Belt's Politics." 40: 107-13.

Corrigan, Richard, and Rochelle L. Stanfield. 1981. "Rising Energy Prices — What's Good for Some States Is Bad for Others." *National Journal*, March 22, pp. 468-74.

Deak, Edward J., and Edward Heinze. 1978. "New England and the Southeast: Interregional Effects of Regional Change." *New England Journal of Business and Economics* 4(Spring): 1-15.

DeLome, Charles D., Jr., and Norman Wood. 1981. "Quantifying Environmental Losses from a Regional Water Development Program." *Growth and Change* 12(January): 21-27.

Dowall, David E. 1978. "Fiscal Impact Rationale for Growth Management." *Annals of Regional Science* 12(July): 83-94.

_____. 1980. "An Examination of Population-Growth-Managing Communities." *Policy Studies Journal* 9(Winter): 414-26.

Economic Review. 1982. "The Southeast in 1982: Special Issue." February: pp. 1-55.

Economic Review. 1983. "The Southeast in 1983: Special Issue." February: pp. 1-82.

Fischer, James S. 1979. "Manufacturing Additions in Georgia: Metropolitan-Nonmetropolitan Differences from 1961 to 1975." *Growth and Change* 10(April): 9-17.

Flowers, George A., Jerome S. Legee, Jr., Paul E. Radford, and David H. Wiltsee. 1981. "Targeting Funds for Economic Development in Rural Georgia." *Public Administration Review* 41(July/August): 485-88.

Gilbert, Kathie. 1983. "The Effects of the New Federalism on South Central States." *Texas Business Review*, January/February, pp. 34-38.

Glendening, Parris N., and Patricia S. Atkins. 1979. "City-County Consolidation: Regional Governance's Refound Tool." *Review of Regional Studies* 9 (Fall): 47-63.

Glenn, Norval D., and Charles N. Weaver. 1982. "Regional Differences in Attitudes Toward Work." *Texas Business Review*, November/December, pp. 263-66.

Gordon, Michael R. 1980. "With Foreign Investment at Stake, It's One State Against the Others." *National Journal*, October 18, pp. 1744-48.

Gottschalk, Peter T. 1981. "Regional Allocation of Federal Funds." *Policy Analysis* 7(Spring): 183-97.

Groszyk, Walter S., and Thomas J. Madden. 1981. "Managing Without Immunity: The Challenge for State and Local Government Officials in the 1980s." *Public Administration Review* 41(May/June): 268-78.

Gustely, Richard D., and Larkin Warner. 1982. "Fiscal Aspects of Southwest Regional Growth." *Texas Business Review*, March/April, pp. 57-62.

Hauschen, Larry D. 1979. "Energy and the Outlook for Agriculture in the Southwest." *Voice, Federal Reserve Bank of Dallas*, May, pp. 16-23.

Havemann, Joel, and Rochelle L. Stanfield. 1977. "A Year Later, The Frostbelt Strikes Back." *National Journal*, July 2, pp. 1028-37.

Hekman, John, and Alan Smith. 1982. "Behind the Sunbelt's Growth: Industrial Decentralization." *Economic Review*, March, pp. 4-13.

Jellinek, Steven. 1978. "Controlling Toxic Substances." *EPA Journal*, September, pp. 4-6, 23.

Johnston, Robert A. 1980. "The Politics of Local Growth Control." *Policy Studies Journal* 9(Winter): 427-39.

Jones, William A., and C. Bradly Doss. 1978. "Local Officials' Reactions to Federal Capacity-Building." *Public Administration Review* 38(January/February): 64-70.

Jusenius, Carol L., and Larry C. Ledebur. 1977. "The Northern Tier and The Sunbelt: Conflict or Cooperation?" *Challenge*, March-April, pp. 44-49.

Kahley, William J. 1982. "Southern Fireworks: Will Defense Spending Light Up The South?" *Economic Review*, December, pp. 21-31.

_____. 1982. "International Banking Activity in the Southeast: Rapid Growth and Change." *Economic Review*, October, pp. 13-22.

Kiel, David H. 1982. "An OD Strategy for Policy Implementation: The Case of North Carolina State Government." *Public Administration Review* 42(July/August): 375-83.

Kirschten, Dick. 1981. "America On The Move." *National Journal*, November 14, pp. 2016-24.

Lucke, Robert B. 1982. "Rich States-Poor States: Inequalities in Our Federal System." *Intergovernmental Perspective* 8(Spring): 22-28.

Madison, C. 1981. "Money for Deeper U.S. Coal Ports — Needed or Just More Pork Barrel?" *National Journal*, February 7, pp. 225-28.

Malecki, Edward J. 1982. "Centers of Technology in the Southwest." *Texas Business Review*, January/February, pp. 1-5.

Markusen, Ann R., and Jerry Fastrup. 1978. "The Regional War for Federal Aid." *The Public Interest* 53(Fall): 87-99.

Markusen, Ann R., Annalee Szenian, and Marc Weiss. 1981. "Who Benefits from Intergovernmental Transfers?" *Publius* 11(Winter): 5-37.

McCrackin, Bobbie H. 1982. "Southeastern Employment After the Recession." *Economic Review*, December, pp. 53-64.

McDowell, Bruce D. 1982. "Deregulation — Effects on State Governments." *The Bureaucrat* 11(Summer): 22-32.

McKenzie, Richard B. 1982. "Myths of Sunbelt and Frostbelt." *Policy Review*, Spring, pp. 103-14.

Murphy, Jerome T. 1981. "The Paradox of State Government Reform." *The Public Interest* 64(Summer): 124-39.

Pack, Janet Rothenberg. 1978. "Frostbelt and Sunbelt: Convergence Over Time." *Intergovernmental Perspective* 4(Fall): 8-15.

Peirce, Neal R., and Jerry Hagstrom. 1980. "New Migrants Mean Opportunities — and Problems — for Rural America." *National Journal*, March 29, pp. 508-12.

_____. 1981. "The Cities, Not the States, May Bear the Brunt of Revenue Sharing Cutbacks." *National Journal*, April 19, pp. 636-39.

———. 1981. "Federal Spending Cuts Could Worsen Older Cities' Ability to Borrow Money." *National Journal*, February 7, pp. 216-20.

Perkinson, Leon B. 1980. "Rural In-Migration: Are Migrants Universally Disadvantaged?" *Growth and Change* 11(July): 17-26.

Pfrommer, Carol. 1980. "Southern Regional Development and Waterway Construction." *Texas Business Review*, September/October, pp. 261-63.

Phillips, Kevin. 1978. "The Balkanization of America." *Harper's Magazine*, May, pp. 37-47.

Plaut, Thomas R. 1981. "Migration Trends of the Elderly in the United States and the Southwest." *Texas Business Review*, May/June, pp. 105-8.

Posner, Alan R. 1981. "Export Promotion Policies in Sunbelt States." *Texas Business Review*, July/August, pp. 152-56.

Public Opinion. 1979. "Environmental Protection: An Idea that Has Come and Stayed." August/September, pp. 21-23.

Radin, Beryl A. 1982. "Leaving It to the States." *Public Welfare* 40(Summer): 17-24.

Rees, John. 1982. "Defense Spending and Regional Industrial Change." *Texas Business Review*, January/February, pp. 40-44.

Reid, J. Norman, and William F. Fox. 1980. "Interregional Benefits From Federal Spending: A New Look at an Old Issue." *Policy Studies Journal* 9(Autumn): 95-102.

Reynolds, William. 1979. "The South: Global Dumping Ground." *Southern Exposure*, Winter, pp. 49-56.

Rostow, W. W. 1978. "The South: Regional Development and National Responsibility." *Texas Business Review*, August, pp. 36-39.

Savage, Robert L. 1982. "The Structure of Growth Management in American States." *Publius* 12(Spring): 99-111.

Schram, Sanford F. 1981. "Politics, Professionalism, and The Changing Federalism." *Social Service Review* 55(March): 78-93.

Sease, Douglas R. 1978. "Yankee Go Home: Many Northern Firms Seeking Sites in South Get Chilly Reception; Low-Wage, Nonunion Areas Turn Down Plant Bids Despite Promise of Jobs." *Wall Street Journal*, February 10, p. 1.

Seninger, Stephen F. 1982. "Spending Rules, Tax Expenditure Limitations, and Fiscal Constraints on State Governments." *Annals of Regional Science* 16(July): 1-11.

Senkan, Selim M., and Nancy W. Stauffer. 1981. "What to Do with Hazardous Waste." *Technology Review* 84(November/December): 34-47.

Serow, William J., and Dudley L. Poston. 1982. "Demographic and Economic Change in the South." *Texas Business Review*, January/February, pp. 30-33.

Smith, R. Jeffrey. 1981. "The Waterway That Cannot Be Stopped." *Science*, August 14, pp. 741-44.

Southern City. 1978. "The Sun Belt-Snow Belt Controversy — A Matter of $$ and Sense." July, pp. 3-5.

Southern Growth: Problems and Promise. 1978. "Busbee, Senator Debate." Winter, pp. 1, 3.

Southwick, Lawrence, Jr. 1981. "Public Welfare Programs and Recipient Migration." *Growth and Change*. 12(October): 22-33.

Steinnes, David. 1982. "Do People Follow Jobs or Do Jobs Follow People? A Causality Issue in Urban Economics." *Urban Studies* 19(May): 187-93.

Sternitzke, Herbert S. 1978. "Coastal Plain Hardwood Problem." *Journal of Forestry* 76: 152-53.

Sternlieb, George, and James W. Hughes. 1977. "Regional Market Variations: The Northeast Versus the South." *American Real Estate and Urban Economic Association Journal*, Spring, pp. 44-67.

Sutton, Horace. 1978. "Sunbelt vs. Frostbelt: A Second Civil War?" *Saturday Review*, April 15, pp. 28-37.

Terrell, Paul. 1980. "Beyond the Categories: Human Service Managers View the New Federal Aid." *Public Administration Review* 40(January/February): 47-54.

U.S. News and World Report. 1977. "The Pork-Barrel War Between the States." December 5, pp. 39-41.

Vance, Stanley C. 1977. "The Sunshine Belt: A New Home for Corporate Head-quarters." *Regional Economics and Business*, April, pp. 5-10.

Weissert, Carol S. 1981. "State Legislatures and Federal Funds: An Issue of the 1980s." *Publius* 11(Summer): 67-85.

Williston, Hamlin L. 1979. "The South's Pine Reforestation Problem." *Journal of Forestry* 77: 234-36.

White, Michelle. 1978. "Self-Interest in the Suburbs: The Trend Toward No-Growth Zoning." *Policy Analysis* 4(Spring): 185-207.

Winsberg, Morton D. 1981. "Agriculture and the Interstate: A Note on Locational Impacts in the South." *Growth and Change* 12(July): 47-53.

Zlatkovich, Charles P. 1983. "National and Regional Income Trends During the 1970s." *Texas Business Review*, January/February, pp. 39-43.

BOOKS

Arnold, Victor L., ed. 1980. *Alernatives to Confrontation: A National Policy Toward Regional Change.* Lexington, Mass.: D. C. Heath, Lexington Books.

Dilger, Robert Jay. 1982. *The Sunbelt/Snowbelt Controversy: The War Over Federal Funds.* New York: New York University Press, distributed by Columbia University Press.

Kneese, Allen V., and F. Lee Brown. 1981. *The Southwest Under Stress: National Resource Development Issues in a Regional Setting.* Resources for the Future. Baltimore, Maryland: Johns Hopkins University Press.

Liner, E. Blaine, and Lawrence K. Lynch, eds. 1977. *The Economics of Southern Growth.* Durham, North Carolina: Seeman Printing.

Newby, I. A. 1978. *The South: A History.* New York: Holt, Rinehart, and Winston.

Perry, David C., and Alfred J. Watkins, eds. 1977. *The Rise of the Sunbelt Cities.* Urban Affairs Annual Reviews, vol. 14. Beverly Hills, California: Sage.

Poston, Dudley L., Jr., and Robert H. Weller, eds. 1981. *The Population of the South: Structure and Change in Social Demographic Context.* Austin: University of Texas Press.

MONOGRAPHS

Advisory Commission on Intergovernmental Relations. 1981. *Regional Growth: Interstate Tax Competition.* Washington, D.C.: Advisory Commission on Intergovernmental Relations.

Alonso, William. 1977. *New National Concerns and Regional Policy.* Occasional Papers of the National Bureau of Economic Research, vol. 4, no. 3. Washington: U.S. Government Printing Office.

Berry, Brian J. L., and Donald C. Dahmann. 1977. *Population Redistribution in the United States in the 1970s.* Washington, D.C.: National Research Council and National Academy of Sciences.

Congressional Quarterly. 1979. *American Regionalism: Our Economic, Cultural, and Political Makeup.* Editorial Research Reports on American Regionalism. Washington, D.C.: Congressional Quarterly Press.

Dusenbury, Patricia J., and Thad L. Boyle. 1979. *Southern Cities and the National Urban Policy.* Research Triangle Park, North Carolina: Southern Growth Policies Board.

Focus on Regional Cooperation: North-South Summit. 1978. Report on a conference sponsored by the Northeast-Midwest Congressional Coalition in conjunction with Southern Growth Policies Board. Boston, Massachusetts, August 25-26.

Godschalk, David R., J. M. Bruce Knopf, and Seth G. Weissman. 1978. *Guiding Growth in the South.* Research Triangle Park, North Carolina: Southern Growth Policies Board.

Katzman, Martin T. 1977. *The Quality of Municipal Services, Central City Decline and Middle Class Flight.* Harvard University, Cambridge, Massachusetts: City and Regional Planning.

Liner, E. Blaine. 1978. *The Snowbelt and the Seven Myths.* Research Triangle Park, North Carolina: Southern Growth Policies Board.

National Economic Research Institute. 1979. *Urban Development Action Grants:*

A Study of Regional Influence. Austin, Texas: National Economic Research Institute.

Peterson, David. 1979. *The Relative Need of States and Regions for Federal Aid.* Research Triangle Park, North Carolina: Southern Growth Policies Board.

Quindry, Kenneth E., and Niles Schoening. 1979. *State and Local Tax Ability and Effort.* Atlanta: Southern Regional Education Board.

Southern Growth Policies Board. 1977. *Annual Report, 1977: The South in the Seventies.* Research Triangle Park, North Carolina: Southern Growth Policies Board.

Southern States Energy Board. 1981. *Report of the Task Force on Energy to the Commission on the Future of the South.* Research Triangle Park, North Carolina: Southern Growth Policies Board.

Warman, James C., ed. 1981. *Ground Water Management: Proceedings of a Southeast Regional Conference.* Auburn, Alabama: Auburn University, Water Resources Research Institute.

Weiss, Richard. 1977. *Regional Disparities in Federal Medicaid Assistance.* Washington, D.C.: Northeast-Midwest Institute.

Zabar, Laurence, and Betsy J. Massar. 1978. *Proposed Military Base Realignments: The Regional Impact.* Washington, D.C.: Northeast-Midwest Institute.

GOVERNMENT DOCUMENTS AND REPORTS

Bluestone, Herman, and Robert Coltrane. 1977. *Changes in the Regional Balance of Income and Population in the U.S., 1940-70.* Washington, D.C.: U.S. Department of Agriculture, Economic Research Service.

Booz, Allen and Hamilton, Inc. and Putnam, Hayes and Bartlett, Inc. 1980. *Hazardous Waste Generation and Commercial Hazardous Waste Management Capacity.* Washington, D.C.: U.S. Environmental Protection Agency.

Copenhaver, Emily D., Richard J. Olson, and Patricia L. Rice. 1978. *Regional Environmental-Energy Data Book: Southern Region,* Oak Ridge, Tennessee: Oak Ridge National Laboratory.

Geraghty and Miller, Inc. 1977. *Ground-Water Pollution Problems in the South-eastern United States*. Ada, Oklahoma: U.S. Environmental Protection Agency, Robert S. Kerr Environmental Research Laboratory.

Honea, R. B., E. L. Hillsman, et al. 1979. *Regional Issue Identification and Assessment (RIIA): An Analysis of the Mid-Range Projection Series C Scenario; Executive Summary for Federal Region VI*. Oak Ridge, Tennessee: Oak Ridge National Laboratory.

_____ . 1979. *Regional Issue Identification and Assessment (RIIA): An Analysis of the Mid-Range Projection Series C Scenario; Executive Summary for Federal Regions IV*. Oak Ridge, Tennessee: Oak Ridge National Laboratory.

Seller, L. E., and L. W. Canter. 1980. *Effects of Hazardous Waste Disposal on Ground Water Quality*. Norman: University of Oklahoma, National Center for Ground Water Research.

Shepherd, A. D., M. E. Hodgson, J. Stewart, and K. A. Hake. 1980. *State Water Use and Socioeconomic Data Relating to the Second National Water Assessment*. ORNL Report TM7242. Oak Ridge, Tennessee: Oak Ridge National Laboratory.

U.S. Congress. House of Representatives. Select Committee on Population. 1978. *Consequences of Changing U.S. Population: Population Movement and Planning*. 95th Congress, 2nd session.

U.S. Department of Commerce. 1980. *The High Plains Study*. Washington, D.C.: Department of Commerce.

U.S. Environmental Protection Agency. Office of Research and Development (ORD). 1980. *Environmental Outlook, 1980*. Washington, D.C.: Government Printing Office.

U.S. Environmental Protection Agency, Office of Research and Development, Office of Strategic Assessment and Special Studies. 1980. "Environmental Outlook 1975-2000, Region VI." Unpublished paper.

U.S. Environmental Protection Agency, Region IV. 1978. *Southeast Environmental Profiles, 1977*. Atlanta, Georgia: U.S. Environmental Protection Agency.

U.S. General Accounting Office. 1981. *To Continue or Halt the Tenn-Tom Waterway*. Report #CED-81-89. Washington, D.C.: General Accounting Office.

U.S. President's Commission for a National Agenda for the Eighties. 1980. *Energy, Natural Resources, and the Environment in the Eighties*. Report of the Panel on Energy, Natural Resources, and the Environment. Washington, D.C.: Government Printing Office.

Index

agglomeration economies, 7, 16-19, 30

agricultural lands, protection of, 111

agriculture, 4-5, 14, 28-29

aid to families with dependent children, 166-67

air quality: public opinion about, 114; regulations, 113

Alabama, 9, 19-20, 22, 23, 41, 52, 54, 58, 64, 95, 104, 112, 114, 116, 119-20, 122, 182

Albuquerque, New Mexico, 27

amenities, 22, 24-28, 29-30

annexation, 133, 144-46, 147, 149-50

Appalachians, 24

Arizona, 22

Arkansas, 20, 21, 26, 41, 54, 56, 58, 116, 119, 123, 181, 183

at risk groups, 101-2

Atlanta, Georgia, 16, 217

Austin, Texas, 19

Ballard, Steven, 219

Baton Rouge, Louisiana, 15

Birmingham, Alabama, 95

Biscayne Aquifer, 173

Black Fox Nuclear Power Plant, 120

block grants, 93-94, 102; for child health care, 99; for maternal health care, 99

building code requirements, 146

busbar cost comparisons, 183

business climate, 1, 3, 20, 21, 23-24, 29, 85, 216

Butler, Lisa, 216

California, 18-19, 30, 64

capacity-building, 164, 171-72, 219

capital improvement, 138, 149, 153-55

capital movement (investments, disinvestments): factors causing, 64-66; policies to control, 82-87; significance, 217, 218; theories of, 65-70

Caribbean, 14-15

Carter Administration, 118, 121, 165

Center for Disease Control, 100

child abuse prevention and treatment, 101

Clements, William P., Jr. (Governor of Texas), 198, 200

climate, 1, 3, 24, 26

coal: economic advantages of, 181-82; import costs, 183; utilization, 186 (*see also* lignite)

coastal zone resources management, 111

cogeneration, 192-93

Colorado, 182, 191

community infrastructure, 66

Conference of State Legislatures, 218

Connecticut, 22

Consolidated Coal Company, 185-86

costs: concentration, 18; labor, 7-11, 17-18, 22, 29, 30; of living, 25

crime, 132, 135, 138-39, 141, 142, 152

Cross-Florida Barge Canal, 120

Dallas, Texas, 13, 16, 19, 173, 217

deed restrictions (subdivision regulations), 146

Delta Star Project, 186

237

development, 188-91; and synfuels, 184, 187, 191, 192; for
value-added industries, 184, 190
Little Rock, Arkansas, 26
local markets, 69
locational theory, 66, 72, 74 (*see
also* capital movements, theories)
Louisiana, 11, 13, 15-16, 20,
22, 64, 104, 109, 112, 116,
119, 123, 124, 183

major thoroughfare plan, 151
manufacturing employment, 63, 64,
80
manufacturing industries (*see* industrial development)
markets, 4, 7, 16-17, 21, 22, 29, 30
mass transit, 138, 152-53
McGovern, Daniel, 215, 216-17, 218
Medicaid, 166-67
Mental Health Association, 99
mental health, 98-99
metropolitan areas, 3, 18-19, 24-
25, 27-30
Mexico, 95
Miami, Florida, 16, 27, 97
Miami-Everglades Jetport, 120
Miami-Fort Lauderdale, Florida, 173
migrants and migration, 6, 19, 24-27
(*see also* immigration)
Milwaukee County, Wisconsin, 72
minemouth plants, 183, 184, 192
Minnesota, 22
Mississippi, 13, 41, 44, 47, 54, 56,
100, 104, 109, 114, 116, 123-24,
180-93; Business Permitting Advisory Council, 191; Department
of Energy and Transportation,
180-81; economic development

strategy, 192; energy needs, 181;
lignite resources, 180, 183, 184-
87, 192-93; regional analysis for,
186-87, 189; Research and Development Center, 180-81; research
needs, 187-91; state roles in lignite development, 188, 193
Mississippi River, 13

National Aeronautics and Space Administration, 164
National Association of Counties, 170
National Audubon Society, 118
National Conference of State Legislatures, 168, 172, 174-75
National Governors Association, 170-
71, 174-75
National Institute of Alcohol Abuse
and Alcoholism, 97
National Institute of Drug Abuse,
97
National Institute of Health, 97
National Institute of Mental Health,
97
National Science Foundation, 164-65,
172
National Wildlife Federation, 118-19,
121
natural gas, 11-13, 16
natural resources: aesthetic values,
111; costs and availability, 7-14;
data service, 191; energy costs,
11-13; labor costs, 7-11
neighborhood deterioration, 135, 138,
141, 142, 145, 154, 156, 158
new federalism, 94, 95, 102, 153-54,
163, 166, 172, 175
New Mexico, 9, 11, 20, 24,
26-27, 29, 41, 44, 47, 56, 108-10,

119, 122-23
New Orleans, 15-16
New York, 22
Nigh, George (Governor of Oklahoma), 110, 168
North Carolina, 3, 9, 19-20, 21, 23, 26, 41, 49, 56, 64, 100-1, 104, 109-10, 114, 119, 123, 126, 173
North Dakota, 183
nuclear power, 182, 187
nurses' training, 96-97

Office of Science and Technology Policy, 165, 172
Ogallala Aquifer, 173
oil, 11-13, 16 (see also petroleum)
Oklahoma, 9, 11, 13, 16, 19, 23, 41, 48, 101, 108-10, 116, 119, 122
Omnibus Budget Reconciliation Act of 1981, 93, 96, 99, 100, 101-2
Ontario, Canada, 87
overcrowding, 135
Ozarks, 3, 24, 29

Pacific, 9
petroleum and petroleum products, 14, 16, 17, 29 (see also oil, natural gas)
Phillips Coal Company, 185-86
planning, 150-51, 154, 214, 218
plant closings (factory closings), 63-64 (see also industrial location)
police protection, 142, 147, 152
population, 1, 3, 4, 8, 16, 17, 19, 23-24, 30; metropolitan growth, 43-53; migration, 41, 43; natural

increase, 43-44; nonmetropolitan growth, 43-53; regional growth trends, 38, 40-41; state growth trends, 41, 43
property revaluation, 151
provincialism, 138
Pryor, David, 175
public services/works, 3, 21, 25-26, 29, 83
public/private sector partnerships (leeraging, private sector initiatives), 133, 153-55

racial tensions, 138-39, 141
Raleigh, North Carolina, 19
raw materials, 7, 14-15, 16, 22, 29
Reagan Administration, 93, 95, 100, 163, 166-68, 170-71, 172-73, 174-75
recreation, 3, 26
regional cost differences: effect on capital movement, 72, 74-75; theory, 67
regional growth: costs and benefits, 107
regional markets, 69
regional mobility plan, 154, 156
regionalization (areawide governments), 133, 144, 147-48, 152
reinvestment zone, 154-55, 156
research and development, 10-11, 16, 18-19, 27, 187-91 (see also innovation)
residency: newcomers, 133-35, 138-39, 142, 145-47, 156, 158; old-timers, 134-35, 142, 145-47, 158
residential location: inner city, 134, 135, 138, 139, 141, 142, 144, 147-48, 150, 156; suburbs, 134,

22, 29, 182
Tulsa, Oklahoma, 13, 19

unincorporated areas (*see* residential location)
Union City, Tennessee, 8
unions/activism (*see* labor)
U.S. Agency for International Development, 219
Utah, 182

wage rates (*see* income)
wages and salaries, 1, 3, 4, 6-9, 10-11,

13, 21, 25, 27, 29
Waukesha County, Wisconsin, 72
water: management of, 126; public opinion about, 114
West, 1, 20, 24, 28
Whitmire, Kathryn J., 151
windfall profits tax, 167, 169, 170
Wisconsin, 63, 65, 71-72, 75, 78-79, 80-82
World Bank, 219
Wright, Fielding (Governor of Mississippi), 8

zoning, 145-46, 150-51

About the Editors and Contributors

MARY G. ALMORE is Associate Professor of Urban Studies, Institute of Urban Studies at the University of Texas at Arlington. Until 1973 she was Associate Professor of Psychology at Texas Wesleyan College, Fort Worth, Texas. Dr. Almore has published primarily in the areas of deviant behavior, criminal justice education, and contemporary issues in criminology.

VICTOR L. ARNOLD is the Associate Dean of the Graduate School of Business and Director of the Bureau of Business Research, University of Texas at Austin. His research interests include applied economic systems analysis, business/government interface, natural resource development, and strategic planning design and administration. He also has served at the federal and state levels of government and in the private sector. His accomplishments include: Associate Professor in the LBJ School of Public Affairs; Co-Director of the Mexican Economic Development Project; Executive Director of the Commission on Minnesota's Future; Director of the Development Planning in Minnesota; and Director of Texas 2000 — Governor Clement's long-range planning project for Texas. He has written a number of publications concerned with natural resource utilization and long-range planning and analysis. Among them is his recently published book, *Alternatives to Confrontation: A National Policy Toward Regional Change.*

STEVEN C. BALLARD is the Assistant Director for the Science and Public Policy Program and Associate Professor of Political Science, University of Oklahoma. His fields of interests are policy analysis, utilization of scientific knowledge, energy policy, and natural resource policy. Major publications include coauthorship of *Energy From the West: A Technology Assessment of Western Energy Development* (University of Oklahoma Press) and *Water and Western Energy* (Westview Press); several contract reports on energy and the environment; several journal articles on energy policy, intergovernmental relations, the knowledge utilization process, and methods of policy analysis. He received his Ph.D. in Political Science from Ohio State University (1976).

LISA MATHIS BUTLER, a doctoral student in geography at the University of Oklahoma, has been working as a research assistant for the Science and Public Policy Program since August 1982. She holds a B.S. degree from Colorado State University, attended the University of Edinburgh, Scotland and received a Master's degree in Park Administration with special emphasis on natural resources management from Clemson University. Within geography her specialization is land use and environmental conservation.

DWIGHT F. DAVIS is Senior Program Auditor, Florida Office of the Auditor General. He previously served on the faculty of Texas A & M, University of Oklahoma, and University of Illinois-Chicago Circle. His research interests include program evaluation and political communication. He has published articles in *Administration and Society*, *International Political Science Review*, *American Behavioral Scientist*, and *Experimental Study of Politics*.

ELIZABETH M. GUNN is a Ph.D. candidate in Political Science and a Research Assistant at the Science and Public Policy Program, University of Oklahoma. She was formerly with the Bureau of Government Research and has participated in numerous applied policy research projects. Her current interests include public administration, political economy, and environmental policy.

TIMOTHY A. HALL is a Program Manager on Radian Corporation's Research and Engineering Operations staff, Austin, Texas. He was formerly an Assistant Professor with the Department of Social Sciences at Georgia Institute of Technology. Dr. Hall has published numerous technical reports, chapters, and articles in the areas of energy policy, environmental laws and regulations, and resource development. His articles have appeared in *Policy Studies Journal*, *American Behavioral Scientist*, and the *International Journal of Public Administration*. In addition, he has coauthored three books, *Energy Policy-Making: A Selected Bibliography* (University of Oklahoma Press), *Energy and the Way We Live* (Boyd and Fraiser Publishing Company), and *Energy From the West* (University of Oklahoma Press).

THOMAS E. JAMES, JR. is a Research Fellow with the Science and Public Policy Program and Assistant Professor of Political

Science at the University of Oklahoma, Norman. He has authored numerous articles and papers on program evaluation, urban social reporting, the impact of federal manpower programs, and the generation and utilization of scientific knowledge. His current research is an assessment of ground water problems in the Southeast and the development of policy options for dealing with these problems. He received his Ph.D. in Political Science from the Ohio State University.

DANIEL J. MCGOVERN is a Visiting Assistant Professor of Political Science at the University of Wisconsin-Parkside. He received his Ph.D. from the University of Kansas. His dissertation "Multinational Corporations and European Labor Unions" explores the response of West European workers to capital flight and plant closings. Currently he is involved in a multidisciplinary study of plant closings across the Great Lakes region.

SUSAN A. MACMANUS is a Research Associate in the Center for Public Policy and Associate Professor of Political Science, University of Houston. She has conducted a number of evaluations of the impact of federal programs in Houston for the Brookings Institution, Princeton Center for Urban and Regional Research, Columbia University Conservation of Human Resources Center, National Academy for Public Administration, and the U.S. Departments of Commerce, Labor, Health and Human Services, and Housing and Urban Development. She is the author of several books, including *Revenue Patterns in U.S. Cities and Suburbs* (Praeger 1978) and *The Impact of Federal Aid on Houston in 1978* (Brookings 1983). She has published numerous articles in political science, public administration, and urban journals.

JAMES L. REGENS is Associate Professor of Political Science and Research Fellow in the Institute of Natural Resources at the University of Georgia. He has been a visiting Fellow at Oak Ridge National Laboratory and is currently on leave as the Assistant Director for Science Policy, Office of International Activities, U.S. Environmental Protection Agency. His primary research interests include policy analysis, with a particular emphasis on technology assessment, and energy-natural resource issues.

FRANCES K. RICHARDSON is Associate Professor of Nursing, Harris College of Nursing at Texas Christian University, Fort Worth, Texas. Until 1972 she was a Clinical Specialist in Psychiatric Nursing at St. Joseph's Hospital, Fort Worth, Texas. Ms. Richardson has published primarily in the areas of nursing education and psychiatric nursing.

REBECCA S. ROBERTS is an Assistant Professor of Geography and a Research Fellow with the Science and Public Policy Program at the University of Oklahoma, Norman. Her research interests in resource and economic geography focus on natural resource policy and management and regional economic development; her publications and papers concern land resource evaluation, growth management, land use planning and control, and environmental policy. She holds a Ph.D. in Geography from Oregon State University.

ROBERT W. RYCROFT is Assistant Professor of Public Affairs and Political Science and Deputy Director of the Graduate Program in Science, Technology, and Public Policy, The George Washington University. He received his Ph.D. from the University of Oklahoma and has held research and teaching positions at Oklahoma, Princeton, and the University of Denver. Dr. Rycroft specializes in energy policy, science and technology policy, and technology assessment and policy analysis.